DYLAN THOMAS
A CENTENARY CELEBRATION

Dylan Thomas

A Centenary Celebration

EDITED BY HANNAH ELLIS

B L O O M S B U R Y

LONDON • NEW DELHI • NEW YORK • SYDNEY

A Continuum book

Bloomsbury Publishing Plc
50 Bedford Square
London WC1B 3DP

www.bloomsbury.com

Bloomsbury is a registered trademark of Bloomsbury Publishing Plc

Bloomsbury Publishing, London, New Delhi, New York and Sydney

A CIP record for this book is available from the British Library.

ISBN 9781472903099

10 9 8 7 6 5 4 3 2 1

Typeset by Fakenham Prepress Solutions, Fakenham, Norfolk NR21 8NN
Printed and bound in Great Britain by CPI Group (UK) Ltd, Croydon, CR0 4YY

Contents

Foreword

Terry Jones

I remember my brother, Nigel, first introduced me to Dylan Thomas. I was twelve and he must have been fourteen-and-a-half, when he said to me the BBC were going to present an historic broadcast that evening. It would feature Richard Burton (whom I had never heard of) and it was written by Dylan Thomas (whom I equally had never heard of) and it was called *Under Milk Wood* (a title that meant nothing to me at all). It was 25 January 1954, two months after Dylan's death, though I didn't know it at the time.

My parents didn't want to listen, and as the radio was in the dining room, we were left in possession of it. I remember my brother's reverential silence as 'the play for voices' started, and the rich full tones of Richard Burton's voice filled the loudspeaker – bursting out in a glorious inundation of resonance.

I started out sitting at the dining room table, but by halfway through (or what seemed to me to be halfway through) I was under the table in a delight of table-legs. Maybe I managed to listen until the little town of Llareggub wakes up. Maybe, under my brother's watchful eye, I lasted out the whole broadcast. I can't remember, but I do remember the atmosphere and the characters. And the sheer joy of the words.

Listening to it or reading it now brings tears to my eyes. It's so perfect and yet so funny. 'I will lie by your side like the Sunday Roast', says Mr Mog Edwards to Myfanwy Price, although by the end of *Under Milk Wood* we learn that they live at the opposite ends of town, and neither have really any desire to be together. Other phrases have become part of my life – from the description of Mr and Mrs Floyd, the cockle-pickers, sleeping together 'like two old kippers in a box' to Gossamer Beynon's lament: 'I'll never be refined if I twitch'.

I would also like to celebrate the love expressed in the exchanges between Mr and Mrs Cherry Owen:

CHERRY OWEN
I always say she's got two husbands,
   FIRST VOICE
says Cherry Owen,

CHERRY OWEN
one drunk and one sober.
FIRST VOICE
And Mrs Cherry simply says
MRS CHERRY OWEN
And aren't I a lucky woman? Because I love them both.

And likewise the exchanges between Mrs Beynon and Mr Beynon. I feel they really love each other, despite the spats – I think she secretly likes being teased:

MRS BEYNON
She likes the liver, Ben.
MR BEYNON
She ought to do, Bess. It's her brother's.
MRS BEYNON (Screaming)
Oh, d'you hear that, Lily?
LILY SMALLS
Yes, mum.
MRS BEYNON
We're eating pusscat.
LILY SMALLS
Yes, mum.
MRS BEYNON
Oh, you cat-butcher!
MR BEYNON
It was doctored, mind.

Since then Dylan Thomas became a part of my life. I guess I started reading his poems sometime later. I can't remember when, but they had an impact on me that no other poetry could have had. The earlier poems I found obscure but they thrilled me. No one was doing with words what Dylan Thomas was doing. He wrote: 'I should say I wanted to write poetry in the beginning because I had fallen in love with words … The words alone. What the words stood for was of a very secondary importance …' Maybe that explains the obscurity of the early poems.

Dylan Thomas communicates his excitement at falling in love with words and words and words. I too loved at first sight 'Poem in October' with its 'heron / Priested shore' and its 'Through the parables / Of sun light'. I too fell outright in love with 'Do not go gentle into that good night / Old age should burn and rave at close of day / Rage, rage against the dying of the light'. And I too still love 'Fern Hill' with its prophetic final lines: 'Oh as I was young and easy in the mercy of his means, / Time held me green and dying / Though I sang in my chains like the sea'.

Reading Dylan Thomas is to celebrate life. To enter into a festival of words for their own sake. Dylan Thomas is a unique voice singing in his chains like the sea.

Introduction

Hannah Ellis

Dylan Thomas: A Centenary Celebration has been a 'labour of love' for me, and has signified my own journey of discovery. It has been both exciting and scary finding out about my colourful and extraordinarily talented family.

The death of my mum five years ago, and the birth of my son not long after, have made me more aware of the importance of family, and learning where all our strengths and weaknesses come from. My voyage to learn more about my grandfather started by delving into biographies and quickly finding out that there was much more to understand about Dylan Thomas than the 'legend' would have you believe. I discovered that realizing the truth was far more fascinating than accepting the myths. It was with increasing frustration that I found myself unable to stop the events of 1953 that ended in my grandfather's life being cut tragically short. The questions were endless. What if he had not been given the injection of morphine? What would an opera he planned to write with Stravinsky have been like? How would my mum's life have been different? Would I even be here today?

With an element of embarrassment, I had to admit that I had not read my grandfather's work. What if I didn't like it? What if it was too difficult? So, it was with amazement I found myself reading beautiful and descriptive poetry, surreal and dark short stories, memories of Dylan's childhood in Wales and passionate letters to family and friends. My sheer delight and enjoyment was followed by alarm. If I was only just finding out about the wonderful writing, there must be others of my generation who have not yet experienced it. I suddenly became very aware that I was incredibly lucky to be the grand-daughter of not only a talented wordsmith, but also a sensational actor. Dylan could move audiences with powerful and thoughtful readings, and then, in an instant, cause the same group of people to roll about with laughter, with a quick and witty comment.

However, with the good fortune came a responsibility. One hundred years since my grandfather's birth was just a short while away and there was increasing momentum to find a way to celebrate it. I chose to take on the mantle, have a break from teaching, focus on the centenary and assume a very active role. I would not accept just being a figurehead; I had a vision and wanted to work hard to achieve it. My aims for the anniversary were very clear from the start. I wanted to bring the focus back to Dylan Thomas's work. I wanted it refreshed and revitalized, so new audiences, as well as those already familiar with it, could enjoy it. As a primary school teacher, it was also key for me that we find a way to engage young learners. I visualized using my grand-father's example to give children the confidence to play with words, use rhyme and alliteration and make up a few new words or phrases of their own.

I feel privileged to have been involved in helping create a newfound energy that has relit a love for my grandfather's work, along with a realization that there is also a vulnerable man behind those words. It is so important that we make the most of the amazing opportunity the centenary offers and build a worldwide community that will continue to celebrate Dylan Thomas, and, as a consequence, bring attention to the arts, education and places associated with him. I certainly will be flying the flag the highest. This year, for me, is just the start …

As you make your way through this book, I will be acting as a narrator, with a sprinkling of my opinion and sentiment throughout. However, you will learn the interesting, fascinating, often new, facts about Dylan's life and work from academics, Dylan Thomas experts, biographers, writers, musicians, actors, friends and other family members. My hope is that you will realize the legacy of my grandfather's work and recognize how it has managed to cross different artforms and languages and travel the world.

Dylan as a boy. Courtesy of Susan Deacon

PART ONE

EARLY LIFE – 1914–34

This section looks at my grandfather's early life, 1914 until 1934. It explores the influences and places of his childhood, and the explosion of teenage experimentation and creativity.

> As soon as he was baptized he made for the sea. And there and then, as soon as he came to the sea, he took on the sea's nature and swam as well as the best fish in the sea.
>
> From *The Mabinogion*

It is interesting that my great-grandparents' choice of name for their newly born son was his first bond with the might of the sea, a powerful presence throughout his short life. Dylan Eil Ton, the character from the Welsh mythic tale *The Mabinogion*, simply translates as 'Dylan the second wave'. This unusual, and what turned out to be very apt, name choice, with all its connections with the sea, is why I've decided to start this section with Dr Rowan Williams's beautiful poem, *Swansea Bay*.

In a later broadcast, *Reminiscences of Childhood*, Dylan describes being born in Swansea by the side of a 'long and splendid-curving shore': 'With my friends I used to dawdle on half-holidays along the bent and Devon-facing seashore, hoping for corpses or gold watches or the skull of a sheep or a message in a bottle to be washed up in the wreck'; and 'walking alone over the very desolate Gower cliffs, communing with the cold and the quietness'. The effect of a coastal upbringing had a profound effect on my grandfather's growing imagination. It is no coincidence, in my opinion, that he was always most productive when he was living close to the sea. The harmony of the sea views, sounds and smells inspired some of his most poignant works.

We then travel to where, as he put it in 'Fern Hill', he was 'young and easy' and 'happy as the grass was green'. The first essay of this book is by David N. Thomas. It introduces you to another important place in Dylan's early years, the rural communities of Carmarthenshire, where he stayed with his many aunts and uncles. It was, Dylan once said, his true childhood. The connection with the area ran deep for my grandfather and he continued to visit the Llansteffan peninsula at different periods in his life.

As I read David's essay, I was captivated by all the new and intriguing facts David's hours of meticulous research had uncovered. I particularly liked that there was much more to learn and understand about the 'feckless farmer' Jim Jones than met the critical poet's eye or wondering whether the greying profiles of Dylan's many aunts and uncles help explain why my grandfather was so absorbed, as a teenage poet, with decay and mortality. Certainly, one suggestion made by David will, perhaps, be rather controversial. He is very doubtful that, despite its name, his aunt's farm Fernhill is the true inspiration for his famous poem.

> On one hand, he was in revolt against his father's agnosticism. On the other hand, he was in revolt against the narrow Puritan conventions of his mother's Congregational background, and it was from these tensions that the personality of Dylan Thomas developed.
>
> Bert Trick on Dylan's parents

Wynn Thomas's essay looks at another important influence of Dylan's childhood, the conflicting attitudes from his parents towards religion. Wynn excellently demonstrates Dylan's scepticism of religion through examples in Dylan's own work. For example, in the short story 'The Fight' he depicts his preacher uncle as the pompous Reverend Bevan, while in another story, 'The Peaches', he humorously includes a conversation his cousin Gwilwm is having with God:

> Thou canst see everything we do, in the night and day, in the day and night, everything, everything … O God, mun, you're like a bloody cat.

I find it very ironic that, though the young Dylan was keen to break the spell the preachers had over the Welsh imagination, he himself used the same skills he observed in the pulpit when performing years later. He engaged and delighted audiences with the magical power of language. It is interesting as well that the stories in the Bible were an invaluable resource for his poetry and prose.

> A poem I had printed in the Wales Day by Day column of the Western Mail was pasted on the mirror to make me blush, but the shame of the poem had died … I put it there to make me blush. But nobody came in except my mother.
>
> From *The Fight,* by Dylan Thomas

In Jeff Towns's essay we follow his journey of discovery as he finds further evidence that suggests that Dylan, as a teenager, intended to plagiarize poems. It is intriguing why my grandfather chose to do this, as one of his biographers, Paul Ferris, notes: 'Dylan at that age was writing so many poems that he certainly had no need to steal one'. Different theories exist, including that he was trying to please his parents or that he was focusing fully on his other poems, the ones that filled his remarkable adolescent notebooks. I think I would probably come to a similar conclusion to Jeff. He observed that Dylan 'was a joker ... he was a trickster'. This would fit with a side I very much like about my grandfather – his mischievous and witty sense of humour.

In contrast to his hoodwinking exploits, his teenage years were a time of extraordinary achievement. I find it astonishing, and at times frustrating, that my grandfather sold the cream of this creative work for the equivalent of around £1,200 in 2003. It is equally inconceivable that these notebooks have remained in boxes and never been publicly displayed. Jo Furber's essay follows her expedition to America where she had the opportunity to delve in and explore these notebooks. Jo explains how she 'didn't think [Dylan] could still surprise me like this, but it turns out he can, and with some considerable force'. As her exciting mission continues, she excitedly finds handwritten drafts of what are now very well-known poems with word lists, drawings, rhyme schemes, cigarette burns, crossings-out, coffee stains, annotations, drawings and doodles, underlinings, use of coloured pencil, ink blots and practice signatures. Each poem is dated, numbered, and a few are simply called 'Pome' – again, a hint at my grandfather's playfulness. She concludes that the archive is a 'testament to a precocious talent'.

> To read Dylan, either his prose or his poetry, and especially as he read it, which flowed out in a lovely stream of words, you would think that these words, and these sentence build-ups, came easy to him – but they didn't. They were the result of meticulous craftsmanship.
>
> Bert Trick on Dylan's work ethic

Swansea Bay: Dylan at 100

Rowan Williams

1.
A thumb drawn down, smearing the grey wash,
storm pillars float over a December morning,
the sun still tipping rocks with liquid
out at the headland. In the bay swells urge
this way and that; a dark patch swings
out from the sea wall, pushes the pushing current
sideways, the planes of water tilting by inches
under the lurid morning, heaving this way and that
beneath the mottled skin and pinching it into the long
blade of a wave, the knife under the cloth
ready to slice. Watching, you have no notion
how it all runs, the hidden weights swinging
and striking, passing their messages, hidden
as the pulses under the scalp, behind the eyes,
that sometimes pinch themselves into a sharp
fold, into an edge, as if the buried cranial dances
gathered themselves to cut, for a moment, at
the skull's dry case and break through in white curls.

2.
I sang in my chains. I listened for the pushing swell
of light in the country yards, the undertow
of bliss that still cuts at the cloth, at the bone,
at all the tired shrouds. I listened
for the tide retreating and the small lick and splash
of breeze on the trickles between corrugated sand,
for the silent footfall of pacing birds, processing
to their office. Beyond the bay, the infant-bearing sea
slips further off, the next room is quiet and the sun
whispers hoarsely. When I call in my dream for it,
my voice is small and the knife strains bluntly
at the knotted cloth. Watching the swell again
at whispering liquid sunrise, I have no answer

when I wonder how the world's sand runs
out of grace and the dark moods of the water
jostle each other; I cannot tell if they will gather
ever again, severing the milky web that holds me
mortally. Do not go. Now as I was.

A True Childhood: Dylan's Peninsularity

David N. Thomas

i.m. Colin Edwards, who did what he could

At the centenary of Dylan's birth, it's timely to wonder about his childhood and teenage years. After all, he was an early-onset poet. He published his first collection at twenty, with two more before he was twenty-five. Almost two-thirds of these collected poems had first been written in his teens, prompting one scholar to comment that Dylan was a genius who had already matured by the time he was seventeen. So it seems that the more we know about his early years, the better we might understand both the poetry and the man.

Dylan got off to a good start. His mother, Florence, was attended by Dr Alban Evans, who had already made his mark in Swansea as both a surgeon and a family historian, with a passion for collecting deeds and lineages. His attendance could have cost the Thomases dearly, but Evans was known as a man who 'in a deserving case … was ever willing to modify his fees'. And perhaps especially in Dylan's case because he, like Evans himself, had his roots in the soil of Carmarthenshire. It is, of course, rather fanciful to imagine that, as Florence lay recovering with the baby in her arms, she and the doctor were swapping stories about her Llangain family tree. Could Waunfwlchan, Llwyngwyn and Pencelli-uchaf have been the first sounds that Dylan heard?

Perhaps not, but as he went from baby to boy and further, those sounds and then the words would have become ever more familiar, as relatives descended on Cwmdonkin Drive after a day in the shops, filling the house with Welsh and family news. One Llangain visitor remembered that she was 'always going up there for tea if I was doing a day's shopping in Swansea. We all used to have tea together there'.

Baby delivered, Alban Evans went off to research family papers in the Aeron valley in Cardiganshire, where Dylan himself would later live. It had been a normal birth and mother and baby required no further assistance, though the father had celebrated so well he needed help taking off his boots. Dylan coughed his way through childhood, brought up by an indulgent and ever-protective mother, as well as a nurse and a doting older sister. A family friend later observed that it was 'pretty obvious that Dylan had been brought up very, very, very *annwyl*, as they say in Wales … he was brought up very dearly and closely … sheltered in many ways'.

And there were lots of places to shelter, because he grew up in a very large extended family; it was also a greying family, so that the aunts who looked after him were in their fifties and sixties. Spoiling was the order of the day. A good many of his mother's sisters and cousins had no children of their own; he was the first boy in his mother's close family for over sixteen years, and boys were just as rare on his father's side. All but one of his first cousins were girls, all very much older than him: 'Everybody mothered Dylan; everybody ...'

His mother's family lived mostly in rural west Wales, so that Dylan had two childhoods, one in Swansea and the other farmed out to various aunts in the countryside. There were several of these farmyard mothers, including his favourite aunt, Annie, and her husband, Jim Jones, who lived at Fernhill, a short ride for Dylan by bus or cart from the town of Carmarthen. The farm is often described as remote or isolated, but it was neither; it stood off the main road to Llansteffan, on the lane that went to the shop-and-pubbed settlements of Llangynog and Llanybri. There were also neighbours at Fernhill, almost a dozen farms within a half-mile, as well as Bethesda Chapel and House, though no Eli Jenkins ever preached here. Many more farms were within easy walking distance, as were the forge, post office and shop in the nearby hamlet of Llangain, together with a church and chapel that were at the centre of cultural life.

Fernhill was but one of a number of family farms that Dylan stayed at or visited. He was part of an extensive family network that itself was closely related to a wider farming community. So who were these other relations? What do we know about Annie and Jim's farming neighbours, and the shopkeepers, postmen, blacksmiths, carpenters and farm workers who would have been a part of Dylan's everyday life? Even today, our understanding of this community, and the part it played in the poet's growing-up, is rudimentary.

It's disappointing to reach the centenary knowing so little about Dylan's rural upbringing; material could have been gathered decades ago, when his farming relations and their neighbours were alive. There are a half-dozen universities within easy driving of Carmarthenshire, but professors and research students alike stayed away. This lack of academic interest left Dylan's several biographers in the lurch; they had very little to draw upon in writing about Fernhill, which one of them, FitzGibbon, thought the most important place in Dylan's childhood.

So a rural outing, suggesting both excursion and discovery, seems an appropriate centenary activity. It's also as good a way as any to celebrate the birthday of someone who enjoyed walking so much. I shall start at the bridge over the river Tywi/Towy at Carmarthen. It was the river of Dylan's childhood holidays, and the river of bedtime stories about shipwrecks and drownings, including a cousin, and of the bravery of the lifeboat men, including an uncle, who tried to save them. Not surprisingly, the Tywi appears occasionally in Dylan's writing. Together with its tributaries and landscape, it fills the second half of the Rev. Eli Jenkins's morning prayer. It flows quietly through Dylan's story *A Visit to Grandpa's*, and makes a surprising appearance in his poem 'Over Sir John's Hill'.

It's also the river that connects the two sides of Dylan's family. His paternal grandmother was born upstream of Carmarthen bridge in Llangadog, as was one of his aunties, whose family had once run a pub in the village. Dylan's great-grandfather had also been born here and thought the graveyard so comfy that, in *A Visit to Grandpa's*, he was determined to be buried there. And, in the end, he got his way, brought from Carmarthen along the Tywi valley to the church, and then tucked in nicely next to the graveyard wall, with plenty of space to twitch, without getting his legs wet in the sea or even the river.

Downstream of the bridge, the Tywi belongs to the other side of Dylan's family, the Williamses; it was the birth place of his maternal grandmother, as well as his many cousins, uncles and aunts who, he once wrote, were the 'undeniably mad unpossessed peasantry of the inbred crooked county ...' Perhaps some were mad, and others inbred, but hardly any were peasants or unpossessed. I shall follow the river to the sea. My first stop will be Llangain, shown at the top of the map, where I shall make for Pentrewyman farm, the birthplace of Dylan's uncle, Jim Jones Fernhill.

In his nephew's short story, *The Peaches*, Jim is portrayed as a reluctant and feckless farmer, a man who sold his piglets in the pub for a pint or two. But was

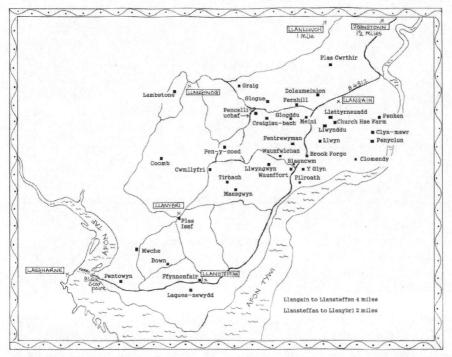

In Dylan's time, the main farms on the Williams side were Pen-y-coed, Maesgwyn, Llwyngwyn, Meini, Llettyrneuadd, Pencelli-uchaf, Plas Isaf, Pentowyn, Mwche, Down and Laques-newydd. On the Jones side, they were Dolaumeinion, Pentrewyman, Penhen, Clyn-mawr, Llwynddu, Llwyn, Church House and Ffynnonfair.

there more to Jim than met the poet's eye? Could local gossip be right, that he was related to a wealthy banking dynasty? As for those poor piglets, would it help us to know that the publican, a cousin, was also a butcher, with his own abbatoir in Llansteffan? So could it have been at all possible that in real life, as Dylan was sitting in the cart outside, Jim was selling the little darlings, not just for a pint, but also to fund his visitor's summer holiday at Fernhill? And while *The Peaches* is clearly about Fernhill, is the poem 'Fern Hill' about another farm altogether?

A life of last straws

'Poor Dad, to die of drink and agriculture'. Rev. Eli Jenkins[1]

I shall set off across Pentrewyman's fields, thinking of eleven-year-old Emily Jones, perhaps a relation, who had come from a neighbouring farm to help clear stones. Jim, just eight years old, was probably one of those working alongside her when she was attacked by a bull. Thrown twenty feet in the air, she fractured a thigh bone, with injuries as well to her stomach and bowel. A surgeon was rushed from Carmarthen and, in due course, she recovered. Was it at this early age that Jim realized that farming was both hard work and dangerous?

Two years later, in 1874, there was another emergency at Pentrewyman. Jim's mother, Rachel, died while giving birth, attended by the elderly widow of a local carpenter. There was no doctor present, and none was rushed from Carmarthen. The baby survived and was named Rachel. Her brother, Jim, was now ten years old and the eldest child. He had lost not only his mother but both his grandmothers as well, but there was precious little time to feel sorry for himself. There were over a hundred acres to farm, and four younger children to feed, including baby Rachel, with only two servants to help – in his mother's day there were four. Jim started work on the farm in earnest. His father re-married; soon there were three more children, and within a few years there were eleven, most of them under twelve. As Jim toiled away, further accidents happened. Within the space of a few months, one neighbour was killed by a bull, and another by lightning while ploughing.

By the time of his marriage to Dylan's auntie Annie in 1893, Jim had probably had his fill of farming. The last straw could well have been the death, in an accident on a farm, of his younger brother, an agricultural labourer, hit by a falling boulder. Jim lived to a ripe old age but could this have been the moment when, like the Rev. Eli Jenkins's father, he lost all ambition and died, in spirit, of too much agriculture? In fact, there was one more blow to come; when Jim's father died in 1906, he left a net estate of over £40,000 in today's terms, but he left nothing at all to his eldest son, not even the smallest token of gratitude for all those years that Jim had worked to keep Pentrewyman going.

There's room for a good deal of speculation about how Jim was affected by his mother Rachel's death. It seems possible, for example, that one legacy

---

[1]   Quotations from the works of Dylan Thomas appear in italics throughout this essay.

was resentment, a grievance about opportunties denied, an 'if only' worm that could have troubled Jim throughout his life. About the time of her death, Rachel's father left Clomendy, the farm on the estuary that had been in the family for more than a hundred years. Now in his late sixties, he retired to Llansteffan with his three unmarried daughters, Rachel's younger sisters. As Jim grew older, and heard more of his family history, did he wonder about how matters might have turned out rather differently?

if only there'd been a doctor present
if only his mother hadn't died
if only she and his father had taken over Clomendy

… then he, as the eldest son, might well have followed on at the farm. And what a prize Clomendy would have been. Just short of two hundred acres, it was 'a very respectable farmhouse' of eleven rooms, 'from situation one of the most desirable in the county', and it included a junior farm bringing in rental income. Clomendy was also close to Penhen, an even larger farm run by his grandmother's family who, the stories went, were on hunting terms with Coomb mansion. Jim would have been well and truly set up to farm as a gentleman. If only …

From Pentrewyman, I shall make my way along the coastal path to Llansteffan. The journey there for a drink was one that Dylan frequently made, usually on the bus, sometimes by bike and often on foot, watching the 'moon ploughing up the Towy' as he walked to the pub. I shall make for the castle, pausing at the graveyard where chesty Grandpa, who later died of bronchitis, was determined *not* to be buried. From the castle, I shall look west towards Pentowyn and Mwche, and the other family farms such as Down and Laquesnewydd. In Dylan's day, the town below was also bursting with relations; some had retired here from their farms, while others ran shops and kept the Williams family pub, the Edwinsford. The castle will also give me a fine view across the tearing estuary towards Ferryside, where some of his mother Florence's other relatives had settled. Both Llansteffan and Ferryside have been modest about their associations with Dylan but, in truth, they have a good deal to shout about.

So has Llanybri, and that's where I'll go next, walking the narrow lanes to the Farmers' Arms. It was one of Dylan's favourite pubs, and the landlady thought the world of him: 'He was a real farmer in his way'. He was also a proper gentleman, she said, though she was taken aback that he and Caitlin would picnic in the pub sitting on the floor: 'Cloth on the floor, and eat their bread and cheese and I think they had an onion with them once here!'

I'm too old for the floor, so it will be a table by the window, with a brown ale and a bowl of Llanybri *cawl*, brimming with lamb from the saltmarsh below. Then I shall sit back and think about other conversations between Dylan and the landlady, such as those about his family:

He talked about his mother, very often about his mother … Oh, he would be saying 'I wouldn't be where I am now only because of mother'.

This would undoubtedly be the moment to consider yet another 2014 celebration. On 7 November, it will be the 200th anniversary of the marriage of Dylan's maternal great-great-grandparents, John and Hannah Williams. They farmed Pen-y-coed, just outside Llanybri, and were followed there by their children and grandchildren. But I shall also raise a glass to Dylan's other set of great-great-grandparents, Evan and Anne Harries, who farmed Plas Isaf, just behind the Farmers' Arms. The family were there until 1906, when their son-in-law, Thomas Phillips, dropped dead in the pub.

And now, as on many walks, we are at risk of getting lost – this time in a thicket of family trees. Thomas was Florence's great-uncle by marriage, and the blood great-uncle of Vera Phillips, Dylan's childhood friend from Swansea. Her husband, William Killick, was tried and acquitted for attempting to murder Dylan. The incident was fictionalized in a 2008 film, *The Edge of Love*. Hollywood's roots, and suckers, are found in the most surprising of places.

So it seems right that I should next take the short walk across the fields from Llanybri to Tirbach, derelict now, but once a thriving farm. I shall think about Dylan and Vera, whose grandfather had farmed here after he, too, had married into Florence's family.

Jim and Annie Jones had also started married life in Tirbach, though Annie had first come here as housekeeper to one of her Williams uncles. He later came to live with them at Fernhill and died there; Annie was the sole beneficiary of his will and was left more than enough to keep the farm afloat for many years. But after paying off his debts, she ended up with very little, and Fernhill slipped slowly downhill thereafter. For Jim, this could have been yet another reason to feel sorry for himself, let down first by his own family and then by the Williamses as well.

Land of his aunties

'They were the background from which he had sprung, and he needed that background all his life, like a tree needs roots'.

Caitlin Thomas on Dylan's aunties

Tirbach would not be a place to linger, with loose dogs about that guard the tilting house. So I shall turn away towards the farm next door, and take myself to Maesgwyn, once farmed by Dylan's great-great-great grandparents, and it's been in the family ever since.

Today, Maesgwyn and adjoining Llwyngwyn are farmed by Dylan's cousin, Heulwen Morris. Here there will be tea and Welsh cakes for another, double celebration. In 2014, we celebrate Heulwen's 80th birthday and, in doing so, we celebrate as well the fact that the Williamses, Dylan's maternal ancestors, have been farming for over two hundred years on the Llansteffan peninsula (*Penrhyn Deuddwr*), the land between two rivers, the Tâf and the Tywi.

This was where Florence's grandparents, great-grandparents and two sets of great-great-grandparents had farmed. It was here, in the fields between Maesgwyn and Fernhill, that she had spent her childhood holidays with her

Heulwen Morris, née Williams, at Llwyngwyn, 2012. Courtesy of Phil Edwards

many cousins. Some of her siblings had been born here, and two had lived here all their adult lives. Three others had retired to the peninsula, while Florence herself had lived there for the best part of the 1940s.

It was the land of his aunties, and being farmed out to them as a boy meant that Dylan spent a significant part of his childhood in a rural community that was largely chapel-going and Welsh-speaking. All of Florence's peninsula relations, including Annie and Jim Jones at Fernhill, spoke Welsh. So did their neighbours and friends: at the 1921 census, 95 per cent of residents in the two parishes around Fernhill were Welsh-speakers. Across the whole peninsula, 13 per cent – more than two hundred people – spoke only Welsh. It was the language of daily life, not just on the farms, but also in the local shops to which Dylan was taken or sent on errands; later, as a teenager, he wrote of 'crying aloud, in broken Welsh' to the postmaster in Llansteffan, though perhaps this is not something we should take too seriously.

We can be sure, however, that almost everywhere on the peninsula the sound of Welsh was ever-present in the ears of the young poet, as both boy and teenager. It was, too, the language of the pulpit. Noting that he went to Sunday school at Smyrna chapel, where the services were always in Welsh, one of his friends said of the Llangain area:

> It was all Welsh – and the children played in Welsh and that's why I say that Dylan must have had a smattering of Welsh in as much as he couldn't speak English when he stopped at Fernhill. I should say that in all his surroundings, everybody else spoke Welsh … as a child, you're bound to pick that up much, much quicker than when you are grown up.

Dylan had been coming here from an early age with his parents, staying for a month at a time in Rose Cottage, Llansteffan, with his mother's half-sister, Anne, and later on, with his other aunt Annie in Fernhill. There were also other aunts and uncles to spoil him, including Florence's first cousins at Llwyngwyn, none of whom had children of their own during Dylan's childhood and teenage years. He stayed for long summer holidays at Fernhill, usually without his parents, and he came, or was sent, at other times of the year, too. It was, Dylan once said, 'my true childhood'.

The peninsula was a rich concentration of relatives, family history and memories, providing a secure sense of place in what would prove to be an unsettled life. Cwmdonkin Drive had been lost to him in 1937 when his parents sold up and left. From then to his death, he lived in twelve different places, as well as at several addresses in London. But here on the peninsula, Dylan was *bachgen y fro*, a local boy, not born here, but someone who belonged and who would always feel his belonging. The farm was home, he once wrote of Fernhill, but so was much of its hinterland.

Because he had been known here since childhood, locals could place him, identifying him as the nephew of this farm or the cousin of that one, the great-grandson of a family that had filled many seats at Capel Newydd, Llanybri, for most of the 1800s. The family were so ubiquitous that even ordinary encounters in Dylan's daily life would bring contact with his relations, helping to affirm his place in the community. The publican at the Edwinsford in Llansteffan, for example, was his mother's cousin, whose daughter had been named after Florence. When Dylan bought meat from Billy Thomas the butcher in Llansteffan or a hat for his mother from the Bowen sisters or cigarettes from Harry Jones or stamps from Henry Jones in Llangain, or took his bike for repair to Daniel Evans at Brook Forge, he was buying from family.

Dylan was a sixth-generation Williams, with gravestones and family Bibles (at least two survive to this day) with genealogical data to prove it. He had so many local connections that he could walk unchallenged on family land across a large part of the sea end of the peninsula. You could do a similar walk today and not meet another soul, but in Dylan's time farming was still labour-intensive and thus more sociable – take a look at the photos in Haydn Williams's excellent book on Llangain. There were always people about, working in the fields and farmyards, so walking brought contact with others and the chance for a chat, about this cousin and that, and all the aunties in between. And Dylan would have had his own bag of tales to tell; his mother was the family historian

Thomas and Anne Williams of Waunfwlchan farm, Dylan's maternal great-grandparents, who married in 1835. Thomas was the son of Pen-y-coed and the grandson of Graig farms. Anne was the daughter of Harries of Plas lsaf and granddaughter of Roberts of Maesgwyn. Between them, Thomas and Anne had nine siblings who also farmed on the peninsula. Their farms, and those of their children, are included on the map. Courtesy of the National Library of Wales

and a good storyteller to boot: 'She was tremendously interesting, because she was full of the lore of Carmarthenshire. She had all sorts of information'.

Dylan also had access to the fields of his quasi-relations, neighbours who were not related by blood or marriage, but who had become so absorbed into family life that they became aunties and uncles. Such were the Harrieses of Pilroath, an imposing mansion that sits at the confluence of Fernhill Brook and the Tywi. It was the farm of Tom Llewelyn Harries JP, a wealthy Welsh-speaking gentleman farmer, like his father before him, with a particular interest in pigs and politics. The Harries and Williams families had always been close; it was a Harries daughter, for example, who looked after Dylan and Caitlin's eldest son, Llewelyn, when he was sent across to spend a large part of each summer on Pilroath – later in life, he took the name of Tom Llewelyn.

Imagine, too, the young Dylan playing in the fields around Fernhill, getting to know Annie's friends and neighbours. Some of the childhood relationships that he made then continued in later life. When he and Caitlin were at Blaencwm, a pair of family cottages, they would walk across to call with Rees Davies at Creigiau-bach ('I was driving them home many times'). He was just a year older than Florence, and had been born and brought up on nearby farms, as had his father and grandfather before him. And, like them, Rees was a general carpenter; between the three of them, they would have been working on the Williams's farms for over a hundred years, making everything from cots to coffins, and much of the equipment needed in the fields.

Rees's farm was just along the lane from Fernhill; it was also right next to Florence's cousins at Pencelli-uchaf, while his fields bordered those of Jim's sister, Rachel, at Pentrewyman (aunt Rach Morgan in *The Peaches*). In his work, Rees travelled from one farm to another, inevitably bringing and taking away family news and local gossip as he did so. He was thus well placed to define for others how Dylan fitted within the genealogy of the countryside. So, too, were door-to-door traders, such as Florence's cousins at the Edwinsford, who took a pony and trap around the farms selling meat. There were several others, bringing groceries, paraffin and other household goods, tying together the threads of community, with news on what was what and who was who.

Working to bring in the harvest, as Caitlin often did, as well as drinking in the kitchen, rather than the bar, at the Farmers' Arms in Llanybri, also helped locals to place Dylan within the narrative of their farming community, as the landlady recalled:

> They wanted to come to my small kitchen ... to enjoy it, to be quiet, for nobody to know they were in there, round the fire in the *gegin* ... he used to like to have Llangain people there ... some of the boys from Llangain, and talking to those always ... so many that I can't remember half their names ... talking about Fernhill. Very often you'd hear him talking to them in there.

In short, Dylan was no Johnny-come-lately from the east. This is something I hope to discuss with Heulwen, as well as the many changes that have happened since his birth. Today, she farms some three hundred acres, but in 1914 (and for all of Dylan's lifetime) the Williamses and their close relatives were working a dozen farms with over a thousand acres between them. The family had carried just enough clout for Florence's half-sister, Anne, to marry into local gentry; she later bought a seven-room house in Llansteffan (Rose Cottage), and another in Ferryside, and was worth £83,000 at her death. Florence's grandfather, Thomas Williams of Waunfwlchan, was a leading figure at Capel Newydd and in his younger days had been an overseer of the poor. It's said he dabbled in the wool trade in Llansteffan. He also owned another property in Llangynog. At his death, his net estate was worth, in today's terms, over £27,000.

Most of the Williamses were tenant farmers, but their farmhouses also told a story of ambition and status: Maesgwyn, Llwyngwyn and Waunfwlchan, for example, had seventeen bedrooms between them, while Mwche was a large country house. It boasted both a dining and drawing room, six bedrooms, two kitchens, scullery and dairy, with extensive farm buildings, including a coach house and saddle room, as well as 'a nice trout stream ... and good Partridge and Wild Fowl Shooting'.

Many of the family farms had live-in servants. Maesgwyn had four, two of whom worked in the house. Jim and Annie Jones had five servants at Pentowyn, including a cook, a domestic position through which Jim seems to have been making a statement about himself. There were only three other dedicated cooks on the whole peninsula, all working in grand country houses.

Yet despite all his farm hands, Jim was still a hopeless farmer, being 'too much of a gentleman there to work', and they were soon on their way to Fernhill,

Robert Phillips and family outside Mwche, c1912. Gwladys, holding the donkey, was a second cousin to both Vera Killick née Phillips and Florence, Dylan's mother. Gwladys and her siblings were at Mwche until the 1980s. Courtesy of Elizabeth Morgan

Maesgwyn, as Dylan knew it, with his aunt, Sarah Evans, outside. Courtesy of Sara Morris

paying rent to the daughter of the so-called Fernhill hangman. It suited Jim better, a small but imposing mansion with just a handful of acres to worry about, but even these he neglected – there was 'no work in him … left Fernhill farm to ruins'. When I read 'Fern Hill' now, I realize that Fernhill's fields could not have been, by any stretch of the imagination or poetic licence, 'fields of praise'.

But Jim continued to play the gent. He was 'big in his ways', affirming his status by choosing to attend church rather than chapel: 'He liked everyone to think that he was Gentleman Jim … he wanted to cut a dash always …' Jim had every reason for swanking it up at church: he was family. One of his first cousins had married the vicar of Llangain, who was also the Rural Dean, a member of the Governing Body of the Church in Wales and much else besides in both church and local affairs, a real man of the cloth, the son of a draper.

Pleasing and unpleasant deaths

'Time has put its maggots on my track'.

Dylan Thomas, age 18

The greying profile of the Williams family might help explain why Dylan was so absorbed, as a teenage poet, with decay and mortality. Having aunties as old as grannies meant that deaths were a recurring element of his growing up. At just sixteen, he was reflecting in his letters on being soaked in morbidity. He described the fragility of life, and the cancer that lay hidden within even the happiest third-former.

By now, he would have learned something about the deaths that had left their mark on Rose Cottage in Llansteffan, where he'd spent his summer holidays with his aunt Anne. Just two years into married life, in 1893, Anne had lost her young daughter (tubercular peritonitis) and husband (acute nephritis) within three months of each other. The next to go was her eldest son, dying of TB in his twenties, followed a year later by Anne's mother, Amy. On the day of Amy's funeral in August 1917, Anne's second son died. Barely out of his teens, he drowned swimming off the beach in Llansteffan where Dylan and his parents would have usually been holidaying, but his mother was at the funeral.

Florence was regularly faced with the prospect of journeying to family funerals; her aunt, Anne Llwyngwyn, died in 1920. Two years later, Anne Rose Cottage died of cancer of the womb, followed by Anna Llwyngwyn, a first cousin who died of nephritis and uraemic convulsions. Then came the death of another aunt Anne, who shot herself with a pistol. There were also two still-births at Llwyngwyn, and the death of a baby cousin in Ferryside. The message would have been very clear to a young poet: birth can be a doublecross, that green fuse could blow at any time.

For Dr Alban Evans, the poet's deliverer, it blew in September 1932, when he drowned in Oxwich Bay. Two months later, Dylan went to the funeral of a teacher from his school, and wondered what his own burial would be like. Two months after that, his favourite aunt, Annie Fernhill, died of heart failure, not of cancer of the womb as Dylan thought. He feigned lack of interest, but there was a surge of death poetry thereafter; family gravestones with their tales of infant and childhood deaths, a suicide and a drowning in the family, diseased lungs and kidneys, an aunt with a diseased womb and babies born dead from the womb (including his mother's stillborn child), as well as a drowned deliverer of babies, all provided part of a maggot-rich harvest for a teenage poet to reap. Not to mention the deaths of the poet's grandparents, all four of whom had gone by the time he was three.

Dylan didn't go to Annie's funeral; if he had, he could have learnt something about the Williamses and their community. She died in February 1933, having seen out her last years in a one-room hovel, kept going by handouts from her cousins. But she wasn't going to go without a show; she was, after all, the fifth generation of Williamses to farm on the peninsula. She had been born close to the Tywi's edge, married a local man, and then lived there for the rest of her life. More than that, Gentleman Jim was also deep Llangain, third-generation on his father's side, and fifth on his mother's, whose family had counted local gentry among their friends. No wonder that Annie's funeral at Capel Newydd was 'largely attended', as reported by *The Welshman*, a once-radical newspaper whose founding publisher had married into Jim's family.

The paper had no doubt that such attendance, in freezing weather, was 'ample testimony to the high esteem in which the deceased was held throughout the neighbourhood'. Annie would have gone on foot, her coffin borne

Annie Jones Fernhill, who died of heart failure in 1933, age seventy. Courtesy of the National Library of Wales

shoulder-high by a relay of bearers along the three miles from her cottage to the gates of the chapel, where the principal bearers were waiting, including Rees Davies who had made the coffin: 'She was a woman who worked hard … oh yes, she was a good woman'. Others would later talk of her kindness: 'Quite educated, jovial, talkative … kind, nicely spoken, gave plenty of welcome, always a cup of tea'. And always a kiss and a hug for her favourite nephew. Annie, wrote Dylan in 'After the Funeral', had a fountain heart that *once fell in puddles/Round the parched worlds of Wales* … And the *parchs* were out in force, Baptist and Methodist ministers sharing duties with the Rural Dean to celebrate Annie's life. After the service, the mourners stood several deep at the graveside, themselves encircled at a respectful distance by a large crowd of local people, all joining together in the Tywi-side hymn, *Bydd myrdd o rhyfeddodau*.

The gathering was 'representative', noted another newspaper. Various dignitaries were present, as well as factory owners and shopkeepers, and one or two ladies of a certain social standing, including Mrs G. Barrett Evans of the Glyn who, at seventy years of age, would have been driven to Capel Newydd by her chauffeur. Her late husband was a cousin of Lady Kylsant of Coomb mansion, a daughter of the Morris banking dynasty. Some would even have wondered if Lady Kylsant herself might have been present, but she was still nursing his Lordship, who had only just come out jail after doing time for fraud.

Miss Lloyd of Plas Llwynddu, one of the finest mansions in the county, was at the graveside. Her brother and his wife, who were first cousins, later moved into the Plas; they were both first cousins to Jim Jones, as was Miss Lloyd herself. It was all rather genetically cosy, but having a grand mansion in the family was not to be sniffed at. The young Dylan was quick off the mark, writing to his sister, who was staying in Fernhill, teasing her about moving in the gayest Llangain society. In truth, they were farmers not gentry, estuary families who had profitably worked the fields along the edges of the Tywi for over a hundred years. Between Llwynddu and the river, they formed the core of Jim's relatives who, in Dylan's childhood and teenage years, were still farming over six hundred acres between them.

Yet, farmers or not, one of the most intriguing questions about Jim Jones remains unresolved. He was a grandson of the Morrises of Clomendy and Penhen, among the most financially astute farming families on the peninsula, who had done well from their interests in a number of local farms, as well as from properties in Carmarthen. But was Gentleman Jim also related through them to the family of David Morris, the founder of the Morris banking business, who had been born and brought up on a nearby estuary farm? If he and the banker were related, then Jim, too, would have been a distant cousin of Lady Kylsant.

The Williamses were well established in farming and chapel circles, but the turnout for the funeral suggests that they were also close to the local political establishment. The district councillor, a relative, was present, as was his predecessor of ten years, Jim's cousin the Rural Dean. The county councillor, Tom Harries of Pilroath, was also there. Past and present chairmen of the parish council turned out, as did its long-serving clerk. He was now in his late sixties, but he braved the cold to be one of the bearers. His standing was all the greater for being a deacon at Smyrna chapel. Through chapel, church and council, the Williamses were well and truly connected to the local power grid.

Whether we look at their political and social connections, or the size of their farmhouses, or the extent of their acreage, it would be wrong to view the Williamses as unpossessed peasantry, as Dylan described them in 1945. By that date, most of them had bought their farms, and were no longer tenants. There were some exceptions, such as Annie and Jim, but on the whole the Williamses had flourished through hard work and astute marriages; so much so that very few of them had felt the need to leave their farms for the mines and industries in the east, though one of Florence's uncles did go west, all the way to Tenafly, New Jersey where, he boasted, he managed the ranch of the banker, J. P. Morgan.

A cowboy in the family? Well, not quite. Banker Morgan didn't have a ranch or any other property at Tenafly, and rancher John Lloyd worked as a labourer on a local farm. Still, it must have been one of Dylan's favourite bedtime stories; and for a young boy on holiday, Lloyd was always worth a visit at his retirement home in Llansteffan, where he enchanted people with his tall American stories about himself, his adventures and the wildlife ('bees were the size of British robins, and the robins as big as blackbirds').

Blaencwm: from rural idyll to dead end

'He would talk about the farm life, but he wouldn't talk about Swansea, that I remember'.

Aeronwy Thomas

Neither Annie's move from Fernhill nor her death brought Dylan's visits to the peninsula to an end. His aunt Polly had moved into Blaencwm, just down the lane from Llwyngwyn, so that's where I'll go next, an easy ramble down a wooded valley, bringing me closer again to the Tywi. Polly had retired here in 1928 and, for the next six years, Blaencwm became Dylan's rural retreat, school and work permitting. He came to escape from his father's rages and discipline, but he found in the countryside the inspiration to write, not just at the cottage but also in the Edwinsford, where the grate 'used to be full of his cigarette packets with his poetry on'.

Scholars have noted that 1933 was a significant year for Dylan's poetry. There were certainly a lot more poems – almost twice as many – and he filled his first three collections with them. It was also the year in which Dylan, still only eighteen, had his first poems published in London.

Paul Ferris has wisely observed that for Dylan, as with many writers, place matters: 'He drew energy from a location … West Wales, imprinted on him as a child, was the place that consistently provoked him to write'. It's reasonable to suppose that the creativity of 1933 had much to do with Dylan being able to spend more time on the peninsula. He had left his job on the *Evening Post* in December 1932; it gave him the freedom, for the very first time, to stay at

Blaencwm whenever he wished, or whenever he needed to escape from the troubles of Cwmdonkin Drive.

The 'Blaencwm effect' goes wider than the number of notebook poems he wrote at the cottage; insight and inspiration discovered on the peninsula would be carried away, so that poems rooted in Dylan's experiences around Blaencwm would be started or continued back in Swansea. December 2014 will be the 80th anniversary of the publication of *18 Poems*, Dylan's first collection. Eight of the poems had been written in the autumn of 1933, when he travelled back and forth between Blaencwm ('a highly poetical cottage') and Swansea ('my nasty, provincial address'). These were the poems, says Ferris, that made him famous.

By early 1934, Dylan was thinking more and more about London, and by the end of the year he was living there. But he still continued to visit Blaencwm. He brought his first serious girlfriend, Pamela Hansford Johnson, to the cottage in 1935. She was enchanted:

> It was idyllic: the purest and sweetest and floweriest countryside. Through the cottage garden ran a little stream edged with rushes and primroses ... a wayside bank so thick with violets and primroses that no green was visible.

Dylan and Caitlin were soon at Blaencwm, after their marriage in 1937, 'staying there much more than holidays, much longer than holidays', noticed Rees Davies. By May the following year, they were living in Laugharne, but the pull of the other side was irresistible. There were excursions across the estuary, for long walks with Glyn Jones, to weddings in Llansteffan and meetings with various writers, including Keidrych Rhys, in Llanybri. Dylan's visits became still more frequent when his parents moved to Blaencwm in 1941, after the bombing of Swansea. Florence was now back in the Williams heartland, with eleven cousins and their families living on farms around her, as well as a good handful of in-laws. Fernhill and Pentrewyman had new occupants, but since both were Florence's cousins, the fields and tracks of Dylan's childhood were still open to him: 'my father obviously felt at home in this part of rural Wales', recalled his daughter, Aeronwy.

Not surprisingly, being at Blaencwm provided the opportunity to think once more about his peninsula upbringing. In August 1944 at the cottage, he finished 'Poem in October', celebrating his thirtieth year to heaven. He writes of the blue, apple-filled days of childhood, and remembers the

> *Forgotten mornings when he walked with his mother/Through the parables/ Of sun light/And the legends of the green chapels ...*

Then he recalls the places in which he played when young, along the banks of Fernhill Brook as it falls through Glog-ddu woods on its way to the Tywi:

> *These were the woods the river and sea/Where a boy/In the listening/ Summertime of the dead whispered the truth of his joy/To the trees and the stones and the fish in the tide.*

As it emerges from the trees, the brook meanders down past his auntie Rach's Pentrewyman. Dylan went to the farm 'constantly because his aunt Rachel was there'. She was now in her fifties and had worked on the farm all her life, taking over completely after her brothers had left to marry. 'She was very nice to everyone ... she was a very good type of person ... it was an open house as such ... you could do what you liked ... it was a very easy-going sort of place'. Rachel may have been specially fond of Dylan; he had been due on 25 October, her fortieth birthday, but he was two days late.

There was also a welcome in the fields from Watt Davies, the farm worker at Pentrewyman. Dylan's two friends from Swansea, who came in the summer to stay at a neighbouring smallholding, remembered that Watt

> was a grand fellow with ... any boys that came along, and so we always went up there then to play or to help with the harvest ... Watt was always letting us have a ride on the horse after we did the haymaking at Pentrewyman ... he was a wonderful jumper and we used to take the first hedge and then the next, and down to the stable ... bareback. All the harness was thrown off and we just had the bridle ... Prince. He was a wonderful horse ...

After work in the fields, there was *cawl*, 'brought out of the saucepan where the grease of it hung from the cabbages to your plate', eaten out of wooden bowls with wooden spoons. Dylan would sometimes stay the night, snuggling up in bed with May, the teenage servant girl. She recalls that Dylan was

> always romping about, and down the river ... he was very fond of going round the trees to get the apples ... in the very hot weather ... we'd be all out together. We'd go down to the sea to fish and look for trout ...

She remembers, too, that 'he liked horses ... he was very interested in horses, always'. He came 'every afternoon, and in the morning to do some riding', leading

> *... the spellbound horses walking warm*
> *Out of the whinnying green stable*
> *On to the fields of praise.*

Dylan rode Prince, the carthorse, crossing the land bareback where, honoured among wagons and carts, he *was prince of the apple towns*, in fields where his aunt toiled long and hard: 'The one that was the worker of the ones I knew was Miss Jones – Rachel'. The fields of praise in 'Fern Hill' could only be hers, and were certainly not those of her brother, Jim.

So when I read 'Fern Hill', I seldom think of Fernhill, but of the playground of family fields that lay between it and Blaencwm, and particularly of Pentrewyman. It was here that Dylan spent his heedless summer days with his two Swansea friends, not at lonely Fernhill where his cousin, Idris, nearing thirty, was far too old for boys' play. It was here on Pentrewyman's one hundred praiseworthy acres that the hay was really house-high, not at Fernhill where much of its fifteen acres had been taken over by reeds and, on the high ground above the house, fern and gorse. It was here on Pentrewyman that the sun of 'Fern Hill' really shone, not at Fernhill, which was a 'dark and dismal' place, so shaded by pine trees that it was rarely struck by the sun. It was here at 'easy-going' Pentrewyman that the house was gay, not Fernhill, and it was here at Pentrewyman that May remembers Dylan searching for pheasants – not surprisingly, since its top fields, close to Fernhill, were always under corn, with much of the rest in hay.

'Fern Hill' also tells us how things were when Dylan's two friends were back in Swansea. It's a lyrical poem about childhood but the worm at its core is the poet's painful memory of being alone in a 'childless land', as he puts it in the poem. The family farms had been empty of children of his own age, as were most of the other farms around Fernhill. It had been, he later said, a lonely place. Florence's family was in particular crisis: between 1870 and 1902, her Llangain relatives produced just thirteen children, and only three of these went on to have children of their own. The families then experienced an extended period of zero childbirth, lasting for thirty years.

It's not difficult to imagine what it was like for Dylan to be on his own as a young boy at Fernhill, a ramshackle house of hollow fear, as he put it, a far cry from the lyricism of 'Fern Hill'. The gloomy, musty rooms were lit by oil lamps and candles, and life there, as in all the family farms, was simple: there was an outside earth closet, with water brought into the house from a dipping well two hundred yards away. Washing oneself was done in the kitchen, and cooking was done on an open fire. The house, noted one official survey, suffered from extreme rising dampness and smelt, wrote Dylan in *The Peaches*, 'of rotten wood and damp and animals'.

But now, in the summer of 1945, married with two children, Dylan struggled to live peaceably with his parents in overcrowded Blaencwm. Perhaps the future would have taken a different turn if, at this critical point in his life, he'd been able to find somewhere on the peninsula to live. If only Miss Griffiths in Llansteffan had been willing to rent him a house. Messages were exchanged and phone calls made, but nothing came of it. His aunt Polly died the following year; if only she had left him her Blaencwm cottage. She had spoiled him all his life but she left it to her siblings. Dylan moved away to a squalid flat in London and then to a wet shack on the banks of a river in Oxford, sustained by dreams of a final escape to America, and pulled back time and again to Blaencwm to care for his ailing parents.

Crossing to the other side

'I bow before shit, seeing the family likeness in the old familiar faeces, but I will not manure the genealogical tree'.

Dylan Thomas

By the time they moved into the Boat House in 1949, Caitlin already understood the link between Dylan's writing and the land of his true childhood on the other side. She installed windows in his shed so that he could look out over the estuary at the family farms, whose fields and saltmarsh stretched from the very tip of the peninsula, filling Dylan's view as he looked across the water. Beyond the ridge, the Williamses and their close relatives were still farming close on a thousand acres, and Caitlin recognized what it meant to him: 'He worked a fanatically narrow groove – the groove of direct hereditary descent in the land of his birth, which he never in thought and hardly in body moved out of'.

Living in Laugharne made visits easier, and he delighted in taking his London guests across on the ferry to Black Scar Point: 'They used to get in the boat across the river estuary and picnic on the other side', recalled one of his Laugharne neighbours. Heulwen's husband remembers them walking down to the family farms from Laugharne. The Farmers' Arms was also a popular outing, crossing by ferry and then a footpath across family land: 'He was coming very often to see me … him and his wife, walking always …', said the landlady. The pubs in Llansteffan were also within walking distance, or by cabin cruiser for an easier journey, and an illegal drink on a Sunday. But this wasn't just about picnics and pubs; it was, too, homage and re-rooting after more than three years away in England, where few, if any, poems had emerged. The peninsula was his true *hen fro*, the old place, and the pilgrims' ferry across was his conveyance to a Wales that was very different to the one he found himself living in at Laugharne.

In September 1953, Dylan and Florence travelled to the other side, taking with them Dylan's American agent, John Brinnin, who wrote about the tour in his book, *Dylan Thomas in America*:

> The day was blue, the country still in its midsummer green. Mrs Thomas entertained us with a flow of anecdotes of gentry and yeomanry, called Dylan's attention to a hundred houses or woodlands or chapels, and seemed altogether delighted in her role of cicerone.

They eventually made their way to Fernhill, where Dylan took them around the rooms, saddened to see that the house had changed for the worse – 'a few overstuffed pieces of mail-order furniture', wrote Brinnin sniffily of the interior. Out in the orchard, they picked apples, while Dylan told stories about the Fernhill hangman. Then they set off for Llwyngwyn, the ancient homestead of Dylan's relatives, said Brinnin colourfully:

> At the top of the rise we turned into a mud-filled farmyard surrounded by big and small buildings stark with new whitewash. A cluster of people, from infants to withered crones, suddenly popped out of half a dozen doors to look at us with curiosity, and then to welcome us.

The party was met not by withered crones, but by Florence's first cousin, Thomas Williams, who took them on a tour of the farm, though Brinnin claimed he 'could not understand a word of our guide's English', and complained about getting his feet wet. Heulwen brought them milk, but Brinnin took her for the milkmaid:

> Inside the bare, scrubbed kitchen with its fireplace big enough for five men to stand abreast in, its hanging sides of bacon, great black iron pots and witches' brooms, we were given large cups of warm milk out of a pail brought in by a red-faced milkmaid. We drank it, bravely, and were surprised to find we liked it.

Heulwen with her father, Thomas Williams, and her mother, Mary Ann, outside Llwyngwyn, 1950s. Courtesy of Heulwen Morris

Then they were led into an adjoining room to meet Thomas's sister, Sarah Evans Maesgwyn. The visitors were told, wrote Brinnin, that Sarah 'was ninety-six years old, quite deaf and unable to speak a word of English'. In fact, Sarah was eighty-two and spoke English well enough. If she'd been ninety-six, she would have been just five years younger than her mother.

Sarah invited them to stay for tea but they declined. They drove back down the lane to Blaencwm, to visit Florence's brother, Bob. Once more, Brinnin's memory lets him down and, in his book, he gets the story about Bob hopelessly wrong, including his name.

Afterwards, Florence took them off to Llanybri, where they stopped at Capel Newydd. Her parents and four of her siblings were buried here, alongside a score and more of close peninsula relatives. She paid her respects at one grave after another, 'pointing out to Dylan names he had probably forgotten … Dylan followed after his mother silently, listening to her little stories of the dead'. The dead also spoke for themselves, though Brinnin says nothing about encountering the imposing tomb that sits next to the Williams graves, that of John Bowen Lloyd Jnr, 'who died at Tenafly N.J. USA 2 Dec 1901 aged 24 years'. Did Florence shiver as she walked past the first of her family to die in America?

As they returned at dusk to the Boat House, she was bright and sprightly, laughing with Dylan 'as they recounted old stories the day's visits had recalled'. In these last few words, Brinnin tells us something important about both Dylan's upbringing and the influences on his writing: Florence's stories about the Llansteffan peninsula and her relatives had been part of his life as child, boy and young man.

A month later, on the day before leaving on his final journey to America, Dylan and Florence crossed once more to the other side, to take tea in the manse with the minister of Capel Newydd. It's also the chapel's 200th anniversary in 2014, so perhaps this is where I shall end my centenary promenade, climbing through the branches of his unmanured genealogical tree. A good many, perhaps most, of the graves to the left of the entrance path belong to Florence's family; a central cluster bears the name Williams, though almost as many others have names such as Harries, Phillips, Lloyd, Francis, Lewis, Davies and Evans, all descending from the Williamses of Graig, Lambstone and Pen-y-coed, the Robertses of Maesgwyn and the Harries of Plas Isaf.

I shall search for the most senior Williams grave that's been found here: that of John Williams (1746–1828) and his wife, Jane (1753–1849) of Graig farm, just across the fields from Fernhill. They were one pair of Dylan's great-great-great-grandparents and, at the moment, this is as far back as we can reliably trace. I shall then make for Sarah Maesgwyn's grave, and uncle Bob's, too, and reflect on how Brinnin got their story so wrong. Sarah died just a few months after Dylan, while Brinnin was working on his book; we know now that, as he was writing, he was drinking heavily, and taking pheno-barbitone, benzedrine and various other drugs. It does explain a lot.

My last stop on this walk will be Annie and Jim Jones's simple grave. A plaque reads 'Relatives of Dylan Thomas'. I've always thought the plaque incongruous, given that so many of the other graves are also those of his relatives. I shall pause here, and wonder yet again: would this have been a better place to bury Dylan, next to his grandparents, aunties and cousins, in the earth that meant so much to him? The ground is comfy here …

you can twitch your legs without putting them in the sea.

Come on home, Mr Thomas.
There's strong beer for tea.
And cake.

Notes, references, bibliography and family trees etc. can be viewed at https://sites.google.com/site/dylanthomaspeninsularity/home

Further reading

Thomas, D. N., *Dylan Remembered 1914–34*, vol. 1 (Bridgend: Seren, 2003).

Thomas, D. N., 'Dylan Thomas' Carmarthenshire Roots', *The Carmarthenshire Antiquary*, 39, 2003

Williams, H., *The Book of Llangain: From Farming Community to Residential Village* (Wellington: Halsgrove, 2007).

Acknowledgements

I am greatly indebted to Alun Davies Llansteffan, Susan Deacon and Haydn Williams Llangain, without each of whom little would have been possible. I have also benefitted greatly from the notes of the Llansteffan family historian, Louie Davies. Many thanks, too, to Eiluned Rees, Gillian Cecchini, Felicity Cleaves, Elizabeth Morgan, Elizabeth Richards, Terry Wells at Carmarthen Archives and Mick Felton and Simon Hicks at Seren Books. I acknowledge my continuing debt to the Colin Edwards archive of interviews at the National Library of Wales. Many thanks as well to Phil Edwards, Delyth Jenkins, Deric John, Stevie Krayer, Dora and Glenys Lewis, Heulwen Morris and Robert Williams. I also appreciate the help of Mark Bowen at Carmarthen Library, Richard Jones at the BMA Library and staff at the National Library of Wales. Finally, thanks to Moira and Chris Sanders at La Jolière, Gathemo, where the last phases of work on the essay were completed.

Marlais[1]

M. Wynn Thomas

'I was born in 1913', quipped the Welsh humorist Gwyn Thomas, 'and the next year was even worse'. 1914: there's not much to be said for it really – except that it was the year Dylan Thomas was born.

Or rather Dylan Marlais Thomas, to give him his full baptismal name. But why bother? Why not stick to the shorter form that has echoed round the world? Well, because it is 'Marlais' that opens a window for us onto Dylan Thomas's 'other' world, the world from which his parents had come, the world of the chapels that had ruled Wales for the century preceding his birth. And in giving that other name, 'Dylan', precedence over 'Marlais', his parents had, however unwittingly, performed two fateful acts: they had attempted to consign that chapel world to their past, and they had burdened their boy with a kind of cultural oxymoron, a conflict in terms, because they had saddled him with two incompatible identities, the one 'chapel', and the other ... well what, exactly?

Dylan: as is now common knowledge even to those Thomas devotees who know little of Wales and its past, the name in its full original form – Dylan Ail Ton – means Dylan son of the wave, and it originates in that great medieval collection of legendary tales, the *Mabinogion*.[2] But why was his father –

---

[1] What follows is a shorter, simpler version of my discussion in '"Marlais": Dylan Thomas and the "Tin Bethels"', in M. Wynn Thomas, *In the Shadow of the Pulpit: Literature and Nonconformist Wales* (Cardiff: University of Wales Press, 2010), 227–55.

[2] The story of his birth to Arianrhod, his baptism, and his identification with the sea (modern scholars speculate he may have originated as a Celtic sea-god) is briefly told in the Fourth Branch of *Pedair Cainc y Mabinogi*. See Meic Stephens, ed., *The New Companion to the Literature of Wales* (Cardiff: University of Wales Press, 1998). The first language of both of Thomas's parents was Welsh, but – typical of many of the new upwardly mobile Welsh 'bourgeoisie' of their period – they declined to pass the language on to their son, no doubt viewing it as socially disadvantageous. Yet D. J. Thomas is recorded as having taught Welsh literature in adult education evening classes. In Welsh 'Dylan' is pronounced 'Duh' (as in 'done') and 'lan' as in 'land' or 'Ann', but the parents seem to have connived at an anglicized pronunciation of the name, with some acquaintances subsequently recalling it to have been 'Dillon' and others 'Dullon'. A revealing essay could be written about the sociocultural

because it is he I darkly suspect – attracted to that name? Well, because in 1914 it was a choice that signalled a defiant identification with the 'new culture' that had seized Welsh Wales and begun to sweep the chapel culture aside. In the disapproving eyes of the more conservative chapel faithful, 'Dylan' was a 'pagan' name, a name redolent of the suspect, sensuous, 'Celtic' past of Wales that nineteenth-century chapel culture had effectively disowned. When T. Gwynn Jones won Wales's most prominent prize for poetry – the chair at the National Eisteddfod – in 1902, for his great poem 'Ymadawiad Arthur' (the departure of Arthur), he controversially heralded the arrival of this 'new culture', the product not of the chapels but of the 'new learning' of university intellectuals – of whom Dylan Thomas's father was, after all, one.

But if 'Dylan' was pagan, what then of 'Marlais'? As scholars have noted, this was a 'family' name – the name of a revered great-uncle on his father's side, who was a chapel minister. But he was no ordinary minister, nor was his chapel an ordinary Nonconformist chapel. Gwilym Marles (whence Marlais) was a Unitarian minister – that is, a minister with that suspect denomination that denied the Trinity, and insisted that Christ was not the Son of God but fashioned by Him to be the most perfect of human beings. Scholars have also correctly recorded that Marles became a kind of folk hero in his locality in the middle of the nineteenth century for his heroic stand on behalf of the ordinary farmers of Cardiganshire who were being threatened with eviction by their absentee English Anglican landlords.[3] One such farming family actually fled to the United States to escape persecution, and a generation later produced one of the greatest architects of the twentieth century in Frank Lloyd Wright.[4] But admired social activist though Gwilym Marles became, he remained a highly suspect figure in the eyes of his mainstream rural society. First, because the dominant chapel sects – the Presbyterians (Welsh Calvinistic Methodists), the Independents and the Baptists – refused even to acknowledge that the Unitarians constituted a truly Christian church; and second, because even among his fellow Unitarians Gwilym Marles was regarded as a man whose opinions bordered on heresy.

implications of issues such as these relating to the name. A further complication is that 'Marlais' (Már-laee-ss) is actually far more difficult for an English tongue to pronounce than Marles (pronounced Már-less), and yet the poet's anti-Welsh parents chose the former.

[3] For a concise summary of Marles's life and career, see the entry on William Thomas (Gwilym Marles) in *Welsh Biography Online* (National Library of Wales website). His role in the rebellion against landlords is discussed in Nansi Martin, *Gwilym Marles* (Llandysul: Gomer, 1973). Also in Aubrey Martin, *Hanes Llwynrhydowen* (Llandysul: Gomer, 1977).

[4] See D. Elwyn Davies, *'They Thought for Themselves': A Brief Look at the History of Unitarianism in Wales and the Tradition of Liberal Religion* (Llandysul: Gomer, 1982); D. Elwyn Davies, *Cewri'r Ffydd: Bywgraffiadur y Mudiad Undodaidd yng Nghymru* (Llandysul; Gomer, 1999); John Gwili Jenkins, *Hanfod Duw a Pherson Crist* (Liverpool: Hughes Evans a'i Feibion, 1931).

But more of that later. First, let's clarify Dylan Thomas's attitude towards the chapel culture whose dark, baleful presence seemed to him, from childhood onwards, to cast a shadow over his Wales. He actually marked his 'coming of age' as a precocious young writer in 1934 by going on a pilgrimage to Aberystwyth to meet Caradoc Evans, who had become the bête noir of the chapels after he'd portrayed them in a notorious short story collection he sarcastically entitled *My People* (1915) as crude, grasping, hypocritical and lecherous Neanderthals. Caradoc's chapel people subscribed with gusto to the popular saying that your Welsh Nonconformist was one who prayed to God on Sunday and preyed on his neighbours every other day of the week. And they lived in a green and peasant land. Having lapped up this satire, the young Thomas wasn't disappointed in Caradoc himself. 'He's a great fellow', he wrote. 'We made a tour of the pubs in the evening, drinking to the eternal damnation of the Almighty & the soon-to be hoped for destruction of the tin Bethels'.[5]

There are echoes in that remark of D. J. Thomas, the poet's father. A confirmed agnostic, he was still wont, as yet another Swansea day turned wet, to exclaim disgustedly 'it's raining again, damn Him'. And his father's distinctive brand of scepticism no doubt came to seem particularly inviting to a young Dylan Thomas who had been subjected by his mother, the daughter of a Congregationalist deacon, to a strong dose of chapel religion administered by her brother-in-law, who was a local minister. He and his nephew didn't get on well, and it's never wise to alienate anyone who might one day become a gifted writer. In due course, Dylan got his revenge by depicting his uncle as the comically pompous Reverend Bevan in 'The Fight': '"Bless our repast this evening", he said, as though he didn't like food at all. But once "Amen" was over, he went at the cold meat like a dog'.[6]

But his revenge on the chapels was much more complete than that. In 'The Peaches', another of the stories about his boyhood and youth that were published under the mockingly modish title *Portrait of the Artist as a Young Dog*, he had great fun at the expense of preachers. There Marlais (that name again), the young towny from anglicized, provincial Swansea, is initiated into the fascinating but bizarre ways of country life in Welsh-speaking, chapel-dominated west Wales. His instructor is his much older cousin, Gwilym, who loves to practise for the ministry in a rickety old barn he's converted into a chapel. Having seated Marlais on a bale of hay, he launches into a peroration high on Welsh *hwyl*, his voice rising and falling mesmerically, until the grand climax is reached: '"Thou canst see and spy and watch us all the time, in the little black corners, in the big cowboys' prairies, under the blankets when we're snoring fast, in the terrible shadows; pitch black; pitch black; Thou canst see everything we do, in the night and day, in the day and the night, everything, everything. Thou canst see all the time. O God, mun, you're like a bloody cat"'.

[5] Paul Ferris, ed., *Dylan Thomas: The Collected Letters* (London: Dent, 1985), 172.
[6] Leslie Norris, ed., *Dylan Thomas: The Collected Stories* (London: Dent, 1983), 160.

In the silence that follows 'the one duck quacked outside', and then: '"Now I take a collection", Gwilym said'.[7]

And Thomas's revenge even took the form of a complete makeover of the rural region of Carmarthenshire and Cardiganshire that was one of the most formidable strongholds of Welsh Nonconformity. In the 'Jarvis Hill' stories he wrote during the thirties, he viewed this area through the magic glass of surrealism, transforming it into a region charged with rampant sexual energies and instinct with ancient, mysterious, pagan forces. This is no place for a God-fearing minister to venture abroad. But venture the old preacher Mr Davies does in 'The Enemies', only to end up in disturbingly strange company. He stumbles upon Mr Owen and his wife, who is a white witch. Seated in their cottage, Mr Davies feels threateningly surrounded by 'the brown body of the earth, the green skin of the grass, and the breasts of the Jarvis hills ... there was creation sweating out of the pores of the trees and the grains of sand on far-away seashores would be multiplying as the sea tolled over them'.[8] In desperation, the minister attempts to fortify himself by saying grace, only for the Owens to accompany him with a sinister *sotto voce* pagan invocation of their own. And, predators that they are, they quickly sense the poor preacher's acute discomfiture: '"He is frightened of the dark," thought Mrs Owen, "the lovely dark." With a smile, Mr Owen thought, "He is frightened of the worm in the earth, of the copulation in the tree, of the living grease in the soil".'[9]

More interesting, though, than Thomas's bold and brash assault on the 'tin Bethels' was his subtle attempt to usurp the traditional role and authority of the preachers as supreme Welsh wizards of the word. The great stars of the Welsh pulpit had, thanks to their eloquence, held formidable sway over the popular mind for several generations before Dylan Thomas's time. Stories were circulated about their preaching prowess and colourful personalities just as 'celeb' stories are endlessly recycled today. Several had their own gimmicks. Matthews Ewenni was famed for 'tearing up a Bible during the sermon, bending backwards over the edge of the pulpit or pulling his coat tails over his head like a hood'.[10] John Elias electrified his congregation by conjuring up the spectacle of an auction of souls. His listeners heard the hoarse whisper of the Devil: 'Strike them down to me, I am ready to take them'. But as the gavel was about to drop, it was dramatically stayed by a quiet interjection: 'I will take them. I will take them as they are, to wash them in My own blood'.[11] No wonder Lloyd George entertained his fellow demagogue of genius, Adolf

---

[7] *Collected Stories*, 128.

[8] *Collected Stories*, 19.

[9] *Collected Stories*, 20.

[10] R. Tudur Jones, *Faith and the Crisis of a Nation: Wales 1890-1914*, trans. Sylvia Prys Jones (Cardiff: University of Wales Press, 2004), 119.

[11] Owen Jones, *Some of the Great Preachers of Wales* (Passmore and Alabaster, 1885), 270.

Hitler, with a string of anecdotes about the charismatic performers of the nineteenth-century Welsh pulpit.

It was these preachers' hold over the Welsh imagination, thanks to their incomparable command and exercise of language, that the young Dylan Thomas sought to break. There's a simple example of his strategy in 'The Peaches', where Thomas follows his comic and subversive parody of Gwilym's preaching skills with an account of budding awareness, as a boy, of his own precocious alternative powers as a secular story-teller: 'There, playing Indians in the evening, I was aware of me myself in the exact middle of a living story, and my body was my adventure and my name'.[12] Here, Thomas's assertion of his exceptional gifts is marginal to the main action, but in one of his strongest poems, 'After the Funeral: In Memory of Ann Jones', the struggle for supremacy between preacher and writer is placed uncompromisingly centre-stage. Here Thomas preens himself on being 'Ann's bard on a raised hearth', a poet whose words are so potent that he is able 'to call all/The seas to service'.[13] His religious opponents, by contrast, are mocked for the 'mule praises, brays' that turn Ann's chapel funeral into a cacophony of pious platitudes. And the dead woman herself is pityingly figured as one who had her whole life crippled by the inhibitions bred by the chapel in her very bones. Imagining Ann as sexually repressed, Thomas, her 'bard', regrets he is able to liberate her only posthumously by animating the dead fox that is the pride of the parlour in which she is decorously laid out, so that 'its stuffed lung ... twitch and cry Love/And the strutting fern lay seeds on the black sill'. Into that last, triumphant, phallic and climactic image is packed all of Dylan Thomas's confidence in his own irresistible, dionysiac way with words. Just as the great sculptor Rodin regarded his chisel as a kind of phallus, so the priapic young Thomas frankly boasted of his pencil as being an artist's best tool.

One of the key strategies in his struggles with the preachers for control of the word, and hence for control over the human imagination, was his bending of biblical language and story to his own subversive purposes. A striking example is the early story 'The Tree', a fantastical modern fairy tale which twists the New Testament story into a grotesque shape.[14] It features a gardener who, rather like Thomas himself, 'loves the bible' as a treasure-trove of fabulous tales. 'But the death of Christ on a tree he loved most'. For the gardener, the crucifixion figuratively encapsulates the whole life cycle of the natural universe, from birth to death. A spellbinding storyteller, he captivates a little boy with tales about how life began with a tree and how Christ ended his life nailed to it. Enchanted, the boy is moved to re-enact the Christian story by tying up an 'idiot' who wanders into the gardener's magic garden and nailing him to the tree that the child is convinced is the tree with which

[12] *Collected Stories*, 132.
[13] Walford Davies and Ralph Maud (eds), *Dylan Thomas: Collected Poems, 1934-53* (London: Dent, 1988), 73.
[14] *Collected Stories*, 5–11.

all life originated in the Garden of Eden. 'The Tree' is thus a commentary on the primal, visceral appeal of biblical stories and their power to capture and corrupt the human imagination once what is figurative in them is read as literal truth. Thomas was himself clearly enchanted all his life by the language, image, rhythm and narrative of the Bible, but rather than ending up in thrall to their primitive magic, as he believed the chapel faithful to be, he treated them as invaluable resources for his poetry. Like the gardener in his story, he 'loved the bible' because it provided him with a wonderful symbolic vocabulary for celebrating what Walt Whitman – one of his heroes – called 'the procreant urge of the world'.

* * * *

Thomas's hostility to the 'Calvinistic capels', as he called them, is therefore far too well documented ever to be doubted. And yet … One of the closest of his friends in the Swansea of his youth was Bert Trick, and Trick insisted, late in his life, that the young Thomas 'was very religious. He felt there was a supreme being with which you could get in touch direct'. Nor was this a casual remark, because Trick proceeded to consolidate and contextualize it very interestingly:

> On the one hand, he was in revolt against his father's agnosticism. On the other hand, he was in revolt against the narrow Puritan conventions of his mother's Congregational background, and it was from these tensions that the personality of Dylan Thomas developed.[15]

So what kind of religious faith was that of Thomas? Well, here again, Trick was quite specific:

> He believed in the freedom of man to be man, that he shouldn't be oppressed by his fellows, and that every man had the stamp of divinity in him, and anything that prevented that divinity having full play was an evil thing.[16]

A hatred of oppression, rooted in the belief that every man bears the stamp of divinity: Thomas's core beliefs, as formulated by Trick, bring us face to face once more with his uncle, the Gwilym Marles whose resistance to the 'alien' landlord oppression of Welsh tenant farmers was rooted in his Unitarian conviction that in Christ one saw not the Son of God but the perfection of the divine potential inherent in every human being.

* * *

And so, we now need to return to Gwilym Marles and get to know him a little better. In one of his late poems, Thomas adopted the persona of a no-good boyo recalling the days 'when I was a windy boy and a bit/And the black spit

---

15 David N. Thomas, ed., *Dylan Remembered*, vol. I (1914–34) (Bridgend: Seren, 2003), 166.

16 *Dylan Remembered*, 164.

of the chapel fold'.[17] Maybe he was recalling his great-uncle Gwilym's stormily
controversial career. As a Unitarian, he was reviled and rejected by the chapel
faithful, who referred to the region of Wales to which the Unitarians were
largely confined as the 'black spot' (possibly recalled in 'the black spit') on the
otherwise fair, unblemished face of Welsh Nonconformity. Their supposed 'sin'
was to have divinized the sinfully human. 'Our faith', the Unitarian newspaper
covering the Swansea area defiantly explained at the very time Dylan Thomas
was writing his poems at Cwmdonkin Drive, 'asserts the natural Divinity of
human nature fresh from the hands of God, which always when true to itself is
Godlike ... so we feel *sure* of the universal Fatherhood of God, and we know of
the Divine Unity. One God and Father of all mankind. That implies the natural
and universal Brotherhood of the whole human race'.[18] This brings out clearly
the central Unitarian tenet that human nature was, in its Christ-like essence,
the very image of the Divine. This was the anthropocentric humanistic creed
to which orthodox churches and denominations of the Christian mainstream
were so fiercely opposed. They insisted on the utter uniqueness of Christ, in
being both human and divine: it was in Christ alone that God had manifested
Himself to fallen man, and it was through the salvific power of Christ alone
that humankind could be redeemed from sin.

The radical social vision of the young Dylan Thomas was, however, rooted
in much the same humanistic conviction as that expressed by the Swansea
Unitarians, and it was likewise powered by liberationist aspirations. In a letter
to Pamela Hansford Johnson he calls for 'Revolution. There is no need to be a
revolution of blood', and he prays 'that all in us of godliness and strength, of
happiness and genius, shall be allowed to exult in the sun'. '*Everything* is wrong
that forbids the freedom of the individual', he adds; 'the churches are wrong,
because they standardise our gods, because they label our morals, because they
laud the death of a vanished Christ, and fear the crying of the new Christ in the
wilderness'.[19] Elsewhere he makes it clear that by releasing language itself from
the shackles of cliché and convention he proposes to awaken the imagination
from its torpor and thus to release the human energies of mind and body that
can refashion the world.

But his great-uncle wasn't only, as a Unitarian, a black sheep of the Welsh
chapel flock. Gwilym Marles came also to be regarded by the Unitarians
themselves as a black sheep of their own fold. Even among rebels, he came to
be viewed as a rebel. Why? Because he gradually embraced a new, progressive
form of Unitarianism that the mainstream faithful regarded as heretical. This
reformed Unitarianism derived from the teachings of the Englishman James
Martineau, but assumed its most influential form in the United States through
the preaching and writing of Theodore Parker, a figure who greatly impressed
Gwilym Marles.

[17]   *Collected Poems*, 148.
[18]   *Monthly Calendar* 30 (April, 1935), 52; *Monthly Calendar* 29 (March 1935), 38.
[19]   *Collected Letters*, 55.

Parker took the Unitarian belief in the divinity of human powers to new extremes by emphasizing that, when fully developed and properly exercised, they offered a more reliable guide to divine truth than even the Scriptures themselves. He further argued that the divine was not only potential within the human individual but also indwelling in the whole natural cosmos. His teaching chimed with the emergent ideas of Ralph Waldo Emerson, shortly to become the father of the American Transcendentalist movement of the mid-nineteenth century that was to leave a permanent mark on modern American consciousness. And in an important address printed in the first issue of Emerson's *Dial*, the organ of the new movement, Parker captured the core of his vision:

> Nature ever grows, and changes, and becomes something new, as God's all-pervading energy flows into it without ceasing. Hence in nature, there is constant change but no ultimate death. The quantity of life is never diminished. The leaves fall but they furnish for new leaves yet to appear, whose swelling germs crowd off the old foliage ... Since God is essentially and vitally present in each atom of space, there can be no such thing as sheer and absolute extinction of being.[20]

The argument is, then, that both the natural and the human worlds are dynamically shaped by a restlessly creative divine energy. The world and humankind are no longer viewed, as in orthodox Christian doctrine, as Fallen and sinful. The whole cosmos is charged with endlessly self-renewing energy, so nothing ever really dies but is simply changed into a different form of life. For anyone who is familiar with Dylan Thomas's work, this great hymn to 'process' – 'the force that through the green fuse drives the flower' – is surely reminiscent of one of his most rhetorically affirmative poems, 'And Death shall have no Dominion'.

> Though they be mad and dead as nails,
> Heads of the characters hammer through daisies;
> Break in the sun till the sun breaks down,
> And death shall have no dominion.[21]

Parker's highly romanticized form of Unitarianism captivated the mind of a Gwilym Marles who was a dedicated nature worshipper, a devoted lover of Romantic poetry both in English and in German, and himself a poet of somewhat modest means and conventional tastes. And in his anger at the way in which divine energies were repressed by humankind, ruthlessly policed by the established social and political order, and destructively disfigured through human mistreatment of the natural world, Marles anticipated the worldview of his great-nephew more than half a century later. Indeed, Dylan Thomas's 'This bread I break' is a sermon on the crucifixion of Christ that is perpetually

[20] *The Dial* I (1840–4) (New York: Russell and Russell, 1961), 59.
[21] *Collected Poems*, 56.

re-enacted through human exploitation of natural resources. In the poem, Thomas's Christ continually cries out against the torture of nature, which He views as a grotesque parody of Holy Communion. He protests that the oat is his very body, and the grape contains his very blood, so that even the process of baking bread and of making wine become expressive of mankind's cannibalistic exploitation of the living natural universe:

> This flesh you break, this blood you let
> Make desolation in the vein,
> Were oat and grape
> Born of the sensual root and sap;
> My wine you drink, my bread you snap.[22]

This apocalyptic sense of the apparent limitlessness of human destructiveness naturally appealed particularly strongly to Thomas during the ominous prewar decade, as Europe inexorably prepared for war. And it was in this context that his imagination was wont to circle obsessively around the two key, twinned, events of the Nativity and the Crucifixion, interpreted in terms reminiscent of the teachings of Marles and his mentor Parker. An early story, 'Gaspar, Melchior, and Balthasaar', eerily anticipates the horrors of aerial warfare shortly to be unforgettably instanced by the Fascist air raid on Guernica. In the midst of the carnage of the aftermath of the bombing of civilians, a little baby is born to a dead woman, turning the narrator into one of the latter-day Three Kings, as 'bitter as myrrh, my blood streamed ... on to the emerging head'.[23]

As for the Crucifixion of Christ, that could take the form of all manner of violent persecutions of the unconventional. It was during that trip to Aberystwyth to visit Caradoc Evans that Dylan Thomas heard the extraordinary story of William Price, the self-styled Unitarian minister and visionary eccentric freethinker who claimed 'druidic' powers and pioneered the modern practice of cremation. In his old age, Price, who vigorously promoted the pleasures of the body, publicly burned at Pontypridd the body of a young son he'd blasphemously named 'Iesu Grist' (Jesus Christ), scandalously born to him of a mother decades younger than himself. Out of this striking historical episode Thomas created the gothic story of 'The Burning Baby', in which he adopts the point of view of the outraged local community that accused Price of incest and 'monstered' him by accusing him of child-sacrifice.[24]

In the radical Unitarian tradition of his great-uncle, Thomas also liked to figure the Nativity as the birth of divine potential in the human imagination. In the workings of his own awakened poetic imagination, he felt he heard 'the crying of the new Christ in the wilderness'. He expressed this vision most potently in a letter he wrote to the *Swansea and West Wales Guardian* following a local protest at a rally held in the town by Oswald Mosley's blackshirt thugs:

---

[22]   *Collected Poems*, 37.
[23]   *Collected Stories*, 21.
[24]   Walford Davies, ed., *Dylan Thomas: Early Prose Writings* (London: Dent, 1971), 23.

The divinity of man is not to be trifled with … the manna of God is not the lukewarm soup and starch of the chapels, but the redhot grains of love and life distributed equally and impartially among us all, and … at our roots of being lies not the greed for property or money, but the desire, large as a universe, to express ourselves freely and to the utmost limits of our individual capabilities.[25]

And like Gwilym Marles, he passionately believed the poet to be specially gifted with the power to broadcast 'the redhot grains of love and life', by virtue of poetry's unique ability to restore the language of the everyday to vigorous imaginative life.

Some sense of this core conviction is captured in 'I Dream'd my Genesis', a poem tracking and enacting the difficult emergence of authentic utterance out of the stifling grip of verbal habit and deadening convention. It is figured as a two-stage process, the original 'nativity' being followed by a 'death' that is eventually conquered through the resurrection of this second Adam into fullness of life at last:

I dreamed my genesis in sweat of death, fallen
Twice in the feeding sea, grown
Stale of Adam's brine until, vision
Of new man strength, I seek the sun.[26]

Thomas was a worshipper of language's 'divine', liberating powers. To discover these powers and release them from their captivity to cliché was his *raison d'être* as a poet. In this respect, at least, his uncle Gwilym Marles would have been proud of him. When the young, word-intoxicated Thomas tells Pamela Hansford Johnson that 'God moves in a long "o"', he is not being altogether facetious after all.[27] His ecstatic psalms to the resources of language are in themselves worshipful examples of what they so intoxicatingly praise, celebrate and glorify:

such sand-storms and ice-blasts of words, such slashing of humbug, and humbug too, such staggering peace, such enormous laughter, such and so many blinding bright lights breaking across the just-awakening wits and splashing all over the pages in a million bits and pieces all of which were words, words, words, and each of which was alive forever in its own delight and glory and oddity and light.[28]

Nevertheless, magnificent magnificat though this be, Thomas was no Romantic, and the naïve belief of an earlier age in language's power to afford the poet direct, unmediated access to spiritual realities could not be his. The child of

---

[25] *Collected Letters*, 143.
[26] *Collected Poems*, 26.
[27] *Collected Letters*, 73.
[28] *Early Prose Works*, 156.

Modernism, he was already being edged, by the currents of thinking of his own time, in the direction of Postmodernism's sceptical view of language as holding the mind captive to its own closed, self-referential system of inherited 'meanings'. He knew that

> from the first declension of the flesh
> I learnt man's tongue, to twist the shapes of thoughts
> Into the stony idiom of the brain,
> To shade and knit anew the patch of words
> Left by the dead who, in their moonless acre,
> Need no word's warmth.[29]

In other words, he accepted there were limits to the extent to which he could 'redeem' language, given it had been definitively shaped by a past that continued to inhere inalterably within it.

But he nevertheless revelled in such modifications to language as he, a gifted poet, *could* effect. And in 'Fern Hill', that seminal expression, in a new nuclear age, of (equivocal) yearning for a more innocent time, which is probably still his best-loved poem, he associated the power of words to summon new life into being with his childhood experience of creating the world anew every day.

> And then to awake, and the farm, like a wanderer white
> With the dew, come back, the cock on his shoulder: it was all
>   Shining, it was Adam and maiden,
>   The sky gathered again
>   And the sun grew round that very day.
> So it must have been after the birth of the simple light
> In the first, spinning place, the spellbound horses walking warm
>   Out of the whinnying green stable
>   On to the fields of praise.[30]

Gwilym Marles might well have warmed to that. But, of course, he would certainly not have warmed to other of his great-nephew's poems that made it abundantly clear how sexuality and the processes of reproduction lay at the very root of human and natural creativity. Kin Dylan Thomas and Gwilym Marles may have been, but close kin they certainly weren't, and of course for all the intriguing resemblances between the poet's vision and the 'renegade' brand of Unitarianism adopted by his great-uncle, Dylan Thomas was evidently no twentieth-century Unitarian.

But, as Bert Trick so diligently insisted, 'religious' he may indeed genuinely have been after a fashion as 'renegade' as that of Gwilym Marles had been in his time. The Prefatory Note he attached to his *Collected Poems* reads as follows:

[29] *Collected Poems*, 22.
[30] *Collected Poems*, 134–5.

I read somewhere of a shepherd who, when asked why he made, from within fairy rings, ritual observances to the moon to protect his flocks, replied: 'I'd be a damn' fool if I didn't!' These poems, with all their crudities, doubts, and confusions, are written for the love of Man and in praise of God, and I'd be a damn' fool if they weren't.

The flippancy of tone, and provocative hint that religion may be no more than superstition, will no doubt persuade some to doubt the sincerity of this dedication. Revealing, though, is the careful balancing of the 'praise of God' with 'the love of Man' – a paralleling that Unitarians would have approved of.

It is a carefully judged formulation that is an almost exact repeat of what Thomas wrote, late in life, about his motivating convictions as poet, when answering the questions of an obscure Texas graduate student. 'The joy and function of poetry', he there wrote, 'is the celebration of man, which is also the celebration of God'.[31] That credo even more closely resembles the kind of Unitarian beliefs that his great-uncle had espoused. And Thomas had absolutely no occasion to grandstand and mislead on this private occasion. Which leads one back to the conclusion that Dylan Marlais Thomas may, after all, have been related to Gwilym Marles through intriguing affinities of the imagination as well as by ties of blood.

---

[31] *Early Prose Works*, 160.

'Borrowed Plumes' –
Requiem for a Plagiarist

Jeff Towns

Immature poets imitate: mature poets steal.

T. S. Eliot[1]

Much has been written about Dylan Thomas's childhood; his life was tragically short – he lived for just thirty-nine years, forcing his many biographers to look very closely at each and every precious year in order to fill their hefty volumes. Critics too, especially those who came at exegesis from a psychoanalytical position, have examined the poet's boyhood to help them in their attempts to explain his poems. For Dylan Thomas himself, his childhood memories were an inspiration for many of his greatest poems and a constant source of material for his prose, and he would draw on his own early 'memories of childhood' in six of the short stories that make up the collection *Portrait of the Artist as a Young Dog* (1940). One of the best-known is 'The Fight', Dylan's account of his first meeting with Daniel Jones, who became his life-long friend, his sometime collaborator, the musician who provided the music for Dylan's radio play *Under Milk Wood*, and later his editor. But it is also the story in which Dylan makes his only reference to his youthful predilection for what his most recent biographer, Andrew Lycett, refers to as 'discreet plagiarism'.

In the story Dylan gives us a detailed description of his 'bedroom by the boiler' and describes how:

> A poem I had printed in the 'Wales Day by Day' column of the *Western Mail* was pasted on the mirror to make me blush, but the shame of the poem had died. Across the poem I had written with a stolen quill and in flourishes: 'Homer Nods'. I was always waiting for the opportunity to bring someone into my bedroom – 'Come into my den; excuse the untidiness; take a chair. No! not that one it's broken' – and force him to see the poem accidentally. 'I put it there to make me blush'. But nobody ever came in except my mother.

---

[1]   T. S. Eliot, *The Sacred Wood*, (London: Methuen, 1920).

His mother Florence would later tell her Swansea friend Ethel Ross that she and D. J. (Dylan's father) were so proud of their son's appearance in 'Wales Day by Day' that they gave Dylan ten shillings, so that they could treasure forever this first remunerative postal order, sent by the paper as payment for the poem. But Dylan's embarrassment was caused by something other than the mawkish sentimentality of the poem. His comments in 'The Fight' are his only nod to an incident which only came to light some forty-five years later, and then only by chance and one man's powers of observation and recall.

In 1971, the same Daniel Jones that Dylan fought with in 'The Fight' edited and introduced a new edition of Dylan's poetry. Up until that point readers were content with the 1952 Dent *Collected Poems 1934–1952*, Dylan's own edition of his poems. Daniel Jones's new edition *The Poems* included extra poems arranged chronologically. The second 'Appendix' to the book comprises a group of twenty-six 'Early Poems' gathered from various sources including Dylan's early notebooks and the pages of the *Swansea Grammar School Magazine*. The section starts with a poem, 'His Requiem'. This is Daniel Jones's note to 'His Requiem':

> (i) 1926 – early 1927. Thomas, born on 27th October 1914 wrote this poem when he was twelve or just over twelve years of age. It was published in the *Western Mail*, 14th January 1927. This was the poem that Dylan was referring to in *The Fight*, the poem he 'had printed in the 'Wales Day by Day' column of the *Western Mail* ... pasted on the mirror to make me blush'.

The real history of this poem came out in a curious fashion. A diligent and observant reader of the *Sunday Telegraph* saw the poem reproduced in that paper's review of Jones's edition in 1971 and recognized it as a poem he had read some four years earlier in *The Boy's Own Paper*, a British paper aimed at younger readers. The author of that poem, however, was given as a Miss Lillian Gard. Although Dylan had made four or five very small changes in his version, his poem is otherwise identical. Further investigation proved that Miss Gard was a regular contributor of poems and stories to children's books and magazines, and she was indeed the true author of the poem.

The newspaper article that revealed the details of this literary theft (see p. 42) ends with a bold statement, with Jones deciding to replace 'His Requiem' with another early poem; the publishers, meanwhile, immediately inserted an explanatory printed slip acknowledging Miss Gard's authorship into all remaining copies and in the subsequent reprints the plagiarized poem was finally excised.

This discovery back in 1971 of a plagiarized poem was down to one man's remarkable observation and memory, but just recently it happened again, and this time the discovery was due to a bizarre coincidence and the new and mighty powers of Google. This has led to other discoveries that make the *Sunday Telegraph*'s bold assertion that 'Daniel Jones ... discounts the possibility of other borrowings' seem a little wide of the mark. It would appear that, during his early teens, Dylan Thomas was a serial plagiarist.

HIS REQUIEM.

Nobody cared a bit, folks said,
When the wicked old man at the gate lay
    dead.

He had no kith, and he had no kin,
And nobody cared his love to win:
Nobody thought of him kindly, none,
For many a cruel thing he'd done;
And many a bitter and angry word
From those thin lips the neighbours heard.
He had lived alone, he had died alone,
With never a friend he could call his own,
Or so folks thought;
And the coffin grim,
With never a mourner mourning him,
Passed through the gate of his garden
    ground.

But hush! a requiem's softened sound
Stole over the silence,
And someone said:
" 'Tis the little brown linnet the old man
    fed."

Swansea.   D. M. THOMAS.

'His Requiem' in the *Western Mail*, 14th January 1927

DYLAN'S POEM WAS NOT HIS

By RICHARD BENNETT

DYLAN THOMAS, the Welsh poet, began his literary career with a poem which was another person's work, it was disclosed last week.

"His Requiem" until now thought to be his first published work, is to be removed from the next edition of a new volume, "Dylan Thomas: The Poems."

It was published under Thomas's name in the *Western Mail* on January 14, 1927, when the embryo poet was 12. It is included among his contributions to periodicals in J. Alexander Rolph's "Dylan Thomas: A Biography."

The long memory of a reader, Mr. Richard Parker, of Torridon Road, Catford, London, started off inquiries by *The Sunday Telegraph* which have shown that the poem was first published in November, 1923, in the *Boys' Own Paper*, under the name of the actual writer, Miss Lillian Gard.

"His Requiem" was reproduced in our review last week of "Dylan Thomas: the Poems" and Mr. Parker remembered seeing it in the *Boy's Own Paper*.

FOUR SMALL CHANGES

Thomas had apparently made four small verbal changes, but the poem he claimed as his own was otherwise identical. Its opening lines read:

Nobody cared a bit, folks said
When the wicked old man at the
*   gate lay dead*

Lillian Gard contributed a number of poems to the magazine in the 1920s. The Lutterworth Press, which published the *Boys' Own Paper* bought the sole rights in everything that appeared in it.

It is understood that Lutterworths is unlikely to take action unless it is proved that Thomas raided other treasures from the journal. There is no guarantee that this one poem was the sole source of his youthful inspiration.

Mr. Daniel Jones, who edited "Dylan Thomas: The Poems," discounts the possibility of other borrowings but he is to replace "His Requiem" in the next edition with another early poem—presumably of cast-iron authenticity.

Dylan Thomas's agent and estate trustee, David Higham, and his publishers, J. M. Dent, have been informed.

The *Sunday Telegraph*'s exposure of Dylan's chicanery

Dylan's first official biographer, Constantine Fitzgibbon, gave us some measure of forewarning of this particular trait in his *Life of Dylan Thomas* (Dent, 1965). Fitzgibbon chooses to include this long episode within parenthesis, but he gives us a detailed account, as 'told' to him by E. F. McInerny, another Swansea Grammar School boy who wrote poems and edited the school magazine. McInerny explained to the biographer that Dylan submitted a poem to him while he was editor and that he recognized it as being from *Arthur Mee's Children's Encyclopædia*, a ten-volume shelf–filler ubiquitous in aspiring middle-class households. The poem, simple and short, was called 'Sometimes' and was written by Thomas S. Jones.

> Across the fields of yesterday
> He sometimes comes to me,
> A little lad just back from play –
> The lad I used to be.
>
> And yet he smiles so wistfully
> Once he has crept within,
> I wonder if he hopes to see
> The man I might have been.

Despite his Welsh-sounding name, Jones was an American poet born at Boonville, New York, on 6 November 1882 (he died in 1932). Jones graduated from Cornell University in 1904 and became a journalist on the *New York Times* from 1904 to 1907. He went on to be the associate editor of *The Pathfinder*. He published several volumes of poetry and the titles give us some indication of his metier: *Path of Dream*, 1904; *From Quiet Valley*, 1907; *Interlude*, 1908; *Ave Atque Vale* (In Memoriam Arthur Upson), 1909; *The Voice in the Silence* (1911). His lifetime's work earned him this contemporary testimonial: 'Mr Jones was a poet of rare delicacy and fineness whose work has gathered to itself a discriminating group of readers'. Dylan Thomas was obviously a proud member of that 'discriminating group'. McInerny considered it his duty as editor to report this attempted deception to the master in overall charge of the school magazine, and the Head of the English department who was also the perpetrator's father, D. J. Thomas.

Although he reported his findings, McInerny's own final judgement was that it was a not a case of literary theft but more an incident of 'total unconscious recall' on Dylan's part. However, this appears to be a very lenient judgement if one considers the trouble and care which Dylan showed in his selection of this poem. It is just the kind of poem that would lie easily on the pages of the *Swansea Grammar School Magazine* and was also consciously dug out from a reasonably good hiding place, buried deep within ten fat volumes. Moreover Thomas Jones was not widely read in the UK, and Arthur Mee's encyclopedia was a didactic work not known for poetry – this all seems to me very similar to young Thomas's usual *modus operandi*.

Subsequent biographers provide more details: Paul Ferris,[2] Dylan's second biographer, gives us chapter and verse. Dylan found the poem in Volume 8 of the *Encyclopædia*, on 'page 5669, where it is one of the "Thousand Poems of All Times and All Countries".' Ferris adds more detail; on being told of the discovery by McInerny, D. J. Thomas exclaimed: 'After this, everything he writes is suspect'.

In his revised 'New Edition' Ferris offers even more details: it was the magazine's co-editor, H. M. V. Thomas, who found the original printing, and McInerny had changed his original charitable 'unconscious recall' opinion when he learned of the *Western Mail* incident and concluded that it was Dylan, 'in an anti-social, devil-may-care mood, like a secret agent fingering a false and superfluous moustache'.

Andrew Lycett[3] in his, the most recent, life of Thomas, introduces the incident lightly: '... Dylan was not above discreet plagiarisation'. But he too finds it hard to explain:

> Why did a bright boy, who clearly knew how to write verse, resort to such deceit? The answer is that this was his way of dealing with the various pressures on him ... It showed Dylan's need to demonstrate his poetic ability to his parents partly to his indulgent mother ... but rather more to his remote father whose laissez-faire attitude to learning in the home belied his firm ambition for his son.

James A. Davies, in his *Reference Companion to Dylan Thomas* (1998), writes of Dylan's other less than attractive childhood traits – petty theft, outrageous foul mouth, wild behaviour – but then he adds: 'Even more serious and puzzling were two clear instances of plagiarism'. Davies then writes of both 'His Requiem' and 'Sometimes', and of the latter he adds: 'When D. J. was informed, he was furious'. He then adds his own comment: 'Oddly, both poems were trifles: Thomas's own light verse of the time is more vigorous and interesting'.

My involvement in this complicated tale began in 2013 when I acquired yet another large collection of Dylan Thomas materials: signed books, photographs, letters and ephemera. Among the collection was a file of letters and photocopies concerned with a group of Dylan Thomas's juvenile poems, in particular a clutch of poems that Dylan's mother found when clearing out a cupboard in the family cottage Blaen Cwm after Dylan's death. She was being helped by a long-standing family friend and her sometime companion, Hettie Owen, who (with her husband Ken) lived at Blaen Cwm. Earlier, Hettie, who was from Port Talbot, had Dylan's 'Uncle Arthur' (D. J. Thomas's brother) staying with her as both a friend and lodger in her home in Arthur Street, Port Talbot.

---

[2] Paul Ferris, *Dylan Thomas The Biography* (London: Dent, 1977; New Edition 1999).
[3] Andrew Lycett, *Dylan Thomas A New Life* (London: Weidenfeld and Nicolson, 2003).

When Florrie announced that she was going to burn the papers and manuscripts, Mrs Owen asked if she could have them. A decade later Kent Thompson, the first of what was to become a continuing stream of American postgraduate students, arrived at Swansea University to further his research on the city's greatest poet. The Hettie Owen file contained numerous letters from the diligent Kent to Hettie and it was apparent that Kent had visited her and been shown the original manuscripts that Hettie had preserved from the bonfire.

The earliest letter is dated 22 November 1966, and Kent writes:

> First and foremost, thank you once again for your kind assistance and hospi-
> tality ... As the saying goes, you have 'contributed to scholarship' and filled
> in those dark gaps in knowledge which slip so ridiculously easily into history.

Further on in the letter we get the first mention of the original juvenile poems: 'The University definitely wants to buy the manuscripts'.

The other letters in the file provide a paper trail of how the group of poems get photographed and offered around to potential purchasers. Swansea University is quickly out of the running. In January 1965 the then Professor of English, Cecil J. L. Price (who another decade on was to become one of my first and best customers – almost the patron of the city's new fledgling Dylans Bookstore) writes Hettie a rather dismissive letter and offers her just 'fifty pounds for the manuscripts of the nine poems'.

Various parties get involved; Kent Thompson suggests 'Sotheby's London', but he also tells Hettie that he has mentioned the manuscripts to Bill Read, an American academic and the partner of John Malcolm Brinnin, who in 1964 had published an early and very well illustrated biography of Dylan – *The Days of Dylan Thomas*. Kent tells Hettie that 'through Bill Reed I have learned of several of those rich Americans who are interested'.

Eventually Dylan Thomas's literary agents David Higham Associates get involved and they broker a cosy deal with their near neighbours, Bertram Rota, a famous London bookselling institution that specialized in Modern Literature in First Edition, Literary Archives, Letters and Manuscripts. Back in 1941 a twenty-six-year-old Dylan Thomas had strolled into Rota's shop with five of his early manuscript notebooks crammed with his early poems both published and unpublished, which they bought. Rota sold them on to the Lockwood Memorial Library of the State University of New York at Buffalo for $140! According to Ferris, that would have been around £70, and he adds, 'whatever Thomas received it was far less than that'. Dylan was then the same age as his literary hero John Keats was when he died, which may have some significance; Dylan had set the deal up earlier in a letter, which ended: 'Will you let me know soon? I should like to sell them, if possible, as I am in need of money'. Rota's ended up buying Hettie's group of poems for £200.

But that is not the end of the trail. Rota's completed the purchase in May 1965. Later in the same year one of the leading, and most legendary and prestigious, American booksellers, the New York-based House of El Dieff Inc.,

SIXTY FIVE

Manuscripts and Correspondence; Paintings and Sculptures;

Drawings and Graphics; Books and Periodicals.

Barrie; Besant; Betjeman; Bodenheim; Boisserée; Bratby; Burns;
Byron; Churchill; Covarrubias; Cummings; Conan Doyle; Fitzgerald;
Flaubert; Flint; France; Franklin; Frost; Gogol;
Graves; Green; Hardy; Henley; Hitler; Homer;
Robert Herrick's Poetical Commonplace Book;
Hugo; Jonson; Joyce; Kennedy; Kitchin;
Lawrence; Lin Yutang; Mansfield; Miller; Moore;
Picasso; Piranesi; Pope; Portraits & Self-Portraits; Robinson;
Rochester; Rouault; Sandburg; Shakespeare; Shaw; Shelley;
Steinbeck; Stendhal; Stevenson; Thomas; Tolstoy;
Lope de Vega; Walpole; Washington; Werfel; Wolmark; Wright

HOUSE OF EL DIEFF, INC.

THIRTY EAST SIXTY-SECOND STREET
NEW YORK, N.Y. 10021

The El Dieff catalogue of 1965

issued one of their elegant and sumptuous catalogues. The title page has a dazzling brief alphabetical list of the literary treasures they have on offer; the penultimate line reads:

Steinbeck; Stendhal; Stevenson; **Thomas**; Tolstoy

The catalogue has three Thomas items, each given a double-page spread, but it is the first that is of interest to this story:

Item 56. Unpublished and Unrecorded Juvenile Poems by Dylan Thomas

Dylan's childhood scribblings, rescued from a cupboard and the threat of bonfire in rural Carmarthenshire, had found their way to the plush cabinets of a swish bookstore on East 62nd Street, New York City, now priced at $2,500.00 – and they sold! They were bought by the Harry Ransom Humanities Research Center at the University of Texas and added into the largest collection of Dylan Thomas manuscripts in existence, where they can be seen and studied today.

For the time being we can leave the fine-paper pages of the El Dieff catalogue (but we shall return). The letters and photocopies in the Hettie Owen folder, although interesting, were to my eager, ever-wishful eyes completely overshadowed by two quite different pages which I found between the modern

Unpublished and Unrecorded Juvenile Poems by Dylan Thomas

THOMAS, Dylan. *Autograph Manuscripts of Five Unpublished Early Poems* (two signed "Dylan," in his mother's hand), 8 pages, 4to, written in ink on ruled exercise paper, with one correction and two marginal notes in pencil, presumably in another hand; *Autograph Manuscripts of Four Unpublished Early Poems*, in fair copies written by his mother and signed by her "Dylan Marlais," with a Swansea address, 7 pages, 4to, written in ink on ruled exercise paper, with some minor corrections; with two family photographs and two letters relating to the manuscripts, v.p., v.d.　　　　　　　　　　　　　　　$2500.00

This important group of hitherto unknown and unpublished juvenilia by one of the major poets of our time was given to a friend during the Second World War by Dylan Thomas's mother. They remained in her possession until early this year. Thomas's extraordinary influence and importance have served to bring to light the greater portion of his existing manuscripts, and the appearance of new work is an event of major significance for collectors and students of the Welsh bard.

The poems in the present collection would appear, on the basis of internal stylistic evidence, to have been written over a considerable period of time. Three of those in Mrs. Thomas's hand might be the work of any youthful poetaster. *Little Dreams* is a moralistic sermon, and *My Party* a wistful day-dream. The *Mishap*, a humorous tale, exhibits a wry point of view. The *Secret Whisky Cure*, also in his mother's hand, is a satirical look at the marriage of a couple who may have been among the Thomas's circle of acquaintances. Written in a romping ballad meter it is sustained for 48 lines and shows a surprising insight into the psychology of the drinker, a subject with which the poet became painfully familiar in later years. The five auto-

graph poems in his own hand are revealing glimpses into the influences and models of his apprenticeship. *The Maniac* is a romantic echo of Keats' *La Belle Dame Sans Merci*, and *Decision* is Tennysonian. *Inspirations* and *La Danseuse* sound most clearly the distinctive note we associate with the poet in his prime. The striking delight achieved by unusual juxtapositions, the beginnings of that richness of vocabulary, the faintly heard Biblical echoes, and the famed verbal complexity. The *Five Limericks* are a delightful romp in an old and honored form.

These poems are decidedly the work of a young man trying out his talents and seeking to find his own inimitable and personal voice, and offer much fruitful study for the development of his style.

The two photographs included show a family group, consisting of the poet's parents, grandparents, two uncles, an aunt, and his sister Nancy as a young child. The other is a small photograph of Dylan's grandfather, in a miniature decorative frame. The two letters provide a record of the provenance and early history of this unusual discovery.

El Dieff catalogue photograph of Thomas's manuscript poems

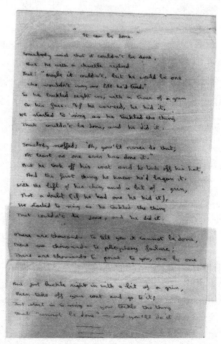

The original manuscript of 'It can be done' in Dylan's schoolboy hand

papers. This paper was ancient, thin, with faded ruled feint, toned brown with age, and bore words scrawled in black ink in a familiar childish hand. Among the copies and modern letters was an original manuscript poem by young Dylan! 'It can be done' – three stanzas of strict rhymed verse of the kind that Dylan was submitting to his school magazine. An original manuscript of an unknown and unrecorded Dylan Thomas poem. What a discovery! I could not explain why it had not gone to America with the others, but that was my good fortune – or so I blindly thought.

Fast-forward just a few weeks, during which time I had carefully transcribed the poem, scanned it and printed it, and I had even begun to mention my new treasure to whoever I met who might be vaguely interested or perhaps a potential customer. Then I was home alone one evening, mooching about, reading, shuffling papers in a desultory fashion, but with the TV on in the background. It was the night of the marathon live annual BBC *Sports Personality of the Year* programme, to which I was paying scant attention. However, my ear was caught by Sue Barker, the presenter, announcing something like '… and now a poem "It Couldn't be Done"'. I turned to the screen as a lone figure began to recite a poem with gravitas and passion, a poem which began to nudge nerve ends in my synapses. I tried to ignore the words but they did sound strangely familiar. The end of his powerful recitation was greeted with rapturous applause and Sue Barker thanked the actor (who I learned was Idris Elba, the star of American police drama 'The Wire'[4]) and acknowledged the author of the poem as being one Edgar Guest. 'Who could that be?' I thought. I tried to return to the book I was reading, but the poem kept bothering me and I could not stop myself from going to my office, finding one of my transcripts of *my* Dylan Thomas poem and heading for my computer. I typed 'Edgar Guest' into Wikipedia and began to read:

Edgar Albert Guest (August 20, 1881, Birmingham England – August 5, 1959 … aka Eddie Guest) was a prolific English-born American poet who was popular in the first half of the 20th century and became known as the People's Poet. In 1891, Guest came with his family to the United States from England. After he began at the Detroit Free Press as a copy boy and then a reporter, his first poem appeared December 11, 1898. He became a naturalised alien in 1902. For 40 years, Guest was widely read throughout North America … Guest penned some 11,000 poems which were syndicated in some 300 newspapers and collected in more than 20 books, including *A Heap o' Livin'* (1916) and *Just Folks* (1917). Guest was made Poet Laureate of Michigan, the only poet to have been awarded the title …

That was quite enough; in a state of incredulous disbelief, another search got me to a printing of Edgar's poem with its original title 'It Couldn't be Done'. The game was up: this was another 'His Requiem'. Dylan had copied the

4   You can still watch this on YouTube: 'It Couldn't be Done': Edgar Guest http://www.youtube.com/watch?v=tlhbAKL3EzE (Accessed 16th January 2013).

poem. I then did a close comparison, and saw that, as well as slightly changing the title from negative to positive, Dylan has made a few other subtle changes (shown here in **bold**).

'It Couldn't Be Done' by Edgar Albert Guest (1881–1959)
[**Thomas: 'It can be done'**]

Somebody said that it couldn't be done,
But, he with a chuckle replied
That 'maybe it couldn't,' but he would be one
Who wouldn't say so till he'd tried. [']
So he buckled right in with the trace of a grin
On his face. If he worried he hid it.
He started to sing as he tackled the thing
That couldn't be done, and he did it.

Somebody scoffed: 'Oh, you'll never do that;
At least no one has done it'; [.]
But he took off his coat and he took off his hat,
And the first thing we knew he'd begun it.
With a lift of his chin and a bit of a grin,
Without any doubting or quiddit,
[**Not a doubt (if he had one he hid it)**]
He started to sing as he tackled the thing
That couldn't be done, and he did it.

There are thousands to tell you it cannot be done,
There are thousands to prophesy failure;
There are thousands to point out to you one by one,
The dangers that wait to assail you.
But just buckle it in with a bit of a grin,
Just take off your coat and go to it;
Just start to sing as you tackle the thing
That 'couldn't be done,' and you'll do it.
[**That 'cannot be done' – and you'll do it**]

So my great discovery turned out to be some kind of fake, but it definitely was not a poem written by Dylan Thomas. A poem in his hand: Yes. Written by him: No. He had copied it out but made a few significant alterations that subtly changed it: by changing the title from negative to positive, by removing the arcane American phrase 'quiddit' – which might have aroused suspicions. If he were just copying out the poem out of admiration to put in his 'favourite poem folder', why make changes? Given his previous form in this area, I could only conclude that this was in preparation for an attempt to pass the poem off as his own. Whether he tried and offered it to his school magazine or some other outlet but had been rejected we do not know, but it does not appear to have been published under Dylan's name.

It was a huge disappointment on many levels, not the least being that it was now hard to see the manuscript having any real monetary value. Although on one level I was amazed and captivated by the synchronicity of the whole Sports Review evening, I felt angry with myself for being duped. Should I not have known of such a prolific versifier as E. A. Guest? Should I have been familiar with Edgar Albert's vast canon? In an attempt to convince myself that I was not at fault, for the next week or two I challenged every literate person I encountered, from well-read customers to professors of English, demanding of them to confess if they had ever heard of Edgar Albert Guest.

I was feeling better when all my questioning brought nothing but blank, incredulous and negative replies, until I was on the phone to a very smart young American rare book dealer[5] who immediately said yes, he knew of such a poet. However, I felt less inadequate when he explained he had never read a word of his poetry but knew him through a wonderful Dorothy Parker rhyming aphorism, which totally disparages any merit in the poetry of Edgar Guest; the sharp-tongued satirist wrote: 'I'd rather flunk my Wassermann test/Than read the poetry of Edgar Guest'.[6]

At least the book dealer's revelation put a smile on my face, and there this story could have ended had I not been concurrently finishing up a book about Dylan's love of the pub and the place of drink in his life. When I was going through the Hettie Owen file I had carefully read all the poems therein and been struck by one of the other early photocopied poems in the file entitled 'The Secret Whisky Cure', a three-page epic ballad, written out by Dylan's mother. The cataloguer at El Dieff obviously had a similar reaction to me and had signalled this poem out for special attention when describing the manuscripts:

> 'The Secret Whisky Cure' … in his mother's hand, is a satirical look at the marriage of a couple, who may have been among the Thomas's circle of acquaintances. Written in a romping ballad meter [sic] it is sustained for 48 lines and shows a surprising insight into the psychology of the drinker, a subject with which the poet became painfully familiar in later years.

The poem ends with a startling and shocking penultimate stanza wherein the whisky drinker, poisoned by his wife so that he cannot drink any more, finds his only respite in a brutal suicide:

> And his wife, when he was sober? – Well, she nagged him all the more!
> And he couldn't drown his sorrow in the whisky as of yore
> So he shot himself in London, and breathed earth no more
> And found rest amongst the spirits from the Secret Whisky Cure.

Well I could certainly use the poem in my book, I thought – a little-known gem that was evidence of Dylan's youthful knowledge of the perils of alcohol. At

---

5 Hosea Baskin of Cumberland Rare Books in Northampton, MA, USA.
6 The Wassermann test is an antibody test for syphilis, named after the bacteriologist August Paul von Wassermann, who discovered it.

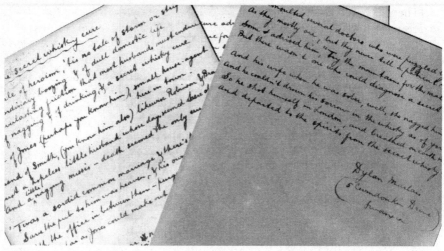

'The Secret Whisky Cure', written out by hand by Dylan's mother

least it would give me some small recompense for my disappointment over 'It Couldn't Be Done'. But it was not to be. I had scanned and typed (and hyped) the poem into the manuscript of my book, but something was making me wary and I could not stop myself going back to Google. Slowly, and with trepidation mounting, I typed 'Secret Whisky Cure' into the box; my hand gingerly moved the mouse, the cursor edged towards the 'search' tab – I double-clicked. The first result showed on the screen:

> The Secret Whisky Cure – Australian Poetry Library. Poets / Lawson, Henry – Tale of nagging and of drinking – and a secret whisky cure. Name of Jones – perhaps you know him – small house – agent here in town …

I had been caught again! But at least I discovered the theft before unwittingly including it, with great aplomb, in my forthcoming book. Even I had heard of Henry Lawson, one of Australia's great swag-man poets. Again I found myself transcribing a poem and highlighting Dylan's few devious and cunning alterations – he leaves out two stanzas from the Lawson original, including the concluding stanza, probably because the opening couplet is too misogynistic, brazen and distasteful to ever have come from the hand of a young boy:

> And the moral? – well, 'tis funny – or 'tis woman's way with men –
> She's remarried to a publican who whacks her now and then …

The most pertinent changes are his blatant efforts to relocate the poem and remove its Australian elements: the 'Sydney Bulletin' becomes the 'Monthly Magazine'; the final dramatic act of the suicide takes place in 'London' not on Manly, a beach just outside Sydney; and the dropping of some curious words or Australian usages – such as 'coalised' and 'Woore' (which I still cannot find a meaning for).

'The Secret Whisky Cure' by Henry Lawson
From the book: *When I was King*
[Dylan's variations in **bold**]

'TIS no tale of heroism, 'tis no tale of storm and strife,
But of ordinary boozing, and of dull domestic life –
Of the everlasting friction that most husbands must endure –
Tale of nagging and of drinking – and a secret whisky cure.
Name of Jones – perhaps you know him – small house-agent here in town –
(Friend of Smith, you know him also – likewise Robinson and Brown),
Just a hopeless little husband, whose deep sorrows were obscure,
[**whose days seemed here obscure**]
And a bitter nagging Missis – and death seemed the only cure.
[**a little nagging missis**]
'Twas a common sordid marriage, and there's little new to tell –
Save the pub to him was Heaven and his own home was a hell:
With the office in between them – purgatory to be sure –
And, as far as Jones could make out – well, there wasn't any cure.
[**was not any cure**]
'Twas drink and nag – or nag and drink – whichever you prefer –
Till at last she couldn't stand him any more than he could her.
Friends and relatives assisted, telling her (with motives pure)
[**no brackets**]
That a legal separation was the only earthly cure.
So she went and saw a lawyer, who, in accents soft and low,
Asked her firstly if her husband had a bank account or no;
But he hadn't and she hadn't, they in fact were very poor,
So he bowed her out suggesting she should try some liquor cure.
She saw a drink cure advertised in the Sydney Bulletin –
[**Monthly Magazine**]
Cure for brandy, cure for whisky, cure for rum and beer and gin,
And it could be given secret, it was tasteless, swift and sure –
So she purchased half a gallon of that Secret Whisky Cure.
And she put some in his coffee, smiling sweetly all the while,
And he started for the office rather puzzled by the smile –
[**and Jones started**]
Smile or frown he'd have a whisky, and you'll say he was a boor –
But perhaps his wife had given him an overdose of Cure.
And he met a friend he hadn't seen for seven years or more –
It was just upon the threshold of a private bar-room door –
And they coalised and entered straight away, you may be sure –
[**agreed and entered**]
But of course they hadn't reckoned with a Secret Whisky Cure.
Jones, he drank, turned pale, and, gasping, hurried out the back way
    quick,

Where, to his old chum's amazement, he was violently sick;
Then they interviewed the landlord, but he swore the drink was pure –
It was only the beginning of the Secret Whisky Cure.
For Jones couldn't stand the smell of even special whisky blends,
And shunned bar-rooms to the sorrow of his trusty drinking friends:
And they wondered, too, what evil genius had chanced to lure
Him from paths of booze and friendship – never dreaming of a Cure.
He had noticed, too, with terror that a something turned his feet,
When a pub was near, and swung him to the other side the street,
Till he thought the devils had him, and his person they'd immure
In a lunatic asylum where there wasn't any Cure.
[**This stanza omitted**]
He consulted several doctors who were puzzled by the case –
As they mostly are, but never tell the patient to his face –
[**but they**]
Some advised him 'Try the Mountains for this malady obscure':
But there wasn't one could diagnose a Secret Whisky Cure.
[**who could**]
And his wife, when he was sober? – Well, she nagged him all the more!
And he couldn't drown his sorrow in the pewter as of yore:
[**in the whisky as of yore**]
So he shot himself at Manly and was sat upon by Woore,
[**So he shot himself in London, and breathed earth no more**]
And found rest amongst the spirits from the Secret Whisky Cure.

And the moral? – well, 'tis funny – or 'tis woman's way with men –
She's remarried to a publican who whacks her now and then,
And they get on fairly happy, he's a brute and he's a boor,
But she's never tried her second with a Secret Whisky Cure.
[**This stanza omitted**]

Once again I had discovered another plagiarized poem, and again, as with
'It can be done', I have not found it published anywhere above Dylan's name,
although I am convinced that these two manuscripts are examples of poems
that he was intending to offer out for publication as his own. Why else effect
these subtle but pertinent changes? This plagiarism seems to be a trait belonging
to Thomas's early to mid-teens and there has never been any suggestion that
any of the poems he included in his published collections were anything other
that entirely his own work. But hold on – what about his prose?

Quite recently I received a note from an old customer and friend, Kerith
Trick. Kerith lived in Norwich and had been a top psychiatrist at St Andrew's
Hospital, which was earlier known as Northampton General Lunatic Asylum
where the Victorian poet John Clare was incarcerated (Kerith was a collector
of Clare's poetry). But Kerith had been born in Swansea, the son of Bert Trick,
often referred to as Swansea's 'communist' grocer and Dylan Thomas's influential friend and political mentor. I invited Kerith to give a lecture on his father

in the 2000 Swansea Dylan Thomas Festival and in it he put the record straight – Bert was never a Communist but was 'always a member of the Labour Party, albeit on the extreme left'. (Dylan suggested that Bert call his son Kerith after the George Moore novel he admired, *The Brook Kerith*.[7])

Kerith's note pointed me towards a remarkable similarity between a famous passage from one of Dylan's most popular stories, now known as 'The Outing', and a passage in an early Sherlock Holmes short story by Arthur Conan Doyle, 'A Scandal in Bohemia' (1891). (Conan Doyle was a favourite author of Dylan's, in particular the Sherlock Holmes stories as they appeared in the *Strand* magazine.)

> Who blows death's feather? What glory is colour?
> I blow the stammel feather in the vein.

'The Outing' was commissioned by the BBC as a television programme – one of only two TV appearances by Thomas, both now sadly lost. Originally called 'A Story', it dates from the last year of Dylan's life. It was televised[8] on 10 August 1953 and subsequently published in the *Listener* in September of the same year (Dylan was to die in New York in November). In 'The Outing' Dylan writes in the voice of his younger self – a young boy forced to accompany his uncle on a typical Welsh, all-male, annual coach outing to the seaside, on a bus full of beer, with stops at every other pub passed, and all manner of shenanigans. Destinations are rarely reached as the pubs become harder to leave. The story begins:

> If you can call it a story. There's no beginning or end and there's very little in the middle. It's all about a day's outing, by charabanc, to Porthcawl, which, of course, the charabanc never reached, and it happened when I was so high and much nicer.

'The Outing' ends with this episode:[9]

> They stopped at the Hermit's Nest for rum to keep out the cold.
> 'I played for Aberavon in 1898,' said a stranger to Enoch Davies.
> 'Liar,' said Enoch Davies.
> 'I can show you photos,' said the stranger.

---

[7] It is also worth noting that once while visiting with Bert, Dylan heard Bert's daughter Pamela ask him 'What colour is glory?' The question so intrigued and beguiled Thomas that he later used it in his notebook poems and finally it appears in *My World Is A Pyramid*, the penultimate poem in Dylan's first collection *18 Poems*: 'Who blows death's feather? What glory is colour?' In this instance Eliot gets it right – mature poets steal.

[8] Critic Reginald Pound wrote in the *Listener* that Dylan's performance 'fell only just short of being a television *tour de force*'.

[9] Which I was pleased to see was recently included in a new anthology, *The First XV – A Selection of the Best Rugby Writing*, Foreword by Gerald Davies, edited by Gareth Williams (Swansea: Parthian, 2011).

'Forged,' said Enoch Davies.
'And I'll show you my cap at home'.
'Stolen'.
'I got friends to prove it,' said the stranger in a fury.
'Bribed,' said Enoch Davies.

And here is the passage that Kerith Trick pointed out to me, which occurs in Conan Doyle's 'A Scandal in Bohemia':

'Then I fail to follow your Majesty. If this young person should produce her letters for blackmailing or other purposes, how is she to prove their authenticity?'
'There is writing'.
'Pooh, pooh! Forgery'.
'My private notepaper'.
'Stolen'.
'My own seal'.
'Imitated'.
'My photograph'.
'Bought'.

There is little or no doubt that Dylan's bar-room exchange echoes profoundly and remarkably the passage from Conan Doyle, but another example of plagiarism? I think not. In this instance I am inclined to give Dylan the benefit of the doubt and to side with Fitzgibbon and agree that what we have here is 'a case of total, unconscious recall'. Or is Dylan living up to Eliot's maxim, 'mature poets steal'?

And what are we to make of all of this – is it terrible? Is it wicked? Should we think any the less of the perpetrator? I am not sure that in the light of these new examples we can dismiss them all, as Fitzgibbon did when he chose to dismiss the poem taken from *The Children's Encyclopædia* as an example of 'a case of total, unconscious recall', or with Fitzgibbon's conclusion that 'Dylan at that age was writing so many poems that he certainly had no need to steal one'.

Paul Ferris concludes his account of 'His Requiem' by seeing it as being provoked by Dylan's overwhelming desire to prove to his father in particular, but to his whole world in general, that he was a poet. Ferris writes:

He would hardly have taken such a risk unless he badly needed to prove – to himself, to his father, to his friends – that he could write acceptable poetry; and unless he was uncertain of his ability to do so.

Andrew Lycett's conclusion is similar:

Why did a bright boy, who clearly knew how to write poems, resort to such deceit? The answer is that it was his way of dealing with various pressures on him ... It showed Dylan's need to demonstrate his poetic ability to his parents, partly to his indulgent mother, who made copies of his work, but rather more to his remote father whose laissez-faire attitude to learning in the home belied his firm ambition for his son.

But what would they have concluded had they too been confronted with 'It couldn't be done' and 'The Secret Whisky Cure'? I would like to propose another explanation. Dylan wrote his first poem for the *Swansea Grammar School Magazine* in 1925 aged eleven. He was still publishing similar light verse in its pages in 1930, when he became editor, and on into 1931 by which time, aged almost seventeen, he had actually left school to work on the local paper. However, if we look at Ralph Maud's *Poet in the Making: The Notebooks of Dylan Thomas* (1967; New Edition 1989), we can see that, by 1930, Dylan Thomas had already begun to compile the four notebooks (now in the Library of New York State University in Buffalo) that were eventually to yield almost half of his published poems, including all the poems that made up his groundbreaking and reputation-building first two books, *18 Poems* (1934) and *Twenty-Five Poems* (1936). Maud writes in his introduction that his study of these notebooks reveals, for the first time, the extent of Thomas's poetic output from his fifteenth to his nineteenth year. It also confounds previous assumptions about the poet's later development by showing, also for the first time, how much of the poetry printed up to his twenty-sixth year was really a reworking of early poems. Maud adds later:

> Indications are that up to this point in [1930] Thomas's poems had been derivative, the borrowed forms dictating the subject and keeping the compositions essentially, albeit enthusiastically, artificial. The poems of this self-assigned homework appeared in the school magazine from 1925, first as precious buddings, later as deftly turned parodies. In April 1930, at the same time as he began the extant Notebooks with *Osiris, Come to Isis*, a serious poem in the Yeatsian manner, Thomas was actually ribbing Yeats in the school magazine with a parody entitled *In Borrowed Plumes*.

My final thoughts are that this massive, never-to-be-repeated, testosterone-fuelled outpouring of searing poems that occurred as Dylan entered his later teens – poems fixated on Dylan's major themes of birth, sex and death – took him away from, and moreover made repulsive, the business of writing anything but these new visceral poems. It was this that drove him to plagiarize poems of this unchallenging kind of lesser work that he was still required, almost obliged, to offer to the school magazine and he felt compelled to have suitable examples to hand. He was bored of writing what he knew was inferior rubbish, so why not pinch it ready-made? And he knew where to look – to the popular folk poets and poetasters from faraway lands; in America and Australia, or buried within the thick pages of *The Boy's Own Paper*, or *Arthur Mee's Children's Encyclopædia*, the better not to be discovered. There is a striking similarity of tone in the poems of Messrs Guest, Lawson, Thomas J. and Miss Gard. He may well have found suitable examples in the anthologies on the shelves of his father's extensive library at 5 Cwmdonkin Drive. More might

II .

W. B. Yeats :

There was a pearl-pale moon that slid
Down oceans of ambrosial sky,
Under the drooping of the day's dusk-lid
Where darkness and her wine-waves lie,
And at that full nocturnal hour
She twined her splendid, curving hair,
And bent her body like a flower,
And glided through the evening air
Light as a cloud, and petal-fair.
She gained the garlanded and leaf-green mound
That tapered like a dove-gray hill,
To sink upon the deep grass without sound,
To press her face upon the lilting ground,
And twine her yellow hair like daffodil.
She raised fine, luscious fruit up to her lips,
Tasted the round grape in full-throated sips,
Smoothed upon her mouth the lovely pear,
When through the darkness coiled about the place,
The terror-scented darkness passion-dim,
A silver spider crawls, and weaves his web about her hair,
And weaves his silken rapture everywhere,
And looks into her wave-wild face,
And wonders why she weeps at him.

D.M.T.

'In Borrowed Plumes'

be sourced in the library at the Grammar School, and there was always his favourite local second-hand bookshop, Swansea's famous 'Ralph the Books', where his lifetime pal, Ralph Wishart, would let him have the run of the shelves and sold him books for pennies.

Having to deal with this sudden explosion of serious poetic creativity, during that moment between Eliot's 'immature' poet and 'mature' poet, Dylan Thomas seems to have felt the need for a little literary misappropriation, about which he displayed little or no conscience.

One final point – let us remember that Dylan Thomas had a very developed and mischievous sense of humour; you only have to look at the very Welsh-looking name he invents for the village where *Under Milk Wood* is set – Llareggub – and then read it backwards to see this in action. He was a joker, a 'trickster', a leg-pulling weaver of fantasies and fallacies. He would no doubt have enjoyed the wicked, guilty ('Homer Nods') pleasures obtained by hoodwinking his readers with a few poems not his own. As late as 1952 he was still giving us a few pointers. Herewith a couple of clues he threw into an intro-duction he gave to a reading at the Massachusetts Institute of Technology in Boston on 3 July 1952.[10] First he expands on his poetic influence and methods when he was a very young reader and writer:

> I wrote endless imitations, though at the time of writing I never thought of them as imitations but rather colossally original … imitations of whatever I happened to be golloping then, Thomas Browne, Robert W. Service, Stevenson, De Quincy, *Eskimo Nell*, Newbolt, Blake, Marlowe, the Imagists, the *Boy's Own Paper* …

The same *Boy's Own Paper* from where, twenty-five years earlier, he had misap-propriated 'His Requiem'. And later in his preamble he admits to his audience that, whenever he likes,

> I can summon my juvenile literary delinquence before me and give it a long periodic sentence.

What would strengthen this theory and make it better would be the existence of some poems by Dylan that bridge these two extremes, but nothing of the sort seems to exist. Fitzgibbon offers another aside unique in his biography, which concerns this and also has a coincidental element. He writes:

> … I cannot, in the school magazine, find any trace of the poems that were to come, though his notebooks show that he was beginning to write 'Dylan Thomas poems' before he left the school.

Then he adds this:

> A German scholar, who researched lengthily in Swansea, did unearth one unsigned poem in the school magazine which gave a transitional clue between Dylan-the-boy and Dylan-the poet. I understand he had to scrap a whole thesis he was writing around this poem. Unfortunately it turned out to have been written by E. F. McInerny.

So the whistle-blower was almost mistaken for a culprit.

And deep in the heart of Texas at the Harry Ransom Humanities Research Center, they still seem to believe that 'The Secret Whisky Cure' originates from Wales and not Australia! The catalogue of the collection describes the poem thus:

> Also notable among the poetry in this collection is a selection of juvenilia, representing some of Thomas's earliest poetic output. There are four fair copies in the hand of his mother Florence – 'Little Dreams,' 'The Mishap,' 'My Party' and 'The Secret Whisky Cure'.

And I am sure that Dylan is quietly chuckling in his grave.

[10] 'I Am Going to Read Aloud' – an introduction to a reading by Dylan Thomas at MIT Boston. Published in *The London Magazine*, September 1956.

'All front page stuff':
Reconstructing Dylan Thomas

Jo Furber

'There's words what d'you want to find *him* for I wouldn't touch him with a barge pole ...'

Return Journey, 326

I am at the Poetry Library, University at Buffalo, New York State. A door opens into a small seminar room with tables pushed into a long oblong. On the table are several conservation boxes, and inside the boxes is what seems to me, after many years studying and exploring Thomas's work and promoting it all over the world, to be some kind of holy grail. The lids are removed from the boxes, and, with a care usually reserved for holding new babies, I begin to explore the pages of Thomas's 1930 Notebook. I have the privilege and responsibility of curating two exhibitions of Dylan Thomas's manuscripts and letters to be displayed at Swansea's Dylan Thomas Centre and the National Library of Wales in Aberystwyth during his centenary year, and exploring the Buffalo Collection is the most exciting and significant stage of my research so far. I am reading Dylan's handwritten drafts of poems produced from the age of fifteen, which, although accessible to researchers, have never been publicly displayed. I didn't think he could still surprise me like this, but it turns out he can, and with some considerable force. One aspect of Thomas that has always fascinated me is the way in which he created various personae throughout his life, and it's especially apparent when viewed through the lenses of *Return Journey*.

... and above medium height. Above medium height for Wales, I mean, he's five foot six and a half. Thick blubber lips; snub nose; curly mousebrown hair; one front tooth broken after playing a game called Cats and Dogs, in the Mermaid, Mumbles; speaks rather fancy; truculent; plausible; a bit of a shower-off; plus fours and no breakfast, you know; used to have poems printed in the *Herald of Wales*. (*Return Journey*, 326; hereafter referred to as *RJ*)

Return Journey's narrator travels through Swansea seeking his younger selves, and in so doing, he attempts to recover a Swansea lost to the Blitz.[1] *Return Journey*, completed and broadcast in 1947, was prompted by the experience of seeing this devastation first-hand, and Thomas researched it meticulously to ensure he had correctly named all the shops and buildings that had been lost. With a greater investigative zeal than that typically shown by the teenage 'newshound Thomas', it is possible for the modern-day Dylan aficionado to follow the steps he pounded into the Swansea pavements and take the same route from the centre of his 'ugly, lovely' town up to Cwmdonkin Park, his 'world within the world of the sea-town'. But my own journey to discover more about the Swansea writing of 'belly-churning Thomas, the Rimbaud of Cwmdonkin Drive' begins some 3,500 miles away. Given the peripatetic nature of Thomas's adult life, and his stature as a writer which led to the exciting but exacting north American lecture tours, and the sheer contradictions, twists and excesses of the Thomas story, this may not be surprising.

In June 1941 the twenty-six-year-old Dylan sold his four surviving poetry Notebooks, plus an early prose Notebook ('the red Notebook') to Bertram Rota, a London dealer, and he in turn sold them on to Buffalo. Thomas's biographer Andrew Lycett writes:

> [f]or over three years [Dylan] had fielded requests from the State University of New York at Buffalo for manuscripts to form the basis of a poetry collection at its new Lockwood Memorial Library ... Bertram Rota was paid just over $140 (or £35) as agent on the deal. Dylan clearly received significantly less. He had sold the cream of his creative work for the equivalent of around £1,200 in 2003. Although his biographer Constantine Fitzgibbon drew over-fanciful parallels with John Keats, who died in his twenty-sixth year, Dylan was indeed sloughing off a youthful skin. A period of intense poetic activity had drawn to an end. Dylan has already written more than eighty per cent of his published verse. (Lycett, 224)

Significantly, it was the first time that the Library had paid for manuscripts, so keen were they to acquire these particular items.

> I seem to remember a chap like you described. There couldn't be two like him let's hope. (*RJ*, 327)

Buffalo's Poetry Collection is of enormous international significance, holding one of the largest collections of poetry first editions, literary magazines and anthologies, and the largest collection of Joyce material in the world. It's appropriate that Dylan's manuscripts are stored alongside those of Joyce's, a writer he so admired. The Dylan Thomas holdings have been enhanced over the years with other manuscripts, most notably an incredible 160-page manuscript of 'Ballad of the Long-Legged Bait' which sets out in page after fascinating

---

[1]   During the Three Nights Blitz on Swansea in February 1941 230 people died. One morning Bert Trick walked towards the offices of the air raid service and bumped into Dylan and Caitlin. 'Our Swansea has died', said Dylan.

page the entire process of writing Dylan's longest poem. It includes word lists, drawings, rhyme schemes, cigarette burns and a few pages near the middle where he is clearly struggling: one section has 'Dylan and Caitlin' written out; another has 'breast and bum' inserted into a couple of different lines. Other notable items include Dylan's letters to Pamela Hansford Johnson, gifted by her to the Collection alongside her diaries from 1934 and 1935, which cover the time when she and Dylan were conducting an intense correspondence, which would eventually develop into his first serious relationship.

> How Dan Jones was going to compose the most prodigious symphony, Fred Janes paint the most miraculously meticulous picture, Charlie Fisher catch the poshest trout, Vernon Watkins and Young Thomas write the most boiling poems, how they would ring the bells of London and paint it like a tart ... (*RJ*, 331–2)

The Notebooks – really school exercise books – reflect Dylan's most prolific period. Started on 27 April 1930 while he was still at Swansea Grammar School, they continue during his brief tenure as a junior reporter at the *South Wales Daily Post*, and the pages explode with poems during the sixteen months in which he worked solely on his writing, distracted only by his acting commitments with Swansea Little Theatre and his long walks on Gower, 'taking my devils for an airing', and informed by his close friendship and collaborations with Swansea friends such as Daniel Jones, Charlie Fisher and Bert Trick. A regular pattern to his days – reading, writing, acting, reading and more writing – is detailed in a letter to Pamela from January 1934, under the heading 'Night and Day: A Provincial Rhythm', which ends with the statement: '[n]ot a very British day. Too much thinkin', too much talkin', too much alcohol' (*Collected Letters*, 102, hereafter referred to as *CL*).

> Oh yes, yes, I remember him well, but I didn't know what was his name. I don't know the names of none of the sandboys. (*RJ*, 335)

This routine, and a lack of financial commitments and responsibilities, ensured that he had the physical and mental space to devote not just to poetry but also to stories and fantastically detailed letters. The Notebooks and letters in particular offer fascinating insights into his ways of writing, as described in a letter to Charles Fisher:

> I write a poem on innumerable sheets of scrap paper, write it on both sides of the paper, often upside down and criss cross ways, unpunctuated, surrounded by drawings of lamp posts and boiled eggs, in a very dirty mess; bit by bit I copy out the slowly developing poem into an exercise book; and, when it is completed, I type it out. The scrap sheets I burn, for there are such a lot of them that they clutter up my room and get mixed in the beer and butter. (*CL*, 209)

The poems in what he described to Geoffrey Grigson in 1933 as 'innumerable exercise books' (*CL*, 33) formed the basis of work published in *18 Poems* (1934), *Twenty-Five Poems* (1936) and contributed to *The Map of Love*

(1939) and were used even as late as 1946's *Deaths and Entrances*. Dated 1930, 1930–2, February 1933 and August 1933, the books demonstrate Dylan Thomas as a meticulous craftsman, who would spend hours, or even days, searching for the right word. They are fascinating objects in themselves, being entirely handwritten, with crossings-out, rhyme-lists, coffee stains, annotations, drawings and doodles, underlinings and use of coloured pencil. When lines or stanzas are crossed out, it's usually in pencil so the pen can still be seen underneath it. There are ink blots, and practice signatures, which offer insights into the development of Dylan's poetic persona. Every Notebook has a start and an end date, and each poem is dated, usually underneath it. Typically, they are numbered and not titled, though a few are simply called 'Pome', and some are marked with symbols. They are testament to a precocious talent: the first draft of 'The hunchback in the park' was written in the 1930–2 Notebook, dated 9 May 1932, when Dylan was seventeen years old. Underneath it, and across two free half-pages, Dylan has written under the heading 'Revised poem. July 1941' the redrafted version that was eventually published in *Deaths and Entrances* five years later. It's an extraordinary record of the development of one of Dylan's best-known poems, and even that revised 1941 version has edits – 'church-black bell' is changed to 'Sunday sombre bell', 'mitching boys' to 'truant boys'. The work of Dylan the craftsman is again evident.

> Then I went on my way from the sea, up Brynmill Terrace and into Glanbrydan Avenue where Bert Trick had kept a grocer's shop and, in the kitchen, threatened the annihilation of the ruling classes over sandwiches and jelly and blancmange. (*RJ*, 336)

The Notebooks were also portable: Bert Trick, described by Dylan as 'a communist grocer with a passion for obscurity and the Powys family', recalls Dylan's first visit to his home in Glanbrydan Avenue, Swansea, where Bert and his wife Nell were spellbound as Dylan opened a Notebook and read his work aloud. Bert would also visit Dylan in Cwmdonkin, and he recalls that:

> [w]e'd start on modern poetry and end up discussing the dialectics of Karl Marx ... It was all terribly exciting ... Many were the times I skipped out of 5 Cwmdonkin Drive, my arms full of books, my head full of stars and feet of feathers. I didn't walk down the hill to my home, I was levitated. There was no need for strong drink, we were intoxicated with words – ideas and words. The magic of language was ours. (Lycett, 81)

This sense of Dylan as an exciting and inspiring companion is echoed in Vernon Watkins's description of his first visit to Cwmdonkin. After Dylan had read to him from a folder labelled 'POMES', Vernon felt 'aware that I was in the presence of a poet of extraordinary genius' (*Portrait of a Friend*, 35). Then,

> Dylan asked Vernon if he used a dictionary. Vernon answered that he occasionally did, but Dylan said 'No, I mean a real dictionary, like this,' and

took down from a shelf a book made of folded sheets of brown paper sewn
together. It was a rhyming dictionary, which he had compiled himself, and to
which he constantly made additions. This, he said, was his Doomsday Book.
(*Portrait of a Friend*, 37)

These evenings with Bert, Vernon and others, and his ongoing correspondence
and exchanging of poems for comment and criticism with Vernon, were crucial
to the development of some of the Notebook poems into their final printed
form in *Twenty-Five Poems*.

Remember when I took you down the mortuary for the first time, Young
Thomas? He'd never seen a corpse before, boys, except old Ron on a
Saturday night ... He went pale green, mun. (*RJ*, 328)

Far from the image of the solitary poet labouring 'by singing light' depicted in
'In my craft or sullen art', Dylan was extremely culturally aware and engaged.
In 1936 he attended the International Surrealists Exhibition in London, and
witnessed Dali nearly suffocating after giving his talk from inside a diving suit;
Dylan himself wandered around with a cup of boiled string, enquiring whether
people would enjoy it 'weak or strong?'. He also, notably, read at an ancillary
poetry event, taking the stage after Paul Eluard. The circles he moved in also
included Arthur Miller, Charlie Chaplin, Shelley Winters and Igor Stravinsky.
He was photographed by, among others, Rollie McKenna, Bill Brandt and Lee
Miller, and painted by Augustus John, Mervyn Levy, Alfred Janes and Gordon
Stuart. He worked at the BBC with Louis MacNeice and John Arlott, and went
to the cricket with both. Moreover, he was an eager collaborator, from the
teenage poems and broadcasts made with Daniel Jones, with whom he formed
the Warmley Broadcasting Corporation, to *The Death of the King's Canary*,
which he worked on with friends including Charlie Fisher and John Davenport,
to those plans in 1953 to write an opera with Stravinsky, which were curtailed
by his early death. On his American lecture tours he would read from the work
of other writers as well as his own. Moreover, he was eager to share his work
with others, and gladly discuss ways of improving it.

No thank *you*, Mr Cheeky, with your cut-glass accent and your father's
trilby! I don't want *no* walk on *no* sands. What d'you say? Ooh listen to him,
Het, he's swallowed a dictionary. (*RJ*, 336)

Dylan was equally generous with the time he spent on the poetry of others.
The letters in the Buffalo archives are fascinating when read alongside the four
poetry Notebooks, and illuminate Dylan's creative processes, his views on his
own poetry, his development of a series of personae, and his insightful critical
appraisal of the work of others. This is especially evident in the correspondence
with Pamela Hansford Johnson. Their regular exchanges of poems and lengthy
and detailed responses to each other's work are fascinating to read, and offer
a comprehensive record of what Dylan was working on and when. In March
1934, for example, he boasts to Pamela (with a typical hint of exaggeration)

that 'the BBC have banned my poetry. After my poem in *The Listener* ('Light Breaks Where No Sun Shines') the editor received a host of letters ... The little smut-hounds thought I was writing a copulatory anthem'[2] (*CL*, 132).

He is unstinting in his praise and – more frequently – his criticism of the work Pamela sent. An early letter from October 1933 states appreciation of 'a beautifully simple' (*CL*, 50) poem, but more frequently, he takes her to task for sloppiness, over-romanticization and lack of conviction, whether describing two lines as 'pearls surrounded not only by the pig's ear but by the whole of his bristling body' (*CL*, 51) or writing that:

> The two prose-poems (I'll allow you that) are very uneven. Much of the writing is, for you, almost criminally wrong, being just what you can do so well but shouldn't. You can lavish the best lavishers in the country off their spates when you want to. But don't you dare do it ... Piece one is remarkable for the number of entirely meaningless & affected words you have managed to drag in. 'Dulcimer', 'Drumdeep', 'Cohorts', & 'Silken Shadowy Girls'. All the damned abracadabra of the Poet's Corner, and as gutless as a filleted herring. (*CL*, 127)

Elsewhere his commentary on her work illustrates his own work ethic:

> ... the talent, which is very easy to see in twenty out of the twenty-four pages of your book, is not enough by itself; the work-woman ... the intellectual, the thinking craftswoman, has not had half enough to do. You must work at the talent as a sculptor works at stone. (*CL*, 139)

These letters to Pamela present a young man trying out a poetic identity while also trying to simultaneously impress and woo the object of his affection. However keen he is to progress their relationship, the need to critique and help her develop her work is continually evident in his well-worked, very considered and extremely readable letters; it's fascinating to explore.

One letter to Pamela boasts a self-portrait in purple and red pencil drawn on the back of the last page, complete with what he describes in *Return Journey* as 'a conscious woodbine'. It's a good example of both the playfulness evident in the Notebooks and the letters, as well as Dylan's self-imaging: near the drawing he has scribbled in pencil, with an attempt at self-deprecation: 'I'm sorry about this. Drawn on the back, and I didn't see it. I don't always draw like that, thank God'. Other letters offer details of his day-to-day life in his 'Glamorgan villa', like this stylized account of a young man negotiating the boredom of provincial Sundays:

> The worms are doing very nicely today. Sunday in Wales. The Sunday-walkers have slunk out of the warrens in which they sleep and breed all the unholy week ... and are now marching up the hill past my window. (*CL*, 135)

---

[2]   Dylan misquotes the offending lines as follows, and the italics are his: 'Nor fenced, nor staked, the *gushers* of the sky / *Spout* to the *rod* divining in a smile / The *oil* of tears'.

Elsewhere there are serious explorations of his poetics:

> Through my small bonebound island I have learnt all I know, experienced
> all, and sent all. All I write is inseparable from the island. As much as
> possible, therefore, I employ the scenery of the island to describe the scenery
> of my thoughts, the earthquakes of the body to describe the earthquakes of
> the heart. (*CL*, 57)

There are also defences of the language of worms, corruption and vermin that
Pamela apparently objected to in the Notebook poems.[3]

For all that Dylan is learning to please various audiences, the week that
Pamela and her mother spent in Swansea in September 1934 was a mixed
experience, to say the least. Pamela's diaries recount time spent working on her
novel, the purchase of a pair of sandals and some yellow shorts, and, despite
some lovely beach walks with Dylan, she notes that she found his mother
Florrie unbearably chatty, that the rain was horrendous, and that she had to
visit a GP in Uplands as she was suffering from hysterics.

> We had reached the last gate. Dusk drew around us and the town. I said:
> What has become of him now? (*RJ*, 338)

Towards the end of *Return Journey*, the narrator has finally retraced his steps
through the years back to Cwmdonkin Park, one of his favourite childhood
haunts, and a place that inspired poems, stories and broadcasts. 'I've known
him by the thousands', the Park Keeper says in response to the narrator's
enquiry, giving an impression that he is just another schoolboy, someone whose
behaviour wasn't unique when he would 'climb the reservoir railings and pelt
the old swans. Run like a billygoat over the grass you should keep off of' (*RJ*,
338). Versions of many of these self-images are presented throughout the
course of *Return Journey* and take their place alongside other images created
by Thomas in his Notebooks and early correspondence. Now, of course, they
jostle with the various images of Dylan that we project on him ourselves. 'Two
typewriter Thomas the ace news-dick' (*RJ*, 330) is still generating news.

Bibliography

Lycett, Andrew, *Dylan Thomas: A New Life* (London: Phoenix, 2003).
Thomas, Dylan, *Return Journey* in *Collected Stories* (London: Phoenix, 2000).
—*Collected Letters* (London: Dent, 2000).
Watkins, Gwen, *Dylan Thomas: Portrait of a Friend* (Talybont: Y Lolfa, 2005).

---

[3] Other advice is offered in a more self-deprecating way: 'The speaking of poetry
should certainly be encouraged. I do hope you read aloud. I myself chant aloud in a
sonorous voice every poem I read. The neighbours must know your poems by heart;
they certainly know my own' (*CL*, 59).

PART TWO

LATER LIFE – 1934–53

This section looks at the second part of my grandfather's life, 1934 until 1953. It shows the contrast between the hectic and demanding times in London and the calmer periods living in peaceful villages and towns in England and Wales.

> She peels off her pink and white skin in a furnace in a tower in a cave in a waterfall in a wood and waits there raw as an onion for Mister Right to leap up the burning tall hollow splashes of leaves like a brilliantined trout.
>
> *Under Milk Wood* by Dylan Thomas

As you read the extract above, it's difficult to contradict Antony Penrose's suggestion that the surrealist movement in London during the 1930s hugely influenced Dylan. Antony's fascinating essay gives us a clear insight into this period of my grandfather's life and how his connection with such a creative circle of friends allowed him to write with the 'wonderful free association his lines hold' and to realize that not everything needs to be 'rationally filtered'. I love the image of my grandfather attending the International Surrealist Exhibition and 'crawling on all fours bearing a teacup filled with string, asking the guests if they want it "weak or strong"'. It's also wonderful to hear about how my grandfather charmed people with amusing anecdotes. I laugh at the reference to him discussing his problems of acid indigestion. This is an ailment I suffer with and have bored many friends and family members with similar tales of woe.

> A year or so later, after the revelations of the German concentration camps, Dylan outlined the idea to me one afternoon in an underground drinking club in Chelsea called the Gateways. The village was declared insane, anti-social, dangerous. Barbed wire was strung about it and patrolled by sentries, lest its dotty inhabitants infect the rest of the world with their feckless and futile view of life. They do not mind at all, though they grumble about the disappearance of the buses. The village is the only place that is left free in the whole world, for the authorities have got it wrong. This is not the concentration camp; the rest of the globe is the camp, is mad, and only this little place is sane and happy.

The Second World War left a deep and haunting mark on my grandfather, as we see in his original plans for *Under Milk Wood* that he discussed with his friend, and later biographer, Constantine Fitzgibbon. It's also very evident in the poem 'Fern Hill', where Dylan looks nostalgically back at more innocent times.

> In the sun that is young once only,
> Time let me play and be
> Golden in the mercy of his means.

We also see the horrors of war through his powerful and evocative broadcast, 'Return Journey'. Between 19 and 21 February 1941, Swansea endured heavy and sustained bombing. Forty-one acres of my grandfather's hometown was obliterated. No less than 857 premises were destroyed. Two hundred and thirty people were killed, 409 injured, and 7,000 were left homeless. Stopped clocks showed the times the bombs fell. My grandfather communicated his heartfelt distress for his lost home as he searched 'through Swansea town cold and early on that wicked February morning'.

> ... he was anti-fascist, anti-fascist most certainly in the sense that fascists were exclusive people ... they wanted to narrow things down ... to me fascism is completely anti-human, and Dylan would have been anti-fascist on these grounds.
>
> Fred Janes on Dylan's political views

My grandfather was a pacifist and the thought of killing another human being was intolerable to him. Despite this, he was very keen to be involved in the war effort and found ways to fight against the aggressive far right extremists. As Paul Jackson shows in his essay, rejecting fascism can take many forms, including 'developing such themes in fiction and plays'. Dylan was aware of this and in a letter commented: '... we wish to enroll ourselves, not merely as nominal members but as active propagandists ... We would wish to propagate, through the columns of all the journals at our disposal, the urgency of bringing together in a common front those who hold similar views to ourselves'. Paul's essay also looks closely at Dylan's work on propaganda films. They have often been referred to as 'hack work' or 'facile', but Paul questions how we judge the work of a writer: 'Is it aesthetic standards alone, or should we include other factors too?' As a historian, he explains that the historical context that writers operate in is vital too, and within their specific historical situation Dylan's films are very successful examples of wartime anti-fascist propaganda. He also observes that, over time, more creativity entered into Dylan's wartime films, and his later scripts were also used to test out ideas and techniques he was developing for scriptwriting after the war.

In September 1944, Dylan went to live for nine months in New Quay, a small seaside town in west Wales. In his chapter, David N. Thomas strongly argues that 'without New Quay, there would have been no *Milk Wood*', but that, he concedes, 'is a matter of judgement, not fact'. He tells the reader that, within months of arriving in New Quay, Dylan had written a radio script about the town, *Quite Early One Morning*, which has many early versions of characters that appear in his later play-for-voices, *Under Milk Wood*. This includes the cleanliness fanatic Mrs Ogmore-Pritchard, who is heard to comment: 'And before you let the sun in, mind he wipes his shoes ...' David humorously remarks: 'To be fair, there were many Mrs Ogmore-Pritchards in New Quay'.

The letter below, written by Dylan while living in the seaside town, surely supports David's argument that the eccentric characters of Llareggub were partly based on New Quay.

> ... I'm so glad you met and like Dai Fred who bottled your ship. Did you come across Dewi, the battery-man? Evan Joshua of the Bluebell? The Norman you know is New Quay's noisiest and least successful fighter; every summer he starts a fight, and every summer some tiny little ape man knocks him yards over the harbour wall or bang through the chemist's window. Did Mrs. Evans the Lion twitch, wink and sip? Did Pat bring his horse in the bar? Jack the Post is an old friend: he once married a pretty widow in London and everything was fine, he said, except that wherever they went they were followed by men in bowler hats. After the honeymoon, Mrs. Jack was arrested for double bigamy. And all the husbands appeared in court and gave evidence as to her good character.

My own visits to New Quay would further back up David's opinion. I can certainly imagine it as described by First Voice, in the prologue to *Under Milk Wood* on a

> spring, moonless night ... starless and bible-black, the cobblestreets silent and the hunched, courters and rabbits wood limping invisible down to the sloeblack, slow, black, crowblack, fishingboat bobbing sea.

It's interesting to note that again, it is a small, peaceful, yet quirky seaside town that helps my grandfather find the space to produce some of his best writing.

Andrew Lycett's essay looks at the role of the patron in Dylan's life. Coincidentally, all three women have the name Margaret. My grandfather, feeling embarrassed by his need for financial assistance, tended to demean these women, but we cannot underestimate the significant part they played in supporting him as a writer, and his extended family as a consequence. If we look briefly at just a few things his most helpful patron, Margaret Taylor, did:

1) She interceded with Graham Greene and a director to publish Dylan's screenplay *The Doctor and the Devils*.
2) She readily acquired a house in the village of South Leigh, Oxfordshire, and found a gypsy caravan so he could work in the garden undisturbed.
3) Realizing his latest ambition to return to the peace and quiet of his native Wales, she paid £3,000 for the Boat House in Laugharne and allowed him to live there for a peppercorn rent.
4) She helped to pay Llewelyn's (Dylan's oldest son) school fees.

It's very difficult to judge the lasting impact of Margaret Taylor's generosity but I know it was something my mum, Aeronwy, was always grateful for. She talked fondly of playing games with Margaret's children, swimming in the river at their home in Oxford and reading stories together. Margaret offered her a stability that was missing elsewhere. As a result, my mum remained friends with Margaret's daughters throughout her life. Andrew recognizes my mum's affection for Margaret Taylor when he quotes from my mum's book, *My Father's Places*: 'I liked Margaret for her boundlessly positive attitude. She made the best of everything and made everything more fun for us children'.

I also find it interesting how profoundly upset Dylan was by his second patron Marged Howard-Stepney's death in early 1953. It is just a few months after his father's death and a few months before his sister dies. In the poem 'Do Not Go Gentle Into That Good Night', we hear Dylan's desperation and despair as his father loses his sight during his long battle with terminal cancer. 'Rage, rage against the dying of the light', he begs. The terrible grief he must have been experiencing helps me understand the reasons he neglected himself in the last few months of his life.

Andrew contemplates whether *Under Milk Wood* would have reached the stage of completion it did without the guidance of his third patron, Princess Marguerite Caetani. He closes the essay with an acute observation which I tend to agree with – that, as well as financial help, 'these women provided the kind of emotional support that Dylan needed as much as any cheque in the post'.

> It looked heavenly: a place to explore, to run around, where we would be living forever. It had verandas and balconies, water-butts, stepped gardens, a large boat shed in the back yard, the harbour and a wall protecting us from the wilds of the friendly estuary beyond. We had fallen upon paradise …
>
> Aeronwy Thomas's impressions when, as a six-year-old child she first saw the Boat House, their new family home in Laugharne.

Another place that was an intense inspiration for my grandfather was Laugharne, in Carmarthenshire, west Wales. In his last-ever broadcast, included in this section, he talks about the unique town. He describes residents 'wandering around like Welsh opium eaters' or 'one Rolls Royce selling fish and chips'. He even comments that he's 'hardly ever stoned in the streets any more, and can claim to be able to call several of the inhabitants, and a few of the herons, by their Christian names'. In giving reasons why people live in Laugharne, he comments that some 'almost certainly come here to escape the international police, or their wives …', though he does finish by saying they are all 'human – often all too human, beings'. And 'there is nowhere like it anywhere at all'.

In a letter to a friend, Dylan calls Laugharne 'the strangest town in Wales'. Jon Tregenna explores Laugharne today, to see if it is still strange, and whether Dylan would know this place if he was still with us. He offers strong evidence to suggest that he would. For example, he tells the reader that 'Laugharne offers sanctuary to those for whom the world is changing too fast … It remains an insular place: many here don't drive, mobile phone reception is patchy at best and the sight of a traffic warden is met with indignation. One local, annoyed at getting a ticket, commented: "If they told us they were coming I wouldn't have parked there"'. Jon explains that it remains 'full of stories ... salacious snippets are gathered, sculpted, embellished and inflated until a story fit for a bar room performance emerges'. He even goes as far as to suggest that, if Dylan were here today, '... he'd garner enough material to write a sequel to *Under Milk Wood* in a weekend'. Roger McGough's poem humorously describes some conversations Dylan may have heard while sitting and listening to the locals in the Brown's Hotel, Laugharne.

In the later life section, I've also included a description by Paul Ferris, one of Dylan's biographers, of a chance meeting with Dylan Thomas in 1949. 'It wouldn't have occurred to me – let alone to him – that twenty-five years later I would be writing his biography'.

I've chosen to include my mum's voice throughout this book. In this part, she follows her parents' footsteps through their wartime haunts in London and allows us to experience vivid recollections of reading with her Dad. She comments, probably with a smile: 'Dad could make lots of other characters from fairytale and nursery rhymes come alive ... It was the best time of the week when Dad opened a book with me'.

My grandfather, Dylan and grandmother, Caitlin are buried in St Martin's Church in Laugharne, marked by a simple white cross. When my mum died in 2009, we scattered her ashes at the Boat House in Laugharne; her four years there with the 'Herons, gulls and pipers encircling her house on stilts' were among her happiest memories.

I finish the section with her poem, 'Later Than Laugharne'.

Dylan Thomas Among the Surrealists

Antony Penrose

In her memoire the Surrealist painter Eileen Agar recalls a dinner party in her home in 1933 or '34 when:

> ... in walked two delightfully refreshing youngsters. Both were poets: one was a shy sensitive plant, the other a ruddy-faced cherub with a snub nose and no chin. Dramatically, as they entered the crowded room all the lights went out, but Dylan squatted on the floor and in a jiffy was reciting limericks in the dark which made everyone present sit up and take notice. This was long before the poet became famous, and he was gay and carefree that evening and hooted when the lights went up again. While Dylan Thomas was deep in flow of bawdy nonsense that kept everyone enthralled ... I managed to grab a pencil and paper (never very far away) and did some lightning drawings of this ugly suckling. Later on, I worked from one of the drawings on a painting which was bought by the Tate Gallery in 1962.[1]

The 'shy sensitive plant' at Agar's party was David Gascoyne, whose book *A short Survey of Surrealism*[2] led him to meet my father, Roland Penrose, in Paris. Penrose had lived in France since 1923, and married the Surrealist poet Valentine Boué in 1925. She introduced him to Paul Éluard and Max Ernst, both of whom were interviewed by Gascoyne. It was Éluard who in turn introduced him to Penrose in about 1935. It was a fortuitous meeting. Penrose had separated from his wife in 1936 and was about to gloomily return to London. He wrote:

> By chance my reluctant return to my native fog coincided with a meeting in the rue de Tournon with Paul Éluard and some other surrealist friends who introduced me to the young English poet, David Gascoyne. It was the encounter of two explorers who had discovered independently the same glittering treasure. David's explosion "Why do we know nothing of this in England?" was echoed immediately by me, who rejoiced in the prospect of converting what had seemed a gloomy retreat into an attack on indifference

[1] Agar, Eileen. *A Look at My Life* p107 Methuen, London. 1988
[2] Gascoyne, David. A Short Survey of Surrealism. Cobden Saunderson, London 1936

and ignorance at home, an affirmation of that which had made life in France so enjoyable and full of purpose.[3]

Surrealism's debut in London came on 11th June 1936. Penrose, closely allied with the art critic Herbert Read, had formed a committee, funded the working capital, organised loans of works from thirteen countries and hired The New Burlington Galleries in Piccadilly. Andre Breton, the 'pope' of Surrealism opened the exhibition to a crowd of about 2,000 people. Dylan Thomas (then aged 22) circulated, crawling on all fours bearing a teacup filled with string, asking the guests if they wanted it "weak or strong". Perhaps he had been inspired to subvert the English tea ritual by Meret Oppenheim's famous object, *Fur Breakfast,* her fur-lined teacup.

By this time Thomas was clearly part of the circle of my father's friends and this was to continue. The next trace that emerges is at the opening of the *Surrealist Objects and Poems* exhibition at The London Gallery 24th November 1937. Penrose had taken over The London Gallery and appointed the Belgian picture dealer and poet Eduard Mesens as its manager. In June of that year Penrose had met and fallen in love with the American surrealist photographer Lee Miller who was to marry Penrose and become my mother. By November she had returned to her husband Aziz Eloui Bey in Cairo. Penrose wrote to her:

> The private view at midnight was a roaring success. There were so many people that for about an hour the place was completely blocked with people packed so tight that they could neither get in nor out. In the rooms upstairs black velvet was served in generous quantities to all who could get to it and after a spectacular fight between a young welsh poet (Dylan Thomas?) and an unknown drunkard who insulted him (one picture smashed) we finally left the gallery at 3.30, but I didn't get to bed until five – I'll tell you about that later.[4]

The London Gallery published a magazine titled The London Bulletin, and it would appear Penrose invited Thomas to contribute a piece for the March 1938 issue, and his request elicited this response from Thomas;

> Blashford
> Ringwood
> Hants
> 21 March 1938

Dear Roland,
    Of course you can count on my support and I'll send you a story or a poem when it's needed. I don't, I suppose, get paid for a contribution? That sounds extremely mean, but I write so slowly and produce so little that it's

[3] Penrose, Roland. *Scrap Book.* p56 Thames & Hudson, London 1981
[4] Letter from Roland Penrose in London to Lee Miller in Cairo dated 26 11 1937. Coll. The Penrose Collection, Farley Farm House. East Sussex.

essential – considering the fact that I try, though always without success, to exist on my writing – I have little money for anything of mine that is published. I really am in a very bad, distressing position now, living on charity, unable to buy for myself even the smallest necessary luxuries, and having little peace of mind from those small and nagging worries to work as well and carefully as I should like. I may have to stop writing altogether very soon – for writing is obviously full-time or not at all – and try to obtain some little, sure work. I'm sorry to write as meanly and wretchedly as this, but the way in which I am forced to live has begun to colour everything. But, of course, if the Gallery Bulletin can't pay, I'll still be very pleased to send you a poem or some prose.

    Best wishes,
      Yours ever
        Dylan T.

('Thomas' is written at the foot of the page in Roland Penrose's hand.)[5]

Sadly no work by Thomas was published in The London Bulletin.

Miller left Eloui Bey in August 1939 and went to London, moving in to Penrose's Hampstead house, 36 Downshire Hill, and started working for *Vogue* magazine as a freelance photographer. Thomas was a frequent visitor to the house. Terry O'Brien, an Australian then in the RAF and married to Timmie, one of Miller's *Vogue* colleagues, wrote:

> We said we would pick him up at the pub near the Langham but when we arrived there was no Dylan, just a message to say he had already gone to Downshire Hill. When we reached there he was apologetic and thirsting for a beer – most of the others, about 10 of them, were drinking Algerian. I found a beer for Dylan and left him with Lee and Timmie, talking about indigestion, when John Lake, who had come up for the night, called me over to talk to someone about camouflage on aircraft. ... During this time Timmie and Lee had remained with Dylan by the window, all in apparent enjoyment of some Welsh mysteries, but when I decided to re-join them they had disappeared. I found Timmie alone downstairs in the kitchen, giggling about the story he was finishing ... and she made him retell it to me. I had to replenish his beer first – he would not take a whiskey.
>
> He had been carrying a schoolboy's leather satchel on arrival and when Roland handed it back to him from the hall hanger Dylan looked at the papers inside and said "Room for a bottle, I see." Roland went back to the sitting room and brought out three, but they finally decided that two was about all the satchel and Dylan maybe, could take.
>
> Another story was about a BBC man taking him to a pub where Dylan had worked a deal with the barman that he would order gin in his beer,

⁵ Dylan Thomas letter to Roland Penrose 21 March 1938. Coll. The Roland Penrose Archive, Scottish National Gallery of Modern Art, Modern Two, Edinburgh.

but it would not be put in his beer, just added to the bill. According to Dylan he drank four pints – or was it fourteen? – and when they left the barman surreptitiously held up his thumb to Dylan confirming that he had the credit waiting. I was told that some BBC man was grabbing every piece of paper Dylan uses, every script, poem, anything, offering to get it typed, and meanwhile he piles up the original Dylan Thomas manuscripts for his pensionable future. When I suggested this to Dylan, he said: "Suits me. They get bits of paper, I get pints of beer."[6]

Evenings at Downshire Hill were not always as jolly for Thomas. Cynthia Thompson who worked for LIFE Magazine had this recollection from about 1943: "I remember Dylan Thomas in the kitchen at Downshire Hill saying: 'I wish I were dead!' Cynthia's husband John (later the editor of The Sunday Telegraph) added: "He (Penrose) probably gave him money like a lot of people did."[7]

Following the Normandy landings in June 1944, Miller, now a war correspondent for *Vogue*, began recording the advance of the American army across Europe. It was 1946 when she returned, having witnessed some of the most horrific moments of the war as a combat photographer. After her experiences, shooting fashion seemed really trivial, but she did enjoy portraiture, particularly with people she liked and could have a drink with both during and after the session. It would seem her session with Thomas on 13 December 1946 fell into this category.

The recent publication of Thomas' collection of writings *Deaths and Entrances* had brought him widespread attention and an excellent review from Cyril Connolly – who was also a friend of my parents. The reason for the Vogue commission was the publication of Dylan Thomas' short story Holiday Memory in their American edition. Studying the contact sheets from the shoot, Miller's style is non-invasive with a minimum of contrivance. Using a background of the studio wall hung with lighting filters and a trestle table with an inkwell and some books she created a sparse set that suggests the simplicity of Thomas' shed in Laugharne. It takes Thomas a while to settle in, and it is the twelfth and last shot on the roll that finds him relaxed. He has lit a cigarette and seems genuinely engrossed in his writing. On the second roll three other takes follow, and then there is a change of set. Miller positions Thomas standing in the corridor outside the studio. The pose looks unnatural so she gets a chair and he sits, tilting back against the wall, relaxed, cigarette in hand nonchalantly gazing at the lens, seemingly lost in thought. This must have appealed to Miller. Here was the friendly but self-absorbed person she knew and liked. She switched from her much loved medium format Rolleiflex and shot five frames on a half plate studio camera. The second frame was the

---

[6] O'Brien, Terrence. Notes for an unpublished memoir. Private collection, England
[7] Thompson, Cynthia and John interviewed by Michael Sweeney 18 11 1997.

winner, and it made a full page in the July 1947 issue of American *Vogue*[8], illustrating Thomas's prose piece *Holiday Memory*. Later it appeared in a feature on Thomas's poetry in the Slovakian publication *Slovenské Pohl'ady*[9], a recognition of the international appreciation of Thomas's poetry at that time.

Some scholars are keen to point out that Thomas repudiated the influence of Surrealism on his work. Certainly in an interview published in Texas Quarterly[10] he disassociated himself from the 'stream of conscious' writing of James Joyce in *Ulysses* and from the surrealist method of delving into the subconscious and freely juxtaposing words with no heed to rational relationship, stating:

> I do not mind from where the images of a poem are dragged up: drag them up, if you like, from the nethermost sea of the hidden self; but before they reach the paper, they must go through all the rational processes of the intellect.[11]

No one can doubt Thomas' honesty in this statement, but one thing that will remain unknown is the level at which the movement influenced his style. Would he have reached the same wonderful free association his lines hold if everything he wrote was rationally filtered? Certainly Thomas, like every other artist, knew an idea that was worth adapting when he saw one and for me the influence of Picasso is something I feel was important to the development of *Under Milk Wood*.

Picasso's play *Desire Caught by the Tail*[12] is essentially a protest – a defiance against the Nazi occupation of France. He wrote it in January, 1941, by which time the full horror of Nazi tyranny had yet to become fully apparent. When it was first performed in March 1944, the French civilians had endured three years oppression, betrayal, shortages of food and energy and a pervasive fear. The French Vichy government worked hand in hand with the Gestapo, targeting Jews, dissidents and others they singled out for vicious and frequently lethal persecution.

In the play we find frequent references to food and its scarcity, and other things that were in short supply like soap, warmth and comfort. Instead we have the frequent occurrence of crude sex, violence, passion, farting, pissing, cold and discomfort, and as to be expected in the harsh times of warfare, we see the importance of chance, represented by the lottery wheel. Fortunate and joyful events occur, only to be brutally reversed. Every incident seems randomly chosen and assembled in a wholly irrational manner.

[8]   Coll *Vogue* archives London
[9]   Coll. Dylan Thomas Museum Swansea
[10] Sinclair, Andrew. *Dylan Tomas Poet of His People* Michael Joseph London 1975. *The Answers called 'Poetic Manifesto'* 1951 *Texas Quarterly* Winter 1961 quoted in full p227–233.
[11] Ibid p323
[12] Picasso, Pablo. *Desire Caught by the Tail*. 1944. Translated by Roland Penrose. Calder & Boyars London 1969

The hero is Big Foot, an artist and poet who lives in a chaotic studio. His friend called Onion is also his rival for Big Foot's passion, The Tart, whose cousin is helpfully named Cousin and friends Fat and Thin Anxiety, Round Piece, the Two Bow-wows, Silence and Curtains are the other members of the cast.

Desire Caught By The Tail with its lush and often sensual language and its pictorial qualities carries no discernible plot line or narrative. Although there was nothing that could give the Gestapo logical cause to use the play as an excuse for their persecution, the performances were held in secret as the enemy would have surely recognised the cry for freedom it contained.

Big Foot's final heroic words assert the defiance of the piece. He declares;

> Light the lanterns. Throw flights of doves with all our strength against the bullets and lock securely the houses demolished by bombs.[13]

The first performance was a reading, directed by Albert Camus, who also read the stage directions, and with Picasso's lover Dora Maar as Thin Anxiety, Zanie Aubier as 'The Tart', Simone de Beauvoir as 'Her Cousin' and Jean Paul Sartre as 'Round Piece'. It was attended by Picasso and Éluard, seated in an audience of about 120. It served to unite and rally people in their darkest moment. The art historian and critic Michel Leiris, in the cast as 'Big Foot', said afterwards that it gave those present a feeling of an affirmation of liberty[14]. It ran in secret for 5 or 6 performances.

Penrose who had championed Picasso's work in England from 1936 translated it into English and it was performed in his London Gallery in 1947, and later mounted by his newly founded ICA – Institute of Contemporary – Arts in 1950 in the Rudolf Steiner Hall with Valentine Dyall as Big Foot and Dylan Thomas as Onion.

The review in Picture Post was appreciative but described Thomas's role as the 'Stage Manager', suggesting perhaps he was also given the lines of stage direction.

The excellent Dylan Thomas website[15] charts the development of *Under Milk Wood* from when Thomas was 17 in 1931, writing an imagined nonsense dialogue between Mussolini and his wife. It seems he was aware from the beginning of the scope offered by a play for voices. *The Londoner* (1946) and *Return Journey* (1947) were significant steps towards *Under Milk Wood*. We will never know how many – if any – ideas he adapted from *Desire Caught By The Tail,* but when comparing the two it is tempting to imagine Thomas at the least found a close affinity with Picasso's work, if not an inspiration.

There is a nice symmetry in that it was the ICA, by now in its premises in Dover Street, where Thomas gave what seems like the only London reading in Britain of *Under Milk Wood*. It was May 1952 and must have been moments

---

[13] Ibid, p62
[14] Ibid p12
[15] www.dylanthomas.com founded by Aeronwy Thomas (1943–2009)

before he left for America to give readings of parts of the work as it progressed through its fraught evolution of re-writes.

Among my parent's records was an LP of Richard Burton's *Under Milk Wood*. As a young teenager it was my introduction to Thomas's work. I loved it. Burton's sure and subtly expressive voice led me through the cobbled streets of Llareggub, meeting and becoming familiar with the village folk and yearning to encounter Polly Garter.

My parents did not tell me of their friendship with Thomas. They told me very little of their previous lives and it always seemed the present was more important to them than the past. Looking back on the evidence that remains it seems their relationship with Thomas was typical of their circle of friends –sometimes they fought, but there was a tremendous bond among them and a sense of excitement at the challenge of rolling back the limitations of public acceptance of the arts and crossing new frontiers. That is what they loved doing and did best, and we are indebted.

Chelsea (in Dylan's Footsteps)

Aeronwy Thomas

Wandering around Chelsea
I look for what was.
The Markham, favourite
watering hole
now a bank or pizza place

Six Bells, where
they drank
during the war
now an American
burger chain
pub garden still
intact.
They preferred the
indoor fug.

Next stop
The Eight Bells,
We'll have a beer.
No open door here,
slammed for a
wedding reception,
an up-market restaurant
now,
renamed Brasserie.

Well, a few steps to,
The Cross Keys
near Cheyne Walk
the church and
Thames.
Stone swans and statuary
on the walls
barely noticed
by the regulars

checking if the beer
had run out,
keen to meet
artistic types
like Theodora Fitzgibbon
a model then,
wife of Dylan's first biographer,
later cookery writer
and chronicler of
those wartorn years.
'The trouble was
drinkers forget
to eat ... she told me ...
so I cooked casseroles
in buckets over a fire
for friends, after hours'.

Today, we all eat
and drink our fill.
Joining us
are Mum and Dad
it's quite a party.
'Don't forget the Anglesea,'
Mum says,
'we drank there too ...
always met someone
from Swansea'.
'It was known as
The Welsh Club,'
laughs Dad.
Unhappily
we move on
or they leave us:
one minute there
holding forth,
to a rapt audience
holding on to their bitters,
then they are gone
who knows where.

In our unexpected meeting
at the Cross Keys
Mother said,
'It only occurred to me
just now seeing you
that we should have stayed

with you, a baby
left under the bombs
born in '43
not kept our pub routine
like clockwork
ignored the warnings
as sirens wailed
every night'.
We walk away to
The Anglesea
nearly at the
Fulham Rd.
known familiarly as
The Welsh Club
near The Queen's Elm
Laurie Lee's haunt
smelling of beer and
blokes
so narrow round the
bar where Dad was
caught in full flow
and audience
by Nicolette, Mother's sister,
to take him away
to view the new baby
Aeronwy Bryn.

She was useless too
forgetting her mission
entranced by a free drink
(she was very pretty)
and his tall tales
and shaggy dog anecdotes
until closing time sounded
We stopped at The Anglesea
longest
as I came to terms
with his negligence
and her's leaving me
as a baby for hours on end
in the glass roofed studio
as air raids raged
and they drank to the dregs
praising
their contribution

to the War Effort
as they valiantly ignored
the falling bombs.

'We should have stayed with you,' she said
'but I'd have lost him and habits are difficult to break.'

Dylan Thomas: The Anti-Fascist Propagandist

Paul Jackson

How do we judge the work of a writer? By aesthetic standards alone, or should we include other factors too? For literary critics, perhaps, assessing the quality of the literary qualities of an artist's writings is the most crucial factor, while for historians exploring the historical contexts that writers operate within is vital too. Dylan Thomas is often seen as an anti-fascist of sorts. Yet the notion of anti-fascism is a complex theme, and one that Dylan's life intersected with in a number of ways: as a young man opposing British Union of Fascist sympathies in Swansea, as a wartime propagandist, and as a horrified spectator to the destructive impact of Nazism and the Holocaust. Examining this quality to Dylan's life is important; both to understand his own politics, and to better assess the ways in which anti-fascism impacted on European culture more widely too. Indeed, as we move further away from the era of fascism, the ways in which Dylan's anti-fascism was of great significance to his identity have become clearer.

But why is it important to study anti-fascist cultures? In general terms, historians of post-war Europe, such as Tony Judd and Dan Stone, have commented on the ways in which the post-1945 era was marked by a wide range of instinctual responses rejecting Hitler, Mussolini and all that their politics entailed. But in his book, *Goodbye to All That?: The Story of Europe Since 1945*, Dan Stone also highlights the recent decline of this anti-fascist attitude, which in turn has led to the opening up of a political space for far right trends to emerge once more. As anti-fascism as an ingrained feature of British and European culture wanes, it becomes ever more important to understand the variety of ways in which anti-fascism manifested itself. Dylan's own engagements with the various anti-fascist cultures of his era offer a telling example of how creative energies of the mid-century period were indelibly marked by a mood rejecting nationalist extremism. In this context, examining such anti-fascist attitudes is more important than working out whether a particular form of anti-fascist material remains 'good' art or not. A historically driven understanding of anti-fascism is far more concerned with establishing whether anti-fascist material was useful, whether it helped in some way with the immense struggle against the Nazi regime in some manner or another. In this essay, I hope to reappraise Dylan in this regard, presenting him as a typically minor, but passionate, anti-fascist activist and intellectual.

To do this I will focus primarily on Dylan's wartime films, an aspect of his oeuvre that often comes across badly in the critical reception of his various writings. Andrew Lycett has discussed this at some length, but in his biography of Dylan emphasizes quotes suggesting he considered his film experiences to be merely 'hack work'.[1] Meanwhile, Paul Ferris dismissed wartime scripts as 'facile' in his brief treatment of this chapter in the Thomas story.[2] The latter is a particularly reductive viewpoint, especially if we consider these film scripts as products of a specific historical situation, created primarily as functional, anti-fascist media, and developed for an immediate purpose rather than for lasting posterity. A more positive assessment of this early film work comes from John Ackerman, who produced the most comprehensive study of Thomas's various scriptwriting experiences, *Dylan Thomas: The Complete Screenplays*. As this chapter will show, in this volume Ackerman is right to stress that, over time, more creativity entered into Dylan's wartime films, and his later scripts were also used to test out ideas and techniques he was developing for scriptwriting after the war.

Before moving on to the films themselves, gaining a sense of Dylan's wider political sympathies is, of course, important to any discussion on how his anti-fascist sympathies can be understood. To do so, it is also important to stress that anti-fascism as a concept comes with many narrow clichés, largely pointing to attempts to prevent fascist organizations marching on the streets developed by radical left-wing activists. Yet such anti-fascist street demonstrations, and clashes, are just one form of what we can consider anti-fascist activity, amply demonstrated by a recent edited volume by leading expert on British anti-fascism of the interwar period, Nigel Copsey.[3] In his estimation, Copsey suggests we should adopt a much looser and more expansive approach to the issue of defining what 'anti-fascism' is, and calls for us to recognize that anti-fascists are simply those people who identify themselves as such in a variety of ways. They come from all political backgrounds, including the political right, and can also develop their actions in a wide range of forms. Anti-fascist cultures ought to be seen as a far more expansive set of activities than simply rowdy street demonstrations. Anti-fascism can also incorporate writing political essays, developing such themes in fiction and plays, and can appear in myriad other cultural forms that, somehow, seek to reject fascism. Moreover, the theme is concerned with how people establish a sense of their own identity too. With this more expansive approach in mind, we can see that in many ways Dylan's own cultural output, and identity, formed in an era

---

[1]   Andrew Lycett, *Dylan Thomas: A New Life* (London: Weidenfeld & Nicolson, 2003), chapter 13.

[2]   Paul Ferris, *Dylan Thomas: The Biography, New Edition* (London: Dent, 1999), 183.

[3]   Nigel Copsey and Andrzej Olechnowicz (eds), *Varieties of Anti-Fascism: Britain in the Inter-War Period* (Basingstoke: Palgrave Macmillan, 2010).

defined by the growth of fascism, followed the world coming to terms with the extremes of genocide that European fascists unleashed during the Second World War. All this raises the question: how can we understand Dylan's wartime propaganda films within a wider set of anti-fascist values, and better comprehend the context within which he created films that are often easily dismissed as holding little to no importance?

In terms of political outlook, there is some debate as to where, precisely, Dylan's sympathies lay. Nevertheless, it is broadly understood that he was a man very much of the radical left, even if he was not a clear-cut case of a Marxist or a Communist. As a young man, Dylan identified with anti-establishment values, and, coming of age in South Wales during the 1930s, it is probably not surprising that he developed this instinctually left-leaning politics. John Ackerman has written on his intuitive leftist attitudes by highlighting that Dylan was not an artist who connected with ideology on a deep, intellectual level in the same way as one can see in poets who went to fight in the Spanish Civil War, such as W. H. Auden or Stephen Spender, during the 1930s. Rather, for Thomas it was a received wisdom taken from aspects of Welsh radicalism that helped to shape his left-wing views.[4] Moreover, he was not simply an emotive left-winger without any ability to formulate sustained political thought, nor should one confuse a reluctance to politicize his poetry with a detached attitude towards politics. Victor Golightly's analysis of Dylan's politics in the 1930s is useful too, stressing his persistent engagement with Marxist viewpoints and figures while in Swansea. Characters such as Bert Trick were particularly important here, and Golightly's discussion on Dylan's Marxist sympathies draws out his active role within such politicized circles.

In this period, such a radical left identity increasingly led to conflicts with the new politics of fascism. Fred Janes recalls Dylan's ambiguous, but distinctly anti-fascist, politics as follows:

> ... he could even feel tremendous sympathy with people who were completely opposite in point of view ... he had this universal outlook ... I think that if Dylan had ever affiliated himself in any close way with the Communist Party – I don't recall his having done this ... – I'm absolutely certain that this would have been in line with what I have just said in that he was anti-fascist, anti-fascist most certainly in the sense that fascists were exclusive people ... they wanted to narrow things down ... to me fascism is completely anti-human, and Dylan would have been anti-fascist on these grounds.[5]

Moreover, one notorious episode in Dylan's experiences in Swansea helped to draw him into worlds where anti-fascism was a clear presence: his role in demonstrating against the British Union of Fascists in July 1934. The BUF was

[4] John Ackerman, *Dylan Thomas: His Life and Work* (Basingstoke: Palgrave Macmillan, 1991), 31.

[5] Fred Janes in David N. Thomas, ed., *Dylan Remembered: Volume Two 1935–1953* (Bridge End: Seren, 2004), 35.

able to mount a 3,000-strong demonstration in Swansea at this time.[6] Talking about his role in opposing this demonstration, in a letter to Pamela Hansford Johnson,[7] Dylan even suggested that he was thrown down some stairs in a confrontation with BUF activists. In reality, this was probably myth-making, but is also a typically anti-fascist type of mythmaking, revelling in a violent confrontation with fascists. He also went on in the letter to boast of writing a seditious article on the BUF. The point here is not whether the story was true, but rather to highlight the way such correspondence shows how Dylan liked to cultivate an anti-fascist profile among his fellow writer friends, and incorporated this into an emerging political identity. In another example on this theme while in Swansea, Dylan openly took issue with a local councillor, Mainwaring Hughes. Hughes defected for a time from the Conservatives to the BUF in the 1930s, and was publicly critical of local Jewish people too. The pair clashed in the pages of the *Swansea Guardian*, a paper hosting a wide variety of left- and right-wing political views. Such examples show how Dylan happily embraced an anti-fascist identity among friends and publicly, even if this was expressed directly in his poetry.

While developing elements of an anti-fascist profile publicly and among his contacts, Dylan also commented on the theme of how he was prepared to use his writing abilities as a means to advance political points. He was a promoter of pacifism too, and a supporter of the left-leaning No More War Movement. Writing to Ithel Davies in 1934 on the way, as a writer, he could contribute to the No More War Movement, he explained:

> ... we believe the present militarist trend of national politics makes it imperative that those who object to War in any shape or form should actively identify themselves with the Movement ... we wish to enrol ourselves, not merely as nominal members but as active propagandists ... We would wish to propagate, through the columns of all the journals at our disposal, the urgency of bringing together in a common front those who hold similar views to ourselves.[8]

So, when examining his later propaganda work, this sort of attitude is important to establish: writing considered less important aesthetically could be militated towards a political goal. Its purpose was different, so Dylan set different standards for it. Looking at his writings more generally, we find different standards set for different types of work. Much of his prose fiction, such as *Portrait of an Artist as a Young Dog* and *Adventures in the Skin Trade*,

---

[6] Victor Golightly, '"Writing with dreams and blood": Dylan Thomas, Marxism and 1930s Swansea', available online at: http://www.dylanthomasboathouse.com/media/9988/Dylan-Thomas-Essay-Victor-Golightly.pdf [last accessed 17 February 2014].

[7] Dylan Thomas in Paul Ferris (ed.), *Dylan Thomas: The Collected Letters, New Edition* (London: Dent, 2000), 173.

[8] Thomas in *Collected Letters*, 192.

were not written with the notoriously careful and precise artistic voice that he developed for poetry. Rather than sweating for days over a single line or even word, copying and recopying drafts, such prose was written quickly, and often for money – as one might well expect from a jobbing writer.

In sum, before war in Europe broke out, we can clearly characterize Dylan's politics as radically left-sympathizing, to the point of holding close links with communists, and also decidedly anti-fascist in outlook too. These qualities came together again in his wartime scriptwriting.

With the turn to war in Europe, we can gain a useful insight into Dylan's initial reactions to the conflict from his friend and early biographer Constantine Fitzgibbon. Fitzgibbon commented on how, for Dylan, the 'war was a personal affront'. Moreover, for Dylan's bohemian, left-leaning circle, as for many of his generation, while they loathed Nazism, they also held similar feelings for the British state and politicians. Blame for the failures of appeasement, and the turn to war, lay with the British establishment every bit as much as with Nazism's ultra-nationalist war of expansion. More worryingly still, despite by this time having a wife and child, Dylan felt that a man of twenty-four would soon be called up to fight. So for an instinctual pacifist – though one perhaps unlikely to be deemed as such by the state – Fitzgibbon sets out how Dylan was thrown into deep crisis by the war.[9] With no money to emigrate, he summarized his attitude to the war in a letter to John Davenport:

> I am trying to get a job before conscription, because my one-and-only body I will not give ... all I want to do is write poems, I'm only just getting going now, and enough money to keep two and a bit alive ... my money-sources ... are diminishing or dying. Soon there will not be a serious paper paying inadequately for serious stories and poems.[10]

Dylan relocated from Wales to London, living cheaply on the hospitality of Davenport, and subsequently came into contact with Donald Taylor, a producer for Strand Films. Via this connection, we see Dylan's wartime propaganda films emerge. In the 1930s, Taylor had become an established figure within the radical Documentary Film Movement, which itself had developed a style of film that combined a progressive political message with accessible, realist depictions of working-class life, some directly filming everyday life such as working-class slums to raise awareness of poor housing standards. As with many other cultural forms during the war, the Documentary Film Movement was lured into developing media that directly opposed fascism.

Taylor and Thomas hit it off instantly, and Dylan was taken on as a scriptwriter, securing his much-needed wartime income. He also took the work seriously – a point often minimized by subsequent commentators. When describing her husband's wartime propaganda work, Caitlin Thomas highlighted that he

---

[9]   Constantine Fitzgibbon, *The Life of Dylan Thomas* (London: Dent, 1965), chapter 10.
[10] Thomas in *Collected Letters*, 464.

'never took the job lightly', and added, 'he was keenly interested in the new techniques he was learning, and he was hoping to move on to other forms of film writing when, as he expected, the film industry revived after the war'.[11] Film had always fascinated Dylan, and he was excited to be working in the industry. Further, so long as he turned in scripts, he could travel to Wales and elsewhere during the war. Meanwhile, London's Café Royal, or its many pubs, hosted numerous Strand Films production meetings, with the bills covered by expenses. Finally, Dylan was also free to work on poetry and other writing projects.

We can focus on Dylan's own films later, but first it is also important to set the wider context of documentary films, and their place within British wartime propaganda, in this period. When turning to the historical literature on film in wartime Britain, we do get a clearer picture of the specific role for documentary film within the government's project for film propaganda more generally. Curiously, historians of wartime propaganda Anthony Algate and Jeffrey Richards emphasize that this period in many ways became a golden age for British filmmaking, with the scrutiny of the newly established Ministry of Information (MoI) often helping to raise the production quality of film. Moreover, although documentary film was initially viewed with scepticism by the first head of the MoI's Film Division, Sir Joseph Ball, from 1940 Sir Kenneth Clark and then Jack Beddington developed a much more positive attitude towards the documentary form of film propaganda. Estimates suggest that, during the war, documentary film represented around three-quarters of all MoI-commissioned films. Although there were efforts to remove any overt left-wing bias, the Documentary Film Movement was well placed to help fill this demand.

In terms of overarching messages, propaganda film either needed to offer escapism or focus on the war effort; while feature films provided opportunities the former, newsreel and especially documentary were ways to develop the latter. Films that the ministry were happy to commission also needed to reject a simple nostalgia for the past, and to present stories evoking the idea of a people's war leading to a renewed Britain, while also celebrating democratic freedoms. Algate's and Richards's analysis also stresses that this agenda, broadly speaking, genuinely resonated with the public's imagination regarding the aims and purposes of the war.[12] Nicholas Reeves's work on this topic also stresses the positive achievements of British films at this time. Though newsreels were less successful, he too emphasizes that both documentary and feature film reached their target audiences, and successfully transmitted the messages that propagandists sought to articulate.[13]

---

[11] Caitlin Thomas with George Tremlett, *Caitlin: A Warring Absence* (London: Secker & Warburg, 1986), 79.

[12] Anthony Algate and Jeffrey Richards, *Britain Can Take It: British Cinema in the Second World War* (London: I. B. Taurus, 2007), chapter 1.

[13] Nicholas Reeves, *The Power of Film Propaganda: Myth or Reality?* (London: Cassell, 1999), chapter 4.

Despite the need to strike a neutral tone, within the culture of documentary-making itself during the war progressive social messages were still pronounced, through the idea of fighting a people's war. This tenor can be seen in many articles written for the specialist journal for the movement in wartime, *Documentary News Letter*. One essay in *Documentary News Letter* from 1942, by the leading light of the Documentary Film Movement John Grierson, typifies the continued radical tone in documentary films of the wartime era. Highlighting the movement's pre-war goal of instilling a radical vision of social change in the mind of the British public, Grierson stressed that the conditions of 'total war may yet appear as the dreadful period of forced apprenticeship in which we learned what we had hitherto refused to learn, how to order the vast new forces of human and material energies to decent human ends'.[14] This publication offers a vital window into how Dylan's films, among many others, were seen within their historical setting and professional context, and will be drawn on later to make assessments of just how well his work functioned in their intended primary purpose of being anti-fascist media.

To summarize, during the war Dylan, the instinctual left-wing anti-fascist, was writing for a branch of government propaganda, documentary film, that itself was defined by the radical politics of the Documentary Film Movement. In this role he could both produce anti-fascist films, and also develop his own skills as a scriptwriter.

With this contextual backcloth established, we can turn to the films themselves. To begin with an early production from 1942, *New Towns for Old*, here we find Dylan telling the wartime story of a town called Smokedale. The film shows how this fictional town had begun to develop new housing projects before the war and, now that German bombing had helped slum clearance, Smokedale could develop radical new plans for its future. The film depicts scale models setting out the project for the town's reconstruction, highlighting their modern qualities, while commentary stresses the need to grasp the unique opportunity to radically restructure the town created by the war. Two central figures discuss this project of reconstruction, emotively linking Smokedale's regeneration to a new future for its children. With the narrative of war-as-progress strongly developed, the film ends with a scene evocative of the Field Marshal Kitchener posters from the First World War: one of the figures points to the camera and tells the audience that they are responsible for the processes of reconstruction, not elite politicians. To help evoke this people's war theme, they are given regional Yorkshire accents.

While easy to dismiss as a piece of workmanlike propaganda, *New Towns for Old* was clearly a success within its historical situation – and this after all was where it was supposed to have an impact. Highlighting this positive

---

[14] John Grierson, 'The Documentary Idea, 1942', *Documentary News Letter* 3:6 (1942), 83–6, 85.

reception, a review in *Documentary News Letter* shows how the film struck the correct tone for the wartime situation:

> Sensibly enough, the film aims not at the detailing of expert opinion but rather at making the citizenry conscious of their own responsibility as regards planning as well as the difficulties involved. The style adopted is pleasant. It consists of dialogue between two men as they walk through the various areas of 'Smokedale' and discuss the things they see. One of the men takes the lead and is virtually the commentator; as he has a particularly attractive Yorkshire accent, everything he says gets home with a punch – notably at the end of the film, when he turns abruptly to the audience and points out that the realisation of the ideas of the planners rests entirely in their own hands.

There was more about the success of the film than just Dylan's script, but this was, of course, crucial to developing the film. Interestingly, all reviews in *Documentary News Letter* concluded with a sentence outlining the propaganda value of the reviewed film. In this case, *New Towns for Old* was summarized as being 'Very good for the Home Front, particularly since the film makes it clear that plans for the future are bound up with the war effort which we are all engaged in here and now'.[15]

A similar theme of post-war reconstruction was developed in the subsequent film *A City Reborn*, which focused on the reconstruction of Coventry through the lens of a returning soldier wanting to start a family. Once again evoking the war-as-progress ideal, conservative attitudes towards change were represented, and critically dismissed, in a scripted pub discussion. In particular, we see Arnold, an older character, criticizing prefabricated houses while others around him challenge this perspective. The theme of styling the war as an opportunity for social progress is augmented by a running commentary that also stresses the need for new houses to replace pre-war slums. Again, this goal would only be achieved through planning and developing a unifying vision of the future.

For the most part, depictions of men tended to dominate these propaganda films, though not always. While *New Towns for Old* and *A City Reborn* focused on the role of men planning a new future for Britain's cities, women's wartime experiences defined *Balloon Site 568*. Examining the process of recruitment to the Women's Auxiliary Air Service, this film took a commonplace scenario and set out an essentially warming story of women making friends, singing songs, and working hard at an important wartime job. The film was again seen as important in its historical context, in particular as it updated an earlier film concerning barrage balloons, *Squadron 992*, made during the phoney war period, that was deemed to have dated quickly. Dylan's version of the film reworked the significant theme of recruiting women to such gendered

---

[15] *Documentary News Letter* 3:6 (1942), 94.

roles, refreshing a central enlisting message. Its propaganda value, according to *Documentary News Letter*, was as follows:

> A job, which the film admits must at times be hard, even depressing, is shown to be an inviting one. Burdensome military discipline is not to be seen – but the girls drop their sing-song in the recreation hut quickly enough when an operational order comes through. The film should bring recruits to the Service ... We have moved a little since *Squadron 992* so pleasantly mirrored our then conception of total war.[16]

As with *New Towns for Old*, it is easy to dismiss the film's script as being essentially functional, emphasizing positive aspects of warfare in a down-to-earth manner. Yet this was crucial to the brief. Moreover, judged alongside the aesthetic standards set by the Documentary Film Movement more generally, this is also in keeping with the way the tradition developed films. Before the war too, this was a movement that cultivated realism and authenticity over escapist flourishes.

The theme of the empire being at war was a further crucial issue for the commissioners of these anti-fascist films. We can get a clear sense of how Thomas followed the line regarding positive representations of empire from a key article in *Documentary News Letter*. Typifying the vision to be cultivated by propaganda film, this essay described how the empire ought to be depicted as follows:

> (a) The colonies, largely inhabited by 'backward' races ruled completely by us under the official principle of Trusteeship – i.e. benevolent rulership until the developments arising from improved education and social conditions enable them to become self governing, (b) the Dominions, largely new areas of the world colonised from Europe, completely independent, with their own Governments, laws and electoral systems; (c) India, Burma and Ceylon, where the issue of independence (i.e. Dominion status) is one of the major problems faced by Britain today.[17]

When we turn to Dylan's film *Battle for Freedom*, from 1942 and designed to show how the empire was pulling together in wartime, we find that it too chimes with these themes. The film engages with all three categories of empire, and so African colonies are presented as less capable, though clearly progressing under the positive stewardship of British rule; as the script stresses, in the future, 'they may achieve full independence and self-government'. Meanwhile, Canada, Australia and New Zealand are heralded as paragons of freedom, the creations of the benevolent British Empire which produced these democratic new nations. Finally, the war with Japan was presented as an existential battle for India's future freedom. As the script stresses, 'a successful Japanese invasion would mean slavery – would mean that the certainty of the

---

[16] *Documentary News Letter* 3:7 (1942), 100.
[17] 'The Empire and Propaganda', *Documentary News Letter* 2:12 (1941), 223.

British promise of India's independence would vanish like smoke'.[18] So *Battle for Freedom*'s propagandistic representations of empire echoed with the wider themes within the wartime media messages too.

Stressing the positive virtues of aspects of government policy can also be seen in *C.E.M.A.*, detailing the work of the newly established Council for the Encouragement of Music and the Arts. On one level, it is yet another workmanlike script that allows for the people's war theme to be strongly developed. *C.E.M.A.* sets out a number of regional scenes populated predominantly by working-class people engaging with, and enjoying, high art, including classical music and theatre. In so doing, it connected with overarching themes of British wartime propaganda, especially celebrating democratic freedoms. Basically, it styles the spirit that the war is bringing out in the British as the antithesis of the totalitarian enemy. *Documentary News Letter* praised the film for its innovative qualities too.[19] The idea of culture responding positively to the war was also developed in the film *Wales – Green Mountain, Black Mountain*, a production extolling the cultural virtues of Wales in wartime. Curiously, Thomas's script was seen as problematic by the British Council, who had commissioned the film for use overseas, because they felt it stressed too strongly Wales's unemployment problems before the war. Despite this radical subtext, it was eventually released by the MoI's Welsh Office.[20]

As we can see, then, although offering a functional aesthetic, within their specific historical situation these films were successful examples of wartime anti-fascist propaganda. The British were painted in positive, progressive light and the enemy was also implicitly evoked. Although defined by a now-dated aesthetic and level of production, as historical documents they reveal and typify major themes in the documentary films made during the war. However, not all of these scripts were so mundane. Humour is also often associated with Dylan's writing, and the film *These Are The Men* was most certainly the funniest of his anti-fascist pieces. The film's publicity synopsis reads: 'A powerful denunciation of the Nazi leadership for their crimes in "setting man against man", visually based on imaginative re-use of Nazi propaganda, especially "Triumph of the Will".'[21] Drawing on Riefenstahl's film was nothing new among British wartime propagandists, and *Triumph of the Will* was often a go-to film used when filmmakers wanted to depict and parody the Nazi regime. Interestingly, the voiceover for *These Are The Men* employs verse rather than a prose script, and it essentially contrasts the virtues of the allies with the evils of Nazi leaders.

Evoking the core people's war theme once more, a narration with a unifying statement of an 'us' fighting an enemy in wartime begins as follows:

[18] Dylan Thomas, 'Battle for Freedom', in John Ackerman, ed., *Dylan Thomas: The Complete Screenplays* (New York: Applause Books, 1995), 32–7.
[19] *Documentary News Letter* 3:9 (1942), 125.
[20] Ferris, *Dylan Thomas*, 183.
[21] Ackerman, *The Complete Screenplays*, 38.

Who are we? We are the makers the workers the bakers
Making and baking bread all over the earth in every town and village,
In country quiet, in the ruins and wounds of a bombed street
With the wounded crying outside for mercy of death in the city,
Through war and pestilence and earthquake
Baking the bread to feed the hunger of history.

This opening section concludes by asking who is to blame for working people enduring the crisis of warfare. The imagery switches away from shots of British bakers, workers, factories and so forth, and draws on stock footage from *Triumph of the Will*. Soon the images settle on Hitler addressing a large crowd, delivering an impassioned speech, with typically histrionic performance to go with it. Hitler's voice was quickly dimmed as a translator was faded in. The conceit here is that, rather than offering Hitler's speech in English, Dylan's script presents the Führer confessing to various sociopathic tendencies, while also mimicking Hitler's flamboyant oratorical style:

I was born of poor parents.
I grew into a discontented and neurotic child.
My lungs were bad, my mother spoiled me and secured my exemption
    from military service.
Consider my triumphant path to power:
(The crowd roars)
I took up art.
I gave it up because I was incompetent.
I became a bricklayer's labourer,
A housepainter,
A paperhanger,
A pedlar of pictures,
A lance-corporal,
A spy on socialists and communists,
A hater of Jews and Trade Unions,
A political prisoner,
But my work was known.
Patriotic industrial magnates financed me.
Röhm and others supported me.
Later I betrayed and murdered Röhm and others.
They had fulfilled their purpose.[22]

An ability to parody contemporary poets came easy to Dylan, and here we see this skill transferred to a populist mockery of Nazism. This strategy is repeated for other leading Nazis too: Goebbels admits to being a failed writer who took out these frustrations on Jews; Göring confesses to being a drug addict and being confined to a lunatic asylum, twice; Streicher divulges his love for

---

[22] Thomas, 'These Are The Men', in Ackerman, *The Complete Screenplays*, 39–44.

animals and torturing Jews; and Hess declares he was wrong to pursue peace by flying to England in 1941. *Documentary News Letter* was particularly keen to emphasize how 'Dylan Thomas's verse frequently cuts like a knife into the pompously bestial affections of this race of supermen.'[23] Out of all the films, this is probably one of the few that genuinely still connects with an audience, primarily because of Dylan's use of humour.

Not all scripts made their way to finished films either, and within this wider body of texts we can again see attempts at greater artistic innovation, though still operating within the confines of propaganda. The clearest example of this – and, in terms of its structure, highly significant for later script-based work – was *The Unconquerable People*. Written in 1944 and based on the theme of resistance across Europe, the script is the first clear attempt by Thomas to narrate with numbered voices, a central quality of *Under Milk Wood*. The surviving draft of the film uses four voices to celebrate heroism and bravery among resistance figures, highlighting the pan-European nature of the movement, and strongly contrasting heroic resisters with venal collaborators. Letters to Taylor reveal that Thomas was also willing to radically alter the script, and remove more overtly literary phrases, in order to help the film reach production. So here again one sees Thomas doing more than simply turning in copy useful to propagandist. Its themes let Dylan identify with a wider sense of anti-fascist resistance, and its structure demonstrates Thomas playing with form too.

We can see the latter quality again in Thomas's most ambitious effort, *Our Country*, which had a predominantly verse script. Contemporary reception of the film was mixed. Damning it with faint praise, *The Times* suggested that *Our Country* failed as an accurate record of the country at war, but offered a 'lovely' portrait of the British people, continuing:

> A sailor returns home on leave after two years of travels over the land, and is fortunate that he possesses a mouth-organ, since much of his time is spent with people who specialise in singing and dancing. That is all very well, and certainly it is implied that they have done a hard day's work, but of the strain of living from day to day, of queues, of the hardships inflicted on the millions of middle-aged women, who should occupy a conspicuous place in the foreground of any account of England in the last five or six years, there is no mention. What is more, the commentary consists of free verse written by Mr. Dylan Thomas, which may be good – a few lines suggests it is – but which is recited with such a monotonous emphasis that it soon ... becomes a barrier between spectator and screen.[24]

This review also offers us a succinct summary of the limited plot. The sailor's journey again picks up on a key theme in many of these films, evoking once more a sense of unity among the peoples of Britain. As a survey of the British

---

[23] *Documentary News Letter* 4:3 (1943), 145–6.
[24] *The Times*, Issue 50179, col. b, (27 June 1945), 6.

Isles at war, sections of the verse also try to develop senses of place – a central development in Dylan's later poetry. Meanwhile, although still stressing the propaganda message, parts of the commentary do develop greater emotive power when compared to earlier wartime scripts.

We can see this, too, in other writings by Dylan responding to the war. As Ackerman has shown, there is also a clear connection between the mood of this script and the tenor expressed in his war poems of this period: 'Among Those Killed in a Dawn Raid was a Man Aged a Hundred', 'A Refusal to Mourn the Death, by Fire, of a Child in London', and 'Ceremony after a Fire Raid'. Indeed, it appears the latter was written at the same time as *Our Country*. Dylan's own recollections of London's war experiences were transformed into film and poetry alike towards the end of the war. So as responses to the impact of the Nazi war efforts, these poems, as well as films like *Our Country*, can be placed within a broadly anti-fascist culture.

Several lines throughout the script also evoke turns of phrase later found in *Under Milk Wood*. We can see this not only in the opening line, 'To begin with a city', echoing 'To begin at the beginning' in *Under Milk Wood*, but elsewhere too – for example in the use of 'dumb':

> *Our Country:* Of the dumb heroic streets.
> *Under Milk Wood:* Of the dumb found town.

Whatever such similarities might suggest regarding the impact of the film script on Dylan's later writing, this does all highlight that, at the very least, he was clearly taking the poetic voice developed in his films more seriously by this point. This issue also comes through in a letter from Dylan to Taylor regarding the premiere of *Our Country*. Dylan argued against the idea of having a printed programme for the film reproducing his verse in printed form. He felt cuts to the film had destroyed some of the continuity of its verse, while such a programme could suggest a level of pretentiousness that he did not want to cultivate. For Dylan, 'Heard spoken to a beautiful picture, the words gain a sense and authority which the printed word denies them'.[25] Nevertheless, adverts for the film, such as those in *Documentary News Letter*, did reproduce sections of the script. Meanwhile, unlike *The Times*, some reviewers were inclined to agree with the idea that there was poetic worth in the film's script. Edgar Ansley's *Spectator* review offers an example of contemporary praise of its poetic qualities:

> *Our Country* breaks free from the bonds of narrative continuity and surface-skimming clichés of normal commentary and plunges into visual impression and poetry ... [it] represents the most exciting and provocative film ... for many a long day.[26]

More negative reviews, though, greeted Thomas's final propaganda film, *A Soldier Comes Home*. Dealing with the complex emotional situation created

---

[25] Thomas in *Collected Letters*, 587–8.
[26] Reproduced in Ackerman, *The Complete Screenplays*, 63.

when a solder temporarily returned to his wife and son, this is probably Dylan's weakest filmed script. Importantly, it was deemed to have failed to develop its characters in a convincing and sensitive manner, and notably was not successful in linking the scenario to important wider themes, such as people's war or war-as-progress. As *Documentary News Letter* stressed, 'the basic idea was obviously never worked out and what might have been a useful film turns out to be an emotionally muddled rough sketch of a film yet to be made'.[27] While this final film may have been less well received, Dylan himself was now moving on too; though, as we will see, the war and its impact left a lasting impression on him.

This chapter has limited its scope primarily to exploring and contextualizing Dylan's wartime films. What comes through is the way these films conveyed the sense of a cross-class British 'us' coming together to fight a fascist 'them'. In this sense they were clearly anti-fascist. Depictions of Britishness and Nazism were defined by the context of the war against fascism. Moreover, as his engagement with this work developed, there is clear progression. While initially limiting scripts to the utilitarian strictures of the Documentary Film Movement style, and conforming to the careful propaganda messages on themes such as war-as-progress, people's war and the role of empire, in later films Dylan engaged a more dynamic set of themes. Moreover, the contract with Strand Films gave Dylan a chance to progress his other writing projects during and after the war. These ranged from delivering popular broadcasts for the BBC to developing new ideas for non-propaganda scripted work after the war, such as *The Doctor and the Devils* and, later on, *Under Milk Wood*.

But as he moved on after 1945, Dylan was indelibly marked by the nature of the war, and the murderous extremes of the Nazi regime. Interviews with people connected to Dylan conducted by Colin Edwards help to reveal this impact, showing how the full, genocidal nature of the Nazi regime came to be understood by Dylan. Elizabeth Ruby Milton recalled the far-from-untypical way Dylan only slowly became aware of the Holocaust, as follows:

> ... at the beginning, nobody knew, nobody would believe that these things were happening ... we used to discuss if it really was happening. And one or two Jewish people were coming in ... artists, sculptors ... into London, coming away from persecution ... and there were a lot of German artists in London ... so there was this conflict. You either had to believe German artists or have sympathy with the Jews ... nobody wanted to believe. Especially somebody as emotional as Dylan.[28]

She then goes on to explain how a sense of disbelief and even cynicism were strategies that Dylan used to help fend off recognizing the full extent of the horrors that the Nazi regime inflicted. He even joked, crassly, about how Jews

---

[27] *Documentary News Letter*, Issue 51 (1945), 8.
[28] Elizabeth Ruby Milton in Thomas, ed., *Dylan Remembered*, 70–1.

went willingly to their deaths. This, too, suggests a coming to terms with a situation that was beyond imagination, typical of those who learned of the Nazi genocide in a mediated, indirect way. On the way the Holocaust became refracted into Dylan's post-war life over time, Mably Owen added:

> … he had an enormous compassion for people. One of the things that affected him most, of course, was the War – and the suffering. And especially the extermination of the Jews and the horrors and the cruelties. He really was shocked by that. I think the war made a tremendously deep impression on him, but his politics were an expression of his immense and enormous and all-embracing compassion for mankind.

Owen continued by stressing: 'he talked a lot about the suffering of the Jews, which seemed to have entered very, very deeply into his feelings and into his imagination'.[29]

War impacted in other ways too. While the Nazi Holocaust revealed to him the extremes of a fascist regime, Dylan was also fearful of nuclear war in the future. His opera project with Stravinsky that was tragically never realized is a further example of Dylan's attempt to engage aesthetically with another of the new terrors of the twentieth century that shaped imaginations in the immediate post-war era.

To sum up, from opposing the stirrings of Mosley and local fascist sympathizers in the 1930s, to writing wartime propaganda in an era of total war, to coming to terms with a radically different and far less innocent post-war world, we can certainly say that fascism impacted on Dylan in a number of ways, both politically and creatively. His anti-fascism was less pronounced than that of other, more overtly political writers, but remains crucial to understanding his life and times. In the post-war years until his untimely death, we can see themes in his work such as pastoral idylls in 'Fern Hill' and evocations of a small-town community in *Under Milk Wood*. In subtle ways, these themes counterpoint the extremes of violence that so horrified Dylan. In order to set his writings within such a historical context, then, as well as his major writings we need to also recognize the importance of his revulsion to war, and terror, too. His wartime films are an important part of this story. So rather than judge them harshly, as dated pieces of art, it is more useful to recognize that they were effective, well-received propaganda material developed in the context of an extreme conflict. Moreover, this was a war that had a most profound and moving impact on Dylan the developing writer.

[29] Mably Owen in Thomas, ed., *Dylan Remembered*, 42–3.

A Postcard from New Quay

David N. Thomas

There's a lot to write home about in 2014. Among other things, it's the sixtieth anniversary of the publication of *Under Milk Wood*, as well as the seventieth anniversary of Dylan's move to New Quay, Cardiganshire, on the west coast of Wales. The two events are linked: without New Quay, there would have been no *Milk Wood* – but that, of course, is a matter of judgement, not fact.

Moving to Cardiganshire wasn't much of a leap into the Welsh-speaking dark; Dylan was already familiar with the county, not least through his friendship with London Cardis and the short stories of Caradoc Evans. He had also stayed on the coast as a teenager on holiday. Later, in his twenties, he came to visit Evans, who lived just outside Aberystwyth, where Dylan's father had been to university. It's a town that pops up in his writing, and *Aberystwyth* is the hymn that Cherry Owen likes to sing when he's drunk, tenor and bass.

I always sing Aberystwyth.[1]

Dylan's first known visits to New Quay itself were in the mid-1930s. He came to see his aunt and cousin, who had moved from Swansea, and to call on Howard de Walden, a major patron of the arts in Wales. He returned during the early 1940s, when he was staying a few miles away in the Aeron valley. By now, the town had already caught his imagination. He wrote a New Quay pub poem, 'Sooner than you can water milk', cream-rich with material that anticipates *Under Milk Wood*.

Sinister dark over Cardigan Bay. No-good is abroad.

Then, in September 1944, Dylan came back for an extended stay, renting a shack called Majoda on the edge of the cliffs. His nine months there, said FitzGibbon, his first biographer, were 'a second flowering, a period of fertility that recalls the earliest days ... [with a] great outpouring of poems', as well as a good deal of other material.

Dylan was so inspired by New Quay that, within months of arriving, he wrote a radio script about the town, *Quite Early One Morning*, described by one scholar as 'a veritable storehouse of phrases, rhythms and details' later used in *Under Milk Wood*. It was undoubtedly the most important precursor of the play, but there were also colourful letter-poems about the town that take

---

[1] Quotations from the works of Dylan Thomas appear in italics throughout this essay.

Majoda, a wood and asbestos shack. Courtesy of David Evans

us further along the road to Llareggub. Considered together, 'Sooner than', *Quite Early* and the letter-poems indicate how firmly *Milk Wood* was being established in the people and places of wartime New Quay.

It's in a wonderful bit of the bay, with a beach of its own. Terrific.

He certainly kept the post office busy, as scripts and letters went back and forth to London. Such was Dylan's enthusiasm for the town that invitations to visit were soon on their way. The Burtons came, father and adopted son. Richard came to drink, while his father, Philip, a BBC producer, used New Quay as the basis of a radio programme about a Welsh village by the sea. Broadcast while Dylan was living there, it was probably another influence that secured New Quay as a significant template for *Milk Wood*.

Even after Dylan had left New Quay, he was still waxing lyrical in his letters. In the summer of 1946, a friend brought her family for a holiday. Dylan had been lauding up the town, as he put it, to encourage her to visit, and he wanted to know if she'd enjoyed herself. Did you meet Jack Pat and his horse, he asks? And Dai Fred who bottled ships? And Evan Joshua of the Blue Bell? Jack the Post? Taffy Jones the stuttering ace? Norman the no-good fighter? And Alastair Graham of the baronetcy of Netherby, the thin-vowelled laird as Dylan called him, whose love of pickled herring and any form of mackerel was as remarkable as his obsessive time-keeping, reminding us of

Lord Cut-Glass ... the lordly fish-head nibbler ... in his fish-slimy kitchen ... scampers from clock to clock.

With this Cardi background, it's hardly surprising that some of the names in *Under Milk Wood* are to be found in New Quay – Maesgwyn farm and the Sailor's Arms, for example. Llareggub's Welshness is also New Quay's, and certainly not Laugharne's, which has long been an English-cultured and English-speaking enclave, too close to anglicized Pembrokeshire for its own Welsh good.

The windy town is a hill of windows. Courtesy of Bruce Cardwell

Llareggub's harbour, sea-going history, terraced streets, hill of windows and quarry are also New Quay's. Douglas Cleverdon, the producer of the radio version of the play, has pointed out that the topography of Llareggub

> is based not so much on Laugharne, which lies on the mouth of an estuary, but rather on New Quay, a seaside town … with a steep street running down to the harbour.

Cleverdon's description of a steep-streeted town helps us appreciate that the various references in the play to the top of the town, and to its 'top and sea-end', refer to toppling, cliff-perched New Quay, not to Laugharne, which has little top and no sea-end at all. The *Rough Guide* agreed, declaring that New Quay 'has the little tumbling streets, prim Victorian terraces, cobblestone harbour, pubs and dreamy isolation that Thomas so successfully invoked in his play'.

Donkeys angelically drowse on Donkey Down

The *Rough Guide* might also have mentioned that, in Dylan's time and long before, New Quay had the donkeys, as well as the Downs by the Black Lion, where they drowsed like angels, though their braying out on the cliffs, complained Dylan, did little for the peace and quiet of Majoda. Llareggub, of course, had Donkey Down, as well as Donkey Street and Donkey Lane, where many of the town's inhabitants lived.

Buttermilk and whippets?

The Fourth Drowned's question is one example of some of the words and phrases that root *Under Milk Wood* in the particularity of New Quay. Jack Patrick of the Black Lion bred whippets and kept cows, and made buttermilk in his dairy next to the hotel.

Do you see me, Captain? the white bone talking? I'm Tom-Fred the donkeyman ... We shared the same girl once ...

Several of the characters in the play derive from New Quay. Besides bottling ships, Dai Fred Davies carved dildos from wood and scrimshaw. He was also the donkeyman on the fishing vessel, the *Alpha*, in charge of the donkey-engine, an auxiliary engine used for lifting and pumping. Local man Dan Cherry Jones inspired the name Cherry Owen. Indeed, Dylan inadvertently uses the name Cherry Jones in one of his drafts of the play. In an early list of *Milk Wood* characters, Dylan describes Cherry Owen as a plumber and carpenter – Cherry Jones was a general builder in New Quay.

That's Willy Nilly knocking at Bay View ... Who's sent a letter to Mrs Ogmore-Pritchard?

Jack Lloyd the postman, mentioned in Dylan's 1946 letter, was also the Town Crier. He provided the character of Willy Nilly, whose practice of opening letters and spreading the news reflects Lloyd's role as Crier, as Dylan himself noted in one of his worksheets for *Under Milk Wood*: 'Nobody minds him opening the letters and acting as [a] kind of town-crier. How else could they know the news?' It is this note, together with our knowledge that Dylan knew Jack Lloyd ('an old friend'), that provide the sure link between Willy Nilly and Lloyd.

To begin at the beginning

It is a spring, moonless evening, starless but not yet bible-black. In the back-to-front sorting room of the post office, Will and Lil Dolau sniff like mice along the seams of a letter from Calcutta. An owl flies out past Bethel chapel, hovers over Brooklands, where Cherry Jones is snoozing, and then settles on the chimney of Mr John the Cake,

that winking bit, that hymning gooseberry, that Bethel-worm

In Manchester House (Est. 1804), May Thomas tidies up the tussore, smoothes the gentlemen's socks and then gently dusts her sister Cissie's painting of Paris in the rain. Next door in Sheffield House, Mr James (Implement Agent and Hot Water Engineer) lets off steam. Across the road in Goytre, the Rev. W. O. Jenkins inches open the blackout curtains so that you, and only you, can see me, Jack Lloyd, letters sorted, in full regalia now, feathered hat and brassy bell.

Voice of a Town Crier

Stand on this spot. This is New Road, old as the hills, high, wet and green, and from this small turning circle next to Mr Shirley Snap, you can see the town below, limping not yet invisible down to the sloeblue, slow and blue belled sea. But hush! Night is falling still. Shadows steal. Milk bottles step out. Dogs bark to earn their keep, farmyards away. New Quay ripples. Mr Jones the bank slips across the street, as he has done every other night of his married life, to have his hair cut.

Come now, past Cnwc-y-Lili and Parc-y-pant, past the ripening wizard and his widow's hollow larch, past outside privy and dripping tap, to find

me, Dylan Thomas,

fast bowler, asleep in wood-and-asbestos Majoda, dreaming of
33, Coronation Street, Llareggub,

and never such praise as any that swamped the decks of his writing shed, sucking him down into the stone grinding dark where the friends of his long drawn out night nuzzle up to him ...

First Writer
Remember me, Dylan?
Fitz! You were the first to see ...
... that many of the characters derive from New Quay.

Second Writer
Do you see me, Dylan? the BBC talking?
I'm Tom-Doug the producer man ... We shared the same studio once ...
Dougie! You did it on the radio!
You wrote the first half in New Quay, then you ran out of ideas when you left.

Woman's Voice
Ivy Williams, Brown's Hotel. Come up and see me, boys, I'm dead.
Dear Ivy! You always knew the truth.
It wasn't really written in Laugharne at all.

Third Writer
Remember me, Dyl? Richard Hughes, novelist, lived in Laugharne.
Dickie bach! King of the blooming castle!
You didn't use actual Laugharne characters.

Oh, my dead dears!

Come away quietly, to trig-and-trim Belle Vue at the top of the town. Listen. It is dark now, and if you gently lift the latch, you will see

me, Mrs Warfield-Darling,

widow of a General, wife of a doctor, friends with the Rockefellers, dreams of a dead poet: 'He liked to talk to ordinary people, and he'd sort them out ... and that, I think, was one of his greatest successes in life ... there were some very wonderful characters there then in New Quay'.

Come closer still. See, there, above the bay in her hanger of desire,

me, Olive Jones Telegwyn,

wife of the stuttering air ace, snores like a German albatross and recites from little slips of paper she found one day by the typewriter and never gave back: 'He was one of us – one of everybody ... that's where he got his material from – a student of humanity'.

Come further now, past dark and brooding Handcuff House, where PC Islwyn Williams snuggles deep under his boot-brush eyebrows, and dreams of jailing

me, Norman London House

for being a no-good boyo, rumbles PC Williams who, notebook now in hand, stamps huffing and puffing down Brongwyn Lane to arrest

me, Sarah Evans the Sailor's for having five children at Maesgwyn

me, Mary Ann Evans Maesgwyn, for having ten children

me, Hannah Evans Maesgwyn, for having eight children

me, Sarah Evans Maesgwyn, for having six children

and me, Phoebe Evans Maesgwyn, for having nine children

It is night over this evangelical snuggery of babies. Look. Only you can see

me, Phoebe, scrubbing the steps of the Memorial Hall.

Listen. Only you can hear

us, Phoebe's children: 'Mam was proud of being Polly Garter. She said Dylan always had his little notebook ... She was quite chuffed to have known Dylan ... She was adamant she was Polly Garter ... Phoebe was great friends with Caitlin ... She used to babysit for them.'

Come quicker now, past Mrs Evans bottled pop, past cobbler, chemist, baker, barber, past Tydur's taxi and his mother's geese, past princely brothel, Bethel and the Sailor's Arms, past Captain Pat Rosehill talking fish with auntie Cat Blue Bell, to ...

Gomer House, paying guests only, where Captain Tom Polly stands watch, with his watch, waiting for the moment to ... *Codi'r latch*! The town watches, too, and smacks its lips as Tom swiftly crosses the street to lift the latch of the Black Lion, pausing only to scowl at Walter Cherry, magistrate and churchwarden, taking bets in Coronation Gardens.

Look, it is opening time, though time doesn't pass here. Look closer still at

me, Jack Pat,

riding master to the gentry, lover of books, whippets, donkeys and poetry, standing beneath a clock that has never ticked nor tocked, drawing the town's first pint. He sighs deeply, thinking of peaches and plimsolls, and of a poet a lot more gorse than gorsedd and all the better for it, too, thank you very much:

> He just mixed with us all … it was just a matter of being with us, under-standing us … he was so interesting that he had one little corner of my house where we used to gather … it seemed to develop into a little Welsh village …

If Dylan's time in the town provided material which he used in *Under Milk Wood*, then his data collection was hardly unobtrusive, as Jack Pat noted:

> He seemed to do his best writing among us local people – he was always with a pad on his knee during convivial hours. Always busy, making notes of any local characters who came in … He was interested in … the people themselves … listening to them and busy with his notes at all times …

Dylan fitted comfortably into the quiet routines of the Black Lion, betting on the horses and playing cards, darts and shove ha'penny with the locals. It was his vegetabledom, as he once described the town. Caitlin agreed, and recognized that it was the kind of place where he could work hard at his writing:

> … it was only with our kind of purely vegetable background, which entailed months on end of isolated, stodgy dullness and drudgery for me, that he was flattened out enough to be able to concentrate …

But Dylan's vegetabledom is only part of the *Milk Wood* story, because the stodgy menu of his daily life was spiced with cultural richness, interesting company and eccentric characters. It was a town of the well-travelled and the well-read, of musicians, writers and painters, and of unassuming intellectuals, cunningly disguised as drapers, publicans and fishermen. Lord of them all was cobbler Glanmor Rees, son of a sea captain, who presided over the town's tobacco parliament in the back of his shop. If science was the topic of the hour, he could call upon his brother-in-law, Evan Jenkin Evans, the distinguished professor of physics at Swansea, sitting out the war in New Quay.

> *there are peas in my ears & my smile is gravy … I am quite happy and am looking forward to a gross, obscene and extremely painful middle-age*

Dylan's first six months in Majoda were as creative as his four years at the Boat House in Laugharne, perhaps more so. He was happy in New Quay; it was, said Caitlin, exactly his kind of place, with the bonus of having some of his childhood friends living in the town. Indeed, there were many people from Swansea in New Quay, who had come after the 1941 blitz; others had left many years before, such as Evan Joshua James, whose son had come close to marrying Dylan's New Quay cousin. Here, perhaps, lies a clue as to why Dylan seemed so settled and so productive: it was home-from-home, the terraces of his childhood Uplands in salty miniature. And New Quay people, of course, knew all about Swansea; it's where they went to welcome home their docking menfolk from the sea.

Jack Patrick outside the Black Lion. Courtesy of Anne Brodie

New Quay was a pretty and beguiling seaside town; one visitor writing in *The Lady* in 1959 thought 'it was like looking down on another *Milk Wood*'. The puppeteer Walter Wilkinson, visiting in 1947, warned about being trapped by its 'beautiful completeness'. New Quay, he wrote, was a cunning contrivance for inveigling travellers into ceasing their travels:

> You are tipped into it from the hills, as a fly is tipped into a jar of syrup; you come to an edge, and over you go, down the slippery slope, through the three or four terraces of cottages on the hillside, by those narrow, steep streets ... down to the hotel in the old sailmaker's works, down to the jetty and the two or three boats jigging on the green water ... The farm fields still come down to the town, and as you walk from the baker to the draper you can talk to a donkey and a horse, poking their heads over a fence into the street.

This small community of just under a thousand people was often portrayed as one of life's backwaters. One popular guide said that 'visitors will find the natives agreeable, courteous and obliging', and at the same time 'refined, brave, industrious, and hardy ...'.

Yet New Quay was a relatively sophisticated seaside town. It had always been something of a place to which the well-heeled retired. During the war, the town also attracted those seeking to escape the cities – smart evacuees, as Wilkinson called them, with new ideas and war earnings. Along the cliff from Majoda was Morfa Gwyn, the home of Major George Reid, part-owner of a company making aviation instruments. The major lived a comfortable life in wartime New Quay, with a stream of houseguests. One resident remembers the Princess of Sarawak walking, in a sari, around the town; in truth, she was minor English aristocracy, related to Sir Charles Vyner de Windt Brooke, the White Rajah of Sarawak. New Quay had all sorts.

Howard de Walden's house parties also brought a range of interesting people to the town, as did those of the thin-vowelled laird, Alastair Graham, nephew of both the Duchess of Montrose and the Countess of Verulam. His visitors included royalty, writers, artists, spies and diplomats. If Graham's embroidery or decorative knots palled, there was always fish and fishing, about which he was passionate, and a discussion about which sort of fish-heads made the best soup (a good cook, he later published a pamphlet of mackerel recipes). When the weather was bad, Graham's library was at hand, as were his mansion's bedrooms, where he hosted dinner-with-sex parties.

How's the tenors in Dowlais?

New Quay was accustomed to accommodating other kinds of visitors. Miners and metalworkers from south Wales came for their annual holiday, and on most fine evenings they held impromptu concerts, usually on the pier. There was a special connection with Dowlais: there had been several marriages with New Quay girls, and the town's men had gone to Dowlais for work. Evan Joshua had been an overseer there, and had encouraged the summer outings to New Quay. Such was the relationship between the two towns that when the church in Dowlais was demolished, its bell was given to New Quay's parish church. No wonder Dylan had the tenors of Dowlais in Llareggub.

Carrying on with that Mrs Beattie Morris up in the quarry

Evan Joshua had returned to New Quay to manage one of the town's quarries. The stone quarry had provided much of the material for the town's buildings but now it was mainly used for picnics, impromptu concerts and love-making, as the *New Quay Chronicle* reported: 'Should Cupid pierce the tender hearts of the lovely maidens and brave young men, the quarry and the lonely cliffs form an unapproachable fortress to guard their faltering confessions'.

New Quay's sailors (and often their wives with them) had sailed across the world. Daniel Parry-Jones noted in 1948 that New Quay was unmistakably Welsh with its own Welsh dialect, but also cosmopolitan:

A blasé, sophisticated visitor from one of our bigger cities might strut down its narrow streets with a contemptuous superior air, but here were dozens of lads who knew intimately the life and ways of all the great maritime cities of the world.

Llareggub's sailors had also travelled the world. Captain Cat had been to San Francisco. His drowned companions had visited Nantucket. It's hardly surprising that Billy Williams of Laugharne, whose little fishing boats seldom went further than Bristol, thought that the inspiration for Captain Cat was a New Quay sailor. The town abounded with sea captains, noted Wilkinson: 'address any gentleman, not an obvious visitor, as captain, and you will be safe'. In Dylan's day, there were over thirty-five retired, ocean-going captains living there, a wonderful gallery of Captain Cats to inspire a writer's imagination. Indeed, one in five of New Quay's men aged twenty and over were master mariners, either retired or serving.

And who brings cocoanuts and shawls and parrots to my *Gwen now?*

Like those of Llareggub, the sea captains of New Quay returned with clothes and costumes from other countries, in which the town's children dressed up on special occasions. There were also spices and teas, banjos and ukuleles, kimonos and erotica, scent from Algiers, crates of dates and Dresden china. New Quay homes were:

> well-laden with curios, paintings, rugs, teak and mahogany furniture, including items with inlaid ivory ... the occasional wild animal pelt, saw-fish 'bills', spears and shields. Canaries and parrots were popular. The few primates brought home rarely survived. New Quay gardens had palm trees and monkey puzzle trees ... almost every New Quay home had paintings of ships in their hallways, made by Italian artists at ports of call like Naples ...

New Quay's gently swilling, maudlin and miscellaneous retired sea captains, as Dylan variously referred to them, had their own daily meeting place, Cnwc Y Glap, at the bottom of the town near the quay, where they gathered to reminisce, just like the drowned sailors who open *Milk Wood*. Tom Polly Davies, who drank with Dylan in the Black Lion, was one of the captains who met here. He had worked as a censor for part of the war, and had been a Government Observer during the Spanish Civil War. Both these roles could have helped to form Dylan's image of Captain Cat as 'The Witness', as he described him in a list of the characters of the play, someone who lifted the latch on Llareggub, revealing the everyday lives and secrets of its inhabitants. And Tom Polly knew all that was going on in New Quay, sitting for hours on a bench outside his house, looking down the main street of the town: 'He didn't miss a thing'. And while Captain Cat lived in Schooner House, Tom Polly lived in Schooner Town – ninety-nine schooners were built or owned in New Quay between 1848 and 1870. Dylan himself provided a significant clue to New Quay's influence on the play when, in an early draft of *Milk Wood*, he described Llareggub as a 'schooner-and-harbour-town'.

Oh, Mrs Ogmore! Oh, Mrs Pritchard!

It was also a town of tailors and drapers. Mrs Ogmore Davies was the wife of a draper at the top of the town. A few doors away lived Mrs Pritchard Jones, wife of a bank manager. They were both rather snobbish and prim. Mrs Pritchard in particular was obsessively clean, 'a real matron-type, very strait-laced, house-proud, ran the house like a hospital ward'. To be fair, there were many Mrs Ogmore-Pritchards in New Quay. The town prided itself on its wholesome air and clean streets. An early guide noted that

> The place has the reputation of being amongst the cleanest in the Principality. The Houses, inside and out, the Streets and Terraces and everything without exception, are kept in a state of spotless cleanliness and high polish.

Wilkinson enjoyed being in New Quay because 'it would seem that the last hundred years have hardly touched the place'. But what had touched the town and its residents, he noted, was the sea; it had claimed the lives of many of its seafarers, and had nibbled at the land: 'where, as a child, you might have walked across the fields, and among the cows, you would now walk on wet sand'. A few hundred yards to the north of Majoda stood the church of Llanina. Dylan scholar John Ackerman has rightly pointed out that the story of the drowned village and graveyard of Llanina 'is the literal truth that inspired the imaginative and poetic truth' of *Under Milk Wood*.

Who milks the cows in Maesgwyn?

To the south, between Majoda and New Quay, stood Maesgwyn farm and the little community of Pentre Siswrn but they, two roads and about sixty acres of farmland, were lost to the sea in the 1940s. It is these drowned houses and fields that inspired the 'imaginative and poetic truth' of the play, as much as those of Llanina, not to mention the sailors in local graveyards who had died at sea or in foreign ports.

If the sea was at the centre of New Quay life, then so was creative endeavour. This was reflected in the lives of its men and women, but it was also a divide within many families:

> One side of the family were seafarers, captains of the fine old windjammers who rounded the Horn. Strong men with powerful personalities and a talent for strong drink and music ... on the other side, are poets, spartan and intellectual.

One of the centres of cultural life in the town was the Memorial Hall. It had seating for 800, as well as rooms for meetings, billiards and reading. It was the venue for concerts and plays, the props for which were borrowed from neighbouring houses. Rogues and Vagabonds, the touring company of Countess Barcynska (Caradoc Evans's wife) put on weekly plays in the hall during the summer. With the cheapest seats a shilling, the Countess brought London's West End to New Quay.

Praise the Lord! We are a musical nation.

Under Milk Wood is a play full of music and song, and Dylan makes clear that Llareggub itself is a town of music-making. So was New Quay, and there was more than enough to wake any Jack Black from the sixpenny hops of their nightmares. The town had a pop group called the Nautical Boys, and a dance band, as well as the New Quay Orchestra and the Dorian Trio. Part-singing was the norm, taught in the chapels and schools. Throughout the war, New Quay had a Ladies Choir, an Operatic Society and a Juvenile Operatic Party, which surely inspired Dylan to write about Llareggub's 'babies singing opera'.

Madame Clara Tawe Jenkins, the old contralto of *Quite Early One Morning*, had her real-life counterparts in New Quay, which 'has the reputation', said the *Welsh Gazette*, 'of being the home of good vocalists ...' The town may have prided itself on its master mariners, but, as far as its women were concerned, it was as importantly a town of talented singers, instrumentalists, music teachers and concert organizers.

the Reverend Eli Jenkins, poet, preacher ... dreams of ... Eisteddfodau. He intricately rhymes, to the music of crwth and pibgorn

Just like Llareggub, New Quay was a town of *eisteddfodau*, competitive festivals of literature, music and drama. The three chapels were at the forefront of most cultural activities. There was barely a week without an operetta, concert, play or visiting choir. New Quay's music-making was also nurtured in the church, which had a choir, and in the Women's Institute. The Spitfire Fund concerts brought them all together in common cause.

The music of the spheres is heard distinctly over Milk Wood.

Towyn, Bethel, Tabernacle and the Memorial Hall are clustered snugly together at the top of the town, close to the Black Lion. As Dylan walked in the blackout from pub to pub, the sounds of rehearsals and performances would have filled the night air, as they did in Llareggub. One visitor had this experience in 'story-book' New Quay in 1953. As she climbed the hill out of the town, Tabernacle's music was all around her, amplified in the double catch of the bay and the town's hills:

I heard singing ... the full-throated sympathetic singing of Welsh hymns ... hundreds of Welsh people were singing with warmth and fervour, sending the harmony of voices and the music of old familiar words challenging across the tide.

The sound of music over the town was especially pronounced on Sundays, because all three chapels and the church started their services at the same time, singing from different hymn sheets yet together.

But in New Quay the pen flourished as much as the baton. Foremost among the town's writers was Elizabeth Mary Jones (Moelona). She published widely, including books for children, translations of Alphonse Daudet's stories, and novels which demonstrated her commitment to feminism and Welsh nationhood. Her husband was one of the town's poet-preachers. Dewi Emrys was another, winner of both the Chair (four times) and Crown at the National Eisteddfod. Like Dylan, he was part of the drinking and reading circle round Alastair Graham.

Portraits of famous bards and preachers ... hang over him heavy as sheep

In seeking inspiration for Eli Jenkins, Dylan may have drawn on the Rev. Orchwy Bowen of Towyn chapel. Formerly a collier, he came to New Quay in 1923. He was 'a saintly character, unworldly,' recalled one of his congregation, 'a Nationalist before it was fashionable to be one, and a pacifist'. Bowen was a familiar figure around New Quay, with 'a shock of long white hair, like Lloyd George's, with intense blue eyes, and the blue scars of a miner'.

Like Eli Jenkins, Orchwy Bowen wrote in strict metre; he had published a collection of poetry, and won several Chairs in Cardiganshire *eisteddfodau*. His sons, one of whom was also a minister, went one better, winning the Chair and Crown in three National Eisteddfods between 1946 and 1950. This was truly a family of bards and preachers in a town of bards and preachers, which celebrated in style in 1948 when Euros Bowen won the National Eisteddfod Crown and Dewi Emrys the Chair.

Orchwy Bowen was a *bardd gwlad*, a country poet, one of many in the county, the most renowned being the Jones family, known as the Cilie poets, after the name of their farm a few miles outside New Quay, not far from the river Dewi. The family played an important part in the cultural and social life of New Quay, as both poets and singers. Wales's national paper went further, describing them as a centre of Welsh culture, after one of the family won the National Chair in 1936.

Walter Wilkinson was clear that New Quay was no 'quaint back number', yet its distinction was that 'History has stood still, or even gone backwards ... it has no railway station, and does not exhibit pictures of itself on hoardings ... It has the merit of not being up-to-date ...'. The town guide did not demur, but added that its 'comparative remoteness does not seem to deter the discriminating holiday maker'.

In *Voice of a Guide Book*, Dylan said much the same of Llareggub, where visitors would find

> *some of that picturesque sense of the past so frequently lacking in towns and villages which have kept more abreast of the times.*

It was a quality that Dylan appreciated. He liked New Quay because it did not attract

> *man-dressed women with shooting-sticks and sketch-books and voices like macaws*

who came from outside to paint a town's natives.

But painters did come to stay, drawn by the sharp light and clear air. Jack Patrick, both well-read and interested in art, made the Black Lion into a hotel to which artists came to stay and exhibit. Grant Murray and Kenneth Hancock, both Principals in their time of the Swansea School of Art, hung their paintings there, as did Augustus John. The Black Lion also made room for local artists. In this town of 'done-by-hand water-colours', New Quay's women stood out as talented painters, such as Margaret Rhydderch and Cissie Phillips, who exhibited successfully in the fourth exhibition of arts and sciences in Brussels in 1938.

There were many women in New Quay in the 1930s and 1940s who were accomplished painters, musicians and writers. They often had the money and, more importantly, the time to develop their talents. Many were married to (or were widows of) master mariners who were at sea for long periods. Some had their children away at boarding school. They were able to pursue their interests, and make a substantial contribution to the cultural life of the town.

If New Quay was cultured and worldly-wise, it was also colourful and bizarre, a town that was surreal as well as sophisticated. Eccentricity and anarchy, which some see as a defining characteristic of *Under Milk Wood*, were found in full measure here. It was a town full of Welsh characters, as Walter Wilkinson noted: '... the people of New Quay are evidently alive, and not turned out all the same, like so many sausages'.

Wilkinson could have mentioned the sailors in the Blue Bell, who played a version of shove ha'penny with their penises to win a Christmas turkey. Then there was Jack Patrick who rode his horse into the bar of the Black Lion and whose donkey, Maisie, regularly got drunk in the Blue Bell; Baps the barmaid who ran away with a vicar; Daniel the Electric who climbed his own lamp-posts to watch women undressing; Johns the aquatic stunt man; Rees the drag artist; and Hell Fire Jones the butcher, who, with cleaver in hand, chased children, not corgis, down New Quay's toppling streets.

Not forgetting, of course, Norman London House, the town's least successful fighter, as Dylan called him. In fact, Norman was an accomplished, all-round no-gooder – he was also a hopeless shopkeeper, and a lazy fisherman as well. His boat was called the *Idle Hour*, and he liked nothing better than dawdling 'away the rodless day', as Dylan described Nogood Boyo in an early draft of *Milk Wood*. He was often to be found hanging around the harbour doing odd jobs on the boats, although 'you never actually *saw* Norman working', remembered one resident.

Wilkinson spent his last day walking along the Dewi, gloomily contemplating his trudge northwards to Aberaeron. He was, he concluded, 'completely demoralised' by New Quay, 'in which I was lazy enough to want to stay for ever among the Lotus-eaters'.

Destination Llaregubb via Elba, South Leigh and New York

'It was written in New Quay, most of it'.

Ivy Williams, Brown's Hotel, Laugharne

Whatever Dylan felt about New Quay, he could not stay at Majoda; his landlord wanted it back for the holiday season. The Thomases left in July 1945, and a few weeks later Dylan gave the first known public airing of the play that was to become *Under Milk Wood*. It comprised

> some rather bawdy songs and verses he had lately been writing, a sort of *vers de société*, except that the society was Welsh and humble ... the verses ... were rich in affection, humour, compassion, and vivifying detail ...

Finding somewhere to live continued to be a problem, but Dylan reassured Caitlin that he 'would live in Majoda again'. He came back to New Quay at least twice in 1946, the first time in March, a visit he records in *The Crumbs of One Man's Year*. Then, in early summer, he was spotted in the Commercial with jazz pianist Dill Jones. A few months later, *Quite Early One Morning* was published.

In April 1947, Dylan and family went to Italy. He ended his holiday on Elba, staying in Rio Marina, a town, like New Quay, of steep streets, quarries and harbour. And, just like summer in New Quay, it was packed with miners taking their annual holiday. According to a Florence writer staying in the same hotel, Rio had a

> very kind and human atmosphere ... Dylan loved this atmosphere ... I think he saw in the landscape, the naked landscape, a souvenir of the Galles, of Wales.

He seems to have been happier here than anywhere else on his Italian tour. His letters from Rio mention the fishers, miners and webfooted waterboys who we find as the fishers and webfoot cocklewomen of the first page of *Milk Wood*.

On their return in August, the Thomases moved to South Leigh outside Oxford. It was here that Dylan continued work on the play. Philip Burton has recalled a meeting that year, when they discussed some of the characters:

> ... the organist in the choir in the church played with only the dog to listen to him ... A man and a woman were in love with each other but they never met ... they wrote to each other every day ... And he had the idea that the narrator should be like the listener, blind ...

Building on the work that had been done at New Quay, the time at South Leigh was a key period in the writing of *Milk Wood*. Dylan began knocking some shape into the play, as Andrew Lycett put it, becoming the first biographer since FitzGibbon to recognize that there was a good deal more to the writing of *Milk Wood* than Laugharne. Distractions at South Leigh were few; there were no poems on the go, and the new round of film scripts had only just begun. In one of these South Leigh films we find the familiar Llareggub names of Daddy Waldo and Polly Probert.

In March 1949, Dylan travelled to Prague to a conference. His interpreter recalls that he 'narrated the first version of his radio play *Under Milk Wood*'. She describes how he portrayed an eccentric organist who played for sheep and goats, and the baker with two wives. Another present at the gathering recalled the Voices in the play.

This testimony from Prague, when taken with that of Burton, indicates that many of the characters of the play were already in place by March 1949, before Dylan moved to Laugharne: the organist, the two lovers who never met but wrote to each other, the baker with two wives, the blind narrator and the Voices. Not to mention Waldo, Polly and Probert. A twenty-eight-page script that dates from around this time includes the two Voices, more than three-quarters of the cast list, and nearly all of the place, street and house names of the play.

It appears from this evidence that most of the first half of *Milk Wood* was first written in New Quay and South Leigh, with revisions and additions done in America in 1953. The work at South Leigh was completed within three years of Dylan leaving New Quay, presumably with Cardiganshire notebooks to hand, and memories still fresh.

Dylan hadn't lived in Laugharne for almost eight years, but now, in May 1949, he returned to live in the Boat House. In July that year, he broadcast *Living in Wales*, in which he recalled New Quay and the Aeron valley. He also recycled his description of Alastair Graham to describe England as a narrow-vowelled jungle. Mrs Mary Evans the Pop, of the Emporium in New Quay, also gets a mention.

By late summer 1952, the BBC still had only the first part of the play, despite having chased Dylan for some two years for the rest of it. That autumn, he was back in Cardiganshire, travelling through the Aeron valley ('the most precious place in the world') to give a poetry reading in Aberystwyth.

In the spring of the following year, he went to New York to give the first cast performance of *Under Milk Wood*. On his arrival, John Brinnin, his agent, realized that the play 'was still far from finished'. One of the actors has recalled that 'we got about half of the script to begin with …'. With the performance only ninety minutes away, Brinnin is clear that even at this late stage 'the final third of the play was still unorganised and but partially written'. Threats to cancel the performance made Dylan buckle down, and he 'finished up one scene after another'. Dylan then added some forty new lines to the second half for the next American reading. The play was now almost complete, and we can safely conclude that most of it had by this point been written in New Quay, South Leigh and New York.

Back in Laugharne, he prepared for his third and final trip to America, but Cardiganshire was still on his mind. He wrote himself a note about writing to Skipper Rymer, who had run the Dolau pub in New Quay. He also accepted an invitation to give a poetry reading in Lampeter in March the following year. He asked for his expenses and a five guineas fee, adding '… what a long time ahead you do plan! I hope we're not all dead by then'.

Oh, angels be careful there with your knives and forks

Dylan was worked to death in New York; *Milk Wood*, he said, had taken the life out of him. He found some respite in the company of the sailors and longshoremen who drank in the White Horse. But at the end he died alone, just like the mariners of New Quay and Llareggub, a stranger in a foreign port, far from home. With their patient in a coma and on a drip, his angels, the Sisters of Charity, had no need of cutlery.

Notes, references and bibliography etc. can be viewed at https://sites.google. com/site/dylanthomasandnewquay/

Acknowledgements

I am especially grateful for the extensive help provided by Griff Jenkins and Phyllis Cosmo-Jones, and for that of the following family members of many of those mentioned in the text: Anne Brodie, Barbara Cassini, Bunny Evans, Wendy Flenard, Nell Highet, Wynford Harries, Jon Meirion Jones, George Legg, Eleanor Lister, Sue Passmore, Gina Potter, Samantha Wynne Rhydderch, John Sayce, Owen and Maura Thomas, Megan Uncles, Ieuan Williams and John and Wendy Williams. Thanks, too, to Roger Bryan, Jennifer Davies, Keith Davies, Peter Davies, Kay Pascoe and Michael Williams for information and much else besides, as well as Cynthia Roberts of Dowlais Library, and, as ever, the marvellous staff of the National Library of Wales. I am, as always, indebted to the Colin Edwards archive of interviews at the National Library.

Further reading

Bryan, R., *New Quay: A History in Pictures* (New Quay: Llanina Books, 2013).
Thomas, D. N., *Dylan Thomas: A Farm, Two Mansions and a Bungalow* (Bridgend: Seren, 2000).
— *The Dylan Thomas Trail* (Talybont: Y Lolfa, 2002).
— 'The Birth of Under Milk Wood', in D. N. Thomas, *Dylan Remembered 1935-1953*, vol. 2 (Bridgend: Seren, 2004).
— 'Conceiving Polly Garter', in D. N. Thomas, *Dylan Remembered 1935-1953*, vol. 2 (Bridgend: Seren, 2004).
Wilkinson, W., *Puppets in Wales* (London: Bles, 1948).

(About) 1949

Paul Ferris

It wasn't much of a meeting, to be honest. Duration ten minutes? Fifteen? Late in 1949, it must have been, when he was revisiting Swansea, probably to talk and read poetry at some venue. He liked going back there, because he was always fond of the town (which didn't start calling itself a city till years later), especially if someone was paying travel expenses and a fee. He was a working poet. Working poets are allowed and even expected to be unashamed about their need for cash.

I was still living in the town, employed by the local newspaper, the *Evening Post*, where he had been a reporter a couple of decades before. A colleague at the paper, who knew him slightly, said: 'He's over at the Met. I'll take you to meet him.'

The Met was the Metropole Hotel nearby, still bomb-damaged from the war. All that remained in working order was a large saloon bar. Rain fell through a broken glass roof into what was once the 'Palm Court', and since a visit to the men's room lay in that direction, you needed an umbrella if one of Swansea's downpours was in progress.

Dylan was standing at the counter, surrounded by people trying to buy him drinks, as if the pint he had in his hand was insufficient. The colleague eventually processed me through the drinkers and introduced us.

He looked a bit weary. How many dozen times, in other towns and other bars, had strangers come and gone, shaking his hand, secretly hoping he would say or do something they could turn into an anecdote? These days he wasn't even safe in his own backyard. It wouldn't have occurred to me – let alone to him – that twenty-five years later I would be writing his biography.

'You must be ...' he said, and paused. He still knew his Swansea, and he knew that the editor of the *Post* was a man called Powell, known to all as 'D.H.I.P'., his initials. 'You must be', said Dylan, delivering the words with spaces between each of them, 'one of D.H.I.P's blue-eyed boys', and turned back to his drink.

That was it, really. He was never safe from his admirers. Or they from him.

The Three Margarets – Dylan Thomas and his Female Patrons

Andrew Lycett

Dylan Thomas had a thing about rich women called Margaret. There were three in his life; they all wanted to help him in various ways, mainly financially, but, feeling embarrassed by his supplicant position, he tended to demean them – which perhaps explains why he used two diminutives of the name to start his list of Bessie Bighead's cows in *Under Milk Wood*:

> Peg, Meg, Buttercup, Moll,
> Fan from the Castle,
> Theodosia and Daisy.

Nevertheless the facts are incontrovertible: during his last decade, before his early death in November 1953, Dylan was regularly indebted to one of three Margarets: Margaret Taylor, wife of the historian Alan (A. J. P.) Taylor; Margaret (or more correctly Marged) Howard-Stepney, scion of a well-heeled Anglo-Welsh family; and Princess Marguerite Caetani, who remained patient and munificent while he struggled to complete his masterpiece *Under Milk Wood*.

All these women were literary groupies of one sort or another. Dylan flirted with them as much as his wife Caitlin allowed, while he used them, sometimes cynically, but often out of dire need, to help bail himself out of his regular pecuniary predicaments.

Margaret Taylor was the most persistent. She was simultaneously the woman who did most for Dylan (as the benefactor of his much-loved Boat House in Laugharne) and the woman who was most often the butt of his barbs. She had met the diminutive Welsh poet when he unexpectedly descended on her then matrimonial home in Didsbury, a suburb of Manchester, in 1935. At the time Alan Taylor was teaching at the university there. Dylan's health had been suffering after a period of overindulgence in London following the success of his first book *18 Poems* the previous year. So a drinking buddy, Norman Cameron, a poet-turned-advertising copywriter who had been at Oxford with Taylor, sent the young Welshman north to recuperate.

Dylan was only supposed to be there a few days. But he liked the creature comforts, including the beer barrel the historian kept on tap, and quickly overstayed his welcome. Taylor became infuriated when Dylan asked to borrow £2 to pay for the return half of his railway ticket which he had lost. He replied bluntly: 'I lend once and, unless repaid, once only.' However his wife Margaret, the brisk, convent-educated daughter of a chief inspector of mines in India, was more sympathetic. Being artistically inclined, she liked Dylan's company, and he enjoyed her attentions, since she fussed over him and tried to make him feel at home.

A few years later, after her husband had moved to Magdalen College, Oxford, Margaret Taylor was reintroduced to Dylan by mutual friends, the poet Stephen Spender and his wife Natasha. By then Dylan was married to Caitlin and had two children, Llewelyn and Aeronwy. When she learnt that the Thomas family had nowhere permanent to live, Margaret invited them to stay in the summerhouse at the bottom of the garden of Honeywell Ford, their tied house in the college grounds by the banks of the river Cherwell. There was no running water, but the children were able to take baths in the main house.

Alan Taylor was not impressed. In his memoir *A Personal History*, he wrote bitterly about Dylan's arrival and its effect on his wife. 'Here at last was the congenial company which university wives had not provided. Every night she went off drinking with Dylan and Caitlin at some local pub. She laid on literary and artistic parties for them where I felt out of place. She pushed Dylan on to the Oxford literary clubs'.

It was not long before Margaret was inviting Dylan's comments on her own pieces of verse. In late 1945 he could be found painstakingly going through a clutch of her poems, advising her not to use similes such as 'ethereal as a dream'; 'phrases like that are written forever in the Oliver Sandys of time', he commented, referring to a popular writer of the time, who was married to the Welsh author Caradoc Evans.

The two of them cooperated on a film script, *The Shadowless Man*, based on an early nineteenth-century German story about a man who sold his shadow. He used his film contacts unsuccessfully to promote this, while she interceded with Graham Greene, a fellow Oxford resident and a director of Eyre & Spottiswoode, to publish one of Dylan's screenplays, *The Doctor and the Devils*.

When Dylan took his family on an extended holiday-cum-working trip to Italy in the spring of 1947, he was often homesick. However Margaret was on call to cheer his spirits by sending him books and papers, so he could indulge his simple pleasures of doing crosswords and checking the cricket scores. Once again her own husband was annoyed when she made it clear that she would rather be in Italy with the Thomases than with him on a visit to Yugoslavia. However, by this time he was used to her flighty behaviour, as she had had a similar crush on the writer Robert Kee, one of his pupils.

While in Italy, Dylan asked Margaret to help him find somewhere to live on his return. She readily acquired a house in the village of South Leigh, a few miles west of Oxford, which she rented out to him for £1 a week. Caitlin noted how Margaret partly furnished the place 'in her usual energetic way, before we even moved in', and then bought Dylan a gypsy caravan so he could work in the garden undisturbed. Caitlin added that, though she herself would never dream of interrupting Dylan while he was working, Margaret would come to South Leigh and go straight to the caravan: 'It was cruel, and it drove Dylan mad. He should have kicked her out, but he was putting up with it because she was now his patron'.

This domestic set-up allowed him to travel easily into Oxford and catch the train to London, where he tried to support his growing family by working for the BBC and writing film scripts for the Ealing and Gainsborough studios. When he found such sorties taking up too much time, Margaret Taylor was again able to assist him in realizing his latest ambition – to return to the peace and quiet of his native Wales. She paid £3,000 for the Boat House in the Carmarthenshire seaside town of Laugharne, which he knew and loved, and, from May 1949, allowed him to live there for a peppercorn rent.

Dylan was delighted. 'This is *it*: the place, the house, the workroom, the time', he wrote ingratiatingly to Margaret on 11 May 1949. 'I can never thank you enough for making this fresh beginning possible by all the trust you have put in me, by all the gifts you have made me, by all your labour & anxiety in face of callous & ungrateful behaviour'.

Caitlin had initially been wary of her, but latterly warmed to her, even if she did regard her as a bit of a joke. After finding a letter in which Margaret told Dylan that 'to sleep with you would be like sleeping with a god', Caitlin concluded that this meant that no consummation had happened. Nevertheless, in a fit of pique, she cut up a taffeta petticoat that Margaret had given her and sent it back. 'I regretted that afterwards,' she wrote, 'because it was a tempting petticoat'.

Margaret's gift to Caitlin shows that, although she was devoted primarily to Dylan, she liked to see herself as the patron of his wider family as well. She regarded Caitlin as her friend and helped to pay Llewelyn's fees as a boarder at the prestigious Magdalen College School. Aeronwy was particularly fond of her, writing in her posthumous memoir *My Father's Places*: 'I liked Margaret for her boundlessly positive attitude. She made the best of everything and made everything more fun for us children'. With her private income and creature comforts, Margaret offered a tantalizing glimpse of a better way of life for a small girl. Aeronwy recalled: 'I saw Margaret looking the way Mother never would: smart, conventional, and, best of all, unobtrusive in eggshell colours of creams and browns, just turning by the garden gate on to the cliff walk. Her hair was long and brown in contrast to Mother's wild fairness. She wore a smart woollen suit nipped in at the waist, fitting snugly over her ample hips and falling into folds of heavy material for such a spring-like day ...'

But even Aeronwy understood that Margaret could be annoyingly intrusive. In an interesting observation on the dynamics of Dylan's family and working practice, she recalled a visit to Laugharne by the professor's wife. When Caitlin discovered that Dylan was not working as usual in his writing shed, she sent her daughter to find him. Aeronwy came across him walking with Margaret. 'I was outraged on my mother's behalf. The afternoons were for writing and my father never went for a stroll except to the pub'.

Because of this complex web of relationships, Margaret felt, as an unofficial family member, that it was her duty to inform Caitlin when she stumbled upon details of Dylan's romance with the American journalist Pearl Kazin, whom he had met on his first visit to the United States in 1950. He was furious at her interference and thereafter his attitude towards Margaret became more contemptuous. He described her as the 'grey fiend' and 'mad Mags'.

Although she had bought a house for herself in Laugharne so as to be close to her protégés, she was happy to dip into her pockets again in the autumn of 1952 when Dylan changed his mind and decided he needed a London pied-à-terre so as to be closer to the publishers and editors who gave him work. So she paid for a flat at 54 Delancey Street in Camden Town (usefully round the corner from where she was living in Park Village East). Dylan unchivalrously described it to an American friend as 'a house an insane woman has bought us'. This arrangement only lasted a few weeks, prior to Dylan and Caitlin going to the United States in early 1952. After they came back in May, their address was again firmly in Laugharne. By then Dylan was looking to another Margaret as a benefactor.

Marged Howard-Stepney first emerged on the scene in Laugharne around 1951. She was a cousin of Frances Hughes, wife of the novelist Richard Hughes, who had helped introduce Dylan to the Carmarthenshire town in the mid-1930s. Caitlin dubbed her Dylan's 'new County wet nurse' because of her privileged background – a family which had grown immensely rich from land-holdings in Carmarthenshire, where her grandfather, an Old Etonian baronet, had been High Sheriff, as well as Liberal MP for Carmarthen Boroughs.

At the time she met Dylan, Marged was emerging from the second of two marriages and was having difficulty coping. Her first husband, Patrick Murray Thriepland, came from a Scottish family (his father had been adopted as an honorary Welshman through marriage and became the first commanding officer of the Welsh Guards in the First World War). After divorcing Patrick in the 1930s, she married Alan Welch, a stockbroker, who tried to develop a dairy farm at her family home, Cilymaenllwyd (known as Cily), near Llanelli, until their parting of ways in 1948.

However, Marged had a history of problems with alcohol and drugs. Before the war she had embarked on a course of psychoanalysis in Switzerland with a leading Jungian therapist, Carl Alfred Meier, who was later President of the C. G. Jung Institute. In 1949/50 she returned to Zurich for further work with Meier, who had become a friend. Since she met Dylan shortly afterwards, she would certainly have discussed this experience with him. However, evidence of any increase in Jungian imagery in his minimal output of later poems is scant. Perhaps his reference to 'the four elements' and 'man a spirit in love' in 'Poem on His Birthday' (1950) is a nod in this direction.

It seems that Dylan first met Marged during a period when he was giving private readings in houses around Laugharne, and one of these was to a group of her friends at Cily. This occurred when his relationship with Margaret Taylor was floundering and he, like Marged herself, was feeling particularly needy. Marged clearly gave him some indication that she might help him financially, for at some time in 1952 (the date is not clear) Dylan wrote her a grovelling letter which started:

> Once upon a time you told me,
> I remember in my bones,
> That when the bad world had rolled me
> Over on the scolding stones,
> Shameless, lost, as the day I came
> I should with my beggar's cup
> Howl down the wind and call your name
> And you, you would raise me up

To his dismay, Caitlin discovered this note, and he was forced to disown it, telling his wife abjectly: 'That letter was horrible, it was dirty and cadging and lying ... It was vile, a conscientious piece of contriving bamboozling dirt, which *nobody* was supposed to see – not you, nor that Marged gin woman'.

Once again Caitlin looked on with a mixture of jealousy and bemusement. She described Marged as 'a really low alcoholic', but she could not help seeing her as a colourful character. One morning, when visiting Laugharne, Marged went for a swim off the Boat House 'dressed in a pearl necklace and a gold watch, but from the waist down she wore absolutely nothing'. Caitlin was terrified she would drown, but this was not the case.

Intriguingly, the Stepney family's long-standing land agent was a man called Alan More, whom Marged treated as a father figure, since her own father had died when she was a baby. More had a reputation for being careful with her money. For this reason he was known as 'Peid', Welsh for 'no' or 'do not' – his general reaction when approached with a request for financial support.

With her wealth, Marged emerged as a possible purchaser of the Boat House in 1952 when Margaret Taylor wanted to pull out. However, 'Peid' was opposed to the idea. By then Marged was seriously addicted to alcohol and drugs, leading to her death from an overdose of sleeping pills in January 1953, a few months before Dylan himself tragically died in New York.

Dylan was upset at her death, describing her to a publisher as 'my best friend in the world'. He told John Malcolm Brinnin, the agent who had arranged his trips to the United States: 'Then a woman – you never met her – who promised me a real lot of money for oh so little in return died of an overdose of a sleeping drug and left no will, and her son, the heir, could hardly be expected to fulfil that kind of unwritten agreement'. He was mistaken in thinking Marged's son, Mark Murray Threipland, had much to do with this, as he was still a student. Rather Alan 'Peid' More was once again the man who made this decision. According to Mark, Dylan wrote to More, but his friendly communication was torn up. More's son Julian was later a writer and lyricist in

London, where he was responsible for such hit musicals as *Irma La Douce*. By a coincidence, Mark Murray Threipland married Molly Pickett, who worked as a stage manager (and assistant to Brinnin) at the Young Men and Young Women's Hebrew Association (the 92nd Street Y) during the final rehearsals of *Under Milk Wood* in 1953.

One result of Marged's death was that the responsibility for shoring up Dylan's finances fell back on Margaret Taylor. But she was now beginning to feel the pinch – one of the reasons why she had been happy for Marged to take on the Boat House. As she explained in a later letter to Dylan's solicitor, Stuart Thomas, the Boat House had represented two-thirds of her capital. She had spent money on its upkeep, but by the end of 1953 it needed a further sum spent, particularly on the verandah. As a result she was in financial diffi-culties herself; her husband had been forced to help her out (and it is clear how reluctant he would have been to do that) and her bank manager had taken away her chequebook. She managed to negotiate an overdraft of £1,000, but, to service this, she had reached an agreement with Dylan that he should pay rent of 30 shillings a week. So after Dylan's death she was very concerned about how she would cope. She approached his estate, asking if it would be prepared to pay £1,200 for the Boat House. This would have meant her taking a consid-erable loss (as indeed had been the case with the South Leigh house, bought for £2,200 and sold for £1,200). But such was the situation the unfortunate Margaret found herself in.

Even after Marged's sad end, Dylan had one more Margaret he could fall back on, and she had none of the personal problems of this Welsh one. Despite her aristocratic-sounding name, Princess Marguerite Caetani was the daughter of a wealthy Connecticut businessman. An aspiring singer, she travelled to Paris, where, shortly before the First World War, she met and married the Prince Roffredo Caetani (also Duke of Sermoneta, a member of one of Italy's oldest families), with whom she shared a passion for music and dance. Living in the French capital after the war, the self-effacing Marguerite was part of a cultural elite which included James Joyce, Colette, and Pablo Picasso. A distant cousin of T. S. Eliot, she started *Commerce*, a literary magazine which published Joyce, Paul Valéry and several modernist writers. Three decades later, after another world war (in which her beloved son Camillo was killed), she and her husband moved to Rome, where she poured her energies into a similar magazine, *Botteghe Oscure* (literally Dark Shops, after a street associated with the family). From 1948 this sombre-looking journal gained a reputation not just for its sparkling contents but also for paying good fees to writers, from Truman Capote to Giuseppe di Lampedusa.

When the Princess first approached Dylan Thomas in the summer of 1949, she endeared herself by sending him a cheque in advance for his poem 'Over St John's Hill', which was published in *Botteghe Oscure IV* in December that year. When they met for drinks in the Connaught Hotel in London that autumn, he interested her in a short story, for which, again sight unseen, she agreed to pay him £50, or half the fee, upfront. (It is unclear which work he was referring to.)

Before long he was begging her for the remainder, saying he was plagued by debts and his wife was ill with worry.

In February 1950 Marguerite sent money directly to Caitlin – another instance of one of Dylan's female patrons stretching out her hand and taking pity on his family. By then Dylan was talking about his forthcoming first visit to the United States. The Princess provided an introduction to one of her contributors, the poet Archibald MacLeish, and to two of her sisters – one of whom, Katherine Biddle, provided Dylan with a bed when he passed through Washington. A poet and patron of the arts herself, Biddle was the wife of a former US Attorney General. While staying with her on 31st Street, Dylan wrote to Caitlin complaining about a 'rich social house' and his 'posh room that is hell on earth'.

After he returned from the United States, his life was more chaotic than usual, with matrimonial problems adding to his financial difficulties. After Princess Marguerite had again obliged with a payment in advance, he sent her a copy of his poem 'In The Giant's White Thigh' in September. His letter thanking her for her cheque was rather more desperate than usual: 'We can pay some bills, and eat,' he stated. 'Thank you, all my life'.

Dylan subsequently wrote to the Princess on 11 November 1950, saying he had written 'a long radio play which will, I am sure, come to life on the printed page as well'. This was his first intimation to her of the play for voices which would become *Under Milk Wood*.

Four months later he informed her about another work-in-progress, a half-finished poem, 'Lament', which he described as 'coarse and violent'. After she sent more money, he promptly completed it, suggesting that if she did not like it, she should 'slam it back' and she might prefer the one he was working on. This was 'Do Not Go Gentle Into That Good Night', which he duly submitted to her. A mooted play in verse seems to have gone by the wayside.

Over the next few months, Dylan continued to work on his other play, the one for radio. He was encouraged by Douglas Cleverdon, a producer at the BBC, which devised a complex system of payments to reward his progress. However he still desperately needed money (he had been forced to sell his 'Poem on His Birthday' which he had promised to *Botteghe Oscure* to a British magazine *World Review* for a paltry £10). So in October 1951 he sent Princess Marguerite a half-finished version of this play, which he called 'Llareggub, a Piece for Radio Perhaps'. After treating her to a long exposition of how it would develop, he asked for £100 to complete it. This truncated text was published in *Botteghe Oscure IX* in April the following year, the first appearance in print of any part of his most famous work.

Thereafter Dylan's domestic problems became so overwhelming that his links with *Botteghe Oscure* fizzled out. He occasionally wrote to the Princess, apologizing for his failure to communicate or provide anything. 'Please forgive me, and try to trust me again', he stated pathetically in November 1952. His last missive to her, written sometime the following year, was never sent. It was a wordy letter complaining how he bound himself 'always into these imbecile grief-knots' from which he had to 'wrestle out and unravel in a panic, like a seaslugged windy Houdini'.

Although Marguerite now had a distinguished stable of writers, including the young Robert Lowell, she remained faithful to Dylan through his troubled final months. As a memorial, she published three of his letters in *Botteghe Oscure XIII* in spring 1954. She died in 1963, and Margaret Taylor in 1980; but Caitlin Thomas outlived them all, reaching the age of eighty before her death in Italy in 1994.

In retrospect, did these three Margarets, with their disparate backgrounds, bring something special to Dylan? Margaret Taylor, the great enthusiast, cannot just be dismissed as a busybody; she provided regular financial assistance to the Thomases, and, without her, Dylan's dream of returning to Laugharne and to his homeland would have come to nothing. Marged Howard-Stepney was never really able to show her backing to Dylan in any meaningful way, but their relationship was surprisingly close – probably because they both realized they were addicts. Marguerite Caetani was a strong stable influence in Dylan's final years; without her, *Under Milk Wood* might never have reached the stage of completion it did.

It is not that his male friends were ungenerous. Vernon Watkins, for example, was always happy to open his purse strings for his fellow poet. At the BBC, Douglas Cleverdon went out of his way to structure Dylan's payments in a helpful way. Other authors, producers, and even publishers did their best to support Dylan when required. However, these three women provided the kind of emotional support that Dylan needed as much as any cheque in the post. His mother Florrie had always been a nurturing influence – a role that Margaret Taylor unconsciously fell into when she first met Dylan. At the same time, the three Margarets never lost sight of another important factor – Dylan's prowess as a poet. As Caitlin said of Margaret Taylor: 'It was a very strange relationship, but primarily it was that she thought he was a genius'. At times when Dylan's self-esteem was low, that sort of confidence in one's abilities can be very seductive.

Select Bibliography

Ferris, P. (ed.), *Dylan Thomas: The Collected Letters New Edition* (London: Dent, 2000).

Lycett, Andrew, *Dylan Thomas – A New Life* (London: Phoenix, 2004).

Sisman, A., *A. J. P. Taylor – A Biography* (London: Sinclair-Stephenson, 1994).

Taylor, A. J. P., *A Personal History* (London: Hamish Hamilton, 1983).

Thomas, C. with Tremlett, G., *Caitlin: Life with Dylan Thomas* (London: Secker and Warburg, 1986).

Thomas Ellis, Aeronwy, *My Father's Places* (London: Constable, 2009).

Laugharne

Dylan Thomas

Off and on, up and down, high and dry, man and boy, I've been living now for fifteen years, or centuries, in this timeless, beautiful, barmy (both spellings) town, in this far, forgetful, important place of herons, cormorants (known here as billy duckers), castle, churchyard, gulls, ghosts, geese, feuds, scares, scandals, cherry-trees, mysteries, jackdaws in the chimneys, bats in the belfry, skeletons in the cupboards, pubs, mud, cockles, flatfish, curlews, rain, and human, often all too human, beings; and, though still very much a foreigner, I am hardly ever stoned in the streets any more, and can claim to be able to call several of the inhabitants, and a few of the herons, by their Christian names.

Now, some people live in Laugharne because they were born in Laugharne and saw no good reason to move; others migrated here, for a number of curious reasons, from places as distant and improbable as Tonypandy or even England, and have now been absorbed by the natives; some entered the town in the dark and immediately disappeared, and can sometimes be heard, on hushed black nights, making noises in ruined houses, or perhaps it is white owls breathing close together, like ghosts in bed; others have almost certainly come here to escape the international police or their wives; and there are those, too, who still do not know, and will never know, why they are here at all; you can see them, any day of the week, slowly dopily, wandering up and down the streets like Welsh opium-eaters, half asleep in a heavy bewildered daze. And some, like myself, just came, one day, for the day, and never left; got off the bus, and forgot to get on again. Whatever the reason, if any, for our being here, in this timeless, mild, beguiling island of a town with its seven public-houses, one chapel in action, one church, one factory, two billiard tables, one St Bernard (without brandy), one policeman, three rivers, a visiting sea, one Rolls-Royce selling fish and chips, one cannon (cast-iron), one chancellor (flesh and blood), one port-reeve, one Danny Raye, and a multitude of mixed birds, here we just are, and there is nowhere like it anywhere at all.

But when you say, in a nearby village or town, that you come from this unique, this waylaying, old, lost Laugharne where some people start to retire before they start to work and where longish journeys, of a few hundred yards, are often undertaken only on bicycles, then, oh! the way edging away, the whispers and whimpers, and nudges, the swift removal of portable objects!

'Let's get away while the going is good,' you hear.
'Laugharne's where they quarrel with boathooks'.
'All the women there's got web feet'.
'Mind out for the Evil Eye!'
'Never go there at full moon!'

They are only envious. They envy Laugharne its minding of its own, strange, business; its sane disregard for haste; its generous acceptance of the follies of others, having so many, ripe and piping of its own; its insular, featherbed air; its philosophy of 'It will all be the same in a hundred years' time.' They deplore its right to be, in their eyes, so wrong, and to enjoy it so much as well. And, through envy and indignation, they label and libel it a legendary lazy little black-magical bedlam by the sea. And is it? Of *course not*, I hope.

* * *

This radio talk was written by Dylan Thomas before he left Laugharne for the last time on 9 October 1953. He and Caitlin caught the bus to Carmarthen and travelled by train to Swansea, where he recorded the talk at the BBC studios before catching a train to London. His recording was broadcast from Laugharne on 5 November as part of a radio programme on the town for the BBC Welsh Home Service. As the producer Anerin Talfan Davies sat down after thanking the townspeople for their co-operation, Caitlin leant across and told him she had just been passed a telegram saying Dylan was in hospital in New York. He died four days later.

If He Were Still With Us
(Dylan's Laugharne – Still Strange)

Jon Tregenna

He'd know this place if he were still with us. This eccentric enclave with more aliases than a Victorian villain. This place formerly known as Larn, Lacharn, Abercorran, Talavan, Tallagharn and Tullungharne; and Talacharn, Talacharne, Tallaugharne, Abercorram and Laugern but latterly known as Laugharne: pronounced Larn. One syllable nine-lettered 'Laugharne': an Anglicization of Talacharn ('a conspicuous headland' in Welsh) as Fychan became Vaughan; Tydyr, Tudor and Llwyd, Lloyd.

He was nineteen and rootless. He'd capsized his nascent career as a local journalist and London's salons weren't ready for his lyrical swagger. The family home, 5 Cwmdonkin Drive in Swansea, where he'd already written two-thirds of his life's work, was a place of bickering, illness and restrictions, and Fern Hill, the west Carmarthenshire farm of his ancestors, was drab and suffocating. Too ambitious for Swansea, too parochial for London and with damp farms no place for tyro poets, he found comfort in lifelong friendships, trips to the seaside, amateur theatre frivolities, Mumbles boozing and a long-distance romance, but was thwarted in his ideals, sweet-toothed, asthmatic and undermined by rain and shop-girls. A planned novel went un-written and whilst he was continually defining the poetic themes of his adolescence – nature, landscape, religion, sex and death – he'd become a man in search of a manor. In May 1934, almost on a whim, he happened upon a place that would become his haven and his home; a place that was neither town nor village but a barnacled township tethered by a weather-worn rope to the ancient shire of Carmarthen. A place called Laugharne.

From a gull's eye view the northerly coast of Carmarthen Bay in South West Wales resembles a jester's three-pointed hat where a trio of rivers meet the sea. To the east, the Gwendraeth, which flows down a Welsh-speaking mining valley and enters at Kidwelly. To the north, the magnificent Towy which meanders through rich farmland and Merlyn's Carmarthen and enters via a channel between Llansteffan and Ferryside. To the west, the Taf, which winds through St Clears – where men once dressed as women to smash tollgates – and enters the bay at Laugharne. Kidwelly, Llanstephan and Laugharne each have impressive Norman castles guarding the mouths of their estuaries, for this is an area that has always had a military importance: guarding the estuaries from the enemy; guarding the English colonizers from the disgruntled Welsh.

He arrived here with a friend. They walked from Llansteffan across the sleepy green-banked peninsula known as Parc Yr Arglwydd – the Lord's Park – and took a ferry the short distance across the Taf. The lean, gnarled ferryman, with a wet liquorice twig of a cigarette welded to his lower lip, moored at the Ferry House, a building site since 2000 but once an inn and cottage. He would have been given a piggy-back the last few yards across the mud, then puffed up the ancient cliff-carved steps. Peering down he would have taken in the Boat House perched on rock at the water's edge. It is a rectangular building with a disused coal harbour and two façades. To the rear, the front: a two-storey Victorian double-fronted house. To the front, the rear: a utilitarian aspect facing the water. In the dock – built in 1913 to receive coal from Kidwelly – a couple of ailing dinghies lolled under a stilted shed. Around the house at ground and first floor levels ran two balconies with the lower one opening out to a platform where a table and chairs could be set. Nineteen years on from this first visit he would be living here. His American agent would sit on that same platform arguing the case as to why he should make one last trip to the United States.

Lawyers recently proved that, in medieval times, soldiers marching from Pembrokeshire to London would have crossed the Taf on massive stepping stones just upriver, as did pilgrims heading from Canterbury to St Davids. Walking in the footsteps of dockers, drovers, pilgrims and soldiers the poet made his way along the cliff path taking in the estuary with its seabirds, wildlife and Sir John's Hill, as yet undefined by his poetry. To the left the great forest of Pembrey and the rainfall pastures of the Gwendraeth Valley. If it was a clear day he would have recognized the hump-backed hills of his adolescent playground, the Gower peninsular, where he ran like a sand-boy and lived like a king. He might not have expected the proximity. Over fifty long miles by road or rail via the then belching smoke-stacks and steel works of Llanelli and Swansea west, but a mere fourteen miles across the calm bay J. M. W. Turner captured in 1831 in fantasy paintings of tumultuous seas, stricken sailors and desperate boats against the background of Laugharne Castle.

Excitement and anticipation accompany the approach to a new town on foot. His mother's family lived on the headland on the other side of the Taf estuary. He must have been told of this strange lawless place: a place where a shipload of rum went down and Laugharneys buried the barrels, but tapped one and got so drunk that no one could remember where they'd buried the hoard; a place where the ball used in the annual football match was called 'The Head of John The Baptist' (the game itself banned by magistrates in 1838 for being too violent); a place where dancing white lights were seen leaving the homes of the dying and making their way to the cemetery. And what would the people be like? The pubs? The welcome? How strange could a place possibly be? He knew that Richard Hughes, the twenty-something millionaire novelist, lived in a house with a castle in the garden. Would he gain an audience? Maybe some supper? Through Hughes he'd meet the painter Augustus John and his lover Caitlin Macnamara, the original hippy wild child and his future wife. Who needed London?

At a widening in the path he happened upon an intriguing garage high on metal stilts – the first garage for the first car in Laugharne and built for a fortune due to its precarious position. Fifteen years later he would write some of his greatest works in there. Onwards and to the right a crude shipbuilder's cottage called White Spot which stands opposite steps leading down to the sea. Further on another former inn – the Travellers Rest – and on again to an opening where several lanes gather outside the imposing gates of the Glanymor estate. At this junction, known as Long Lanes, the track bears left passing Bay View and its sea captain ghost on the right and a small picturesque graveyard on the left. The original footprint of the long-demolished church is now a car-stand belonging to a house, and another of Laugharne's long-lost pubs, the Ball. Ahead he'd see a grand four-storey house called Sea View, where he would later spend the happiest year of his life, and the brown castle walls lurking beyond. Turning right he would walk down Victoria Street – Hangman's Street until the 1860s – where his namesake, the poet, writer and soldier, Edward Thomas, lived at No. 14 for several weeks in 1912. Here he'd have his first glimpse of a fully functioning Laugharne pub, the Three Mariners, but it was around the corner in Brown's Hotel that he had his first ever drink in Laugharne: a mug of coffee.

One thing dawned on him that morning; one thing that was decidedly odd. Maybe not at first … maybe the first few times he'd have thought it was a trick of the ear or the voices of tradesmen and incomers, but the more he eavesdropped the more intrigued he became. Four miles inland is the Welsh-speaking town of St Clears, but Laugharne was described in Norman times as an 'Englishry' and on this first trip he reported in a letter to a faraway love that, whilst this town was surrounded by hundreds of miles of Welsh countryside, '… people here speak in a broad English accent'. Prior to the Normans, the Romans inhabited Laugharne and 2,000 years before them the Bell Beaker people were here; human remains found during 1950s building work at Orchard Park are kept in a small wooden box in St Martin's Church. Further back in 4000BC people were sophisticated enough to ceremonially bury their dead, and thirty millennia before that Neanderthal man looked out across the estuary from nearby Coygan Cave. Hyenas later used Coygan Cave as their lair at a time when woolly rhinoceroses and mammoths roamed the salt marsh.

So here was an ancient place (he was a spiritual man connected to the past); a tidal place (he had the vocabulary and passions of a precocious seaside boy – indeed Dylan is Welsh for 'son of the wave'); a farming place (Laugharne was largely self-sufficient and farming was in his mother's blood); a natural place (he was a keen student of animals and birds); a cosmopolitan place (one that still entices artists and writers); an English enclave in his beloved Wales (English was his mother tongue); and most importantly, a place of stories and story-tellers.

He would recognize much in 2014. Whilst three hostelries – the Farmers, the Corporation and the Green Dragon – have served their last since his drinking

5 Cwmdonkin Drive, Swansea, Dylan Thomas's childhood home and now open to the public. Courtesy of Matthew Hughes, Dylan Thomas Birth Place.

The view from 5 Cwmdonkin Drive. The sea was an ever-powerful presence throughout Thomas's life. Courtesy of Matthew Hughes, Dylan Thomas Birth Place.

Dylan Thomas's childhood bedroom where he wrote early drafts of many of his best-loved poems. It has been restored meticulously. Courtesy of Matthew Hughes, Dylan Thomas Birth Place.

The Uplands area of Swansea, where Dylan Thomas was born, as it would have looked during his childhood. Courtesy of West Glamorgan Archive Service.

Dylan Thomas regularly visited Llansteffan throughout his childhood and continued to return there throughout his life. DiscoverCarmarthenshire.com

The main high street in Swansea town centre before the three nights blitz of 1941 that destroyed it. Courtesy of West Glamorgan Archive Service.

The aftermath of the 1941 blitz. Courtesy of West Glamorgan Archive Service.

Dylan and his family lived in the Welsh town of New Quay, Ceredigion between 1944–45. The sea views and quirky characters were a great inspiration for his poetry and prose. Courtesy of Janet Baxter and Ceredigion County Council.

Dylan Thomas lived in the Welsh town of Laugharne, Carmarthenshire, on and off, for fifteen years. Thomas and his wife, Caitlin Macnamara are buried together in the graveyard of St Martin's Church. DiscoverCarmarthenshire.com

The Thomas family lived at the Boathouse, Laugharne from 1949 until Dylan's death in 1953. The ashes of Dylan and Caitlin's daughter, Aeronwy, were scattered here at her childhood home. An inscription on a bench overlooking the estuary reads, 'The Funny Thing Is I Find Myself Returning Again and Again...' DiscoverCarmarthenshire.com

The Sailors Arms – Courtesy of Sir Peter Blake and Enitharmon Editions.

Mrs Organ Morgan's General shop – Courtesy of Sir Peter Blake and Enitharmon Editions.

The Afternoon Buzzes – Courtesy of Sir Peter Blake and Enitharmon Editions.

Courtesy of Peter Ross

days, he'd be heartened to hear 'last orders' still being called in the Fountain, the New Three Mariners and Brown's Hotel, whilst another alehouse, the Cross, awaits renovation. These are pubs where detectives talk tides with town drunks; where brickies and bankers bicker; where plumbers, poets and Portreeves plot. And he'd know the three Georgian shop fronts which remain on Market Street although the shops behind, built on vaulted medieval cellars, do not. These were shops where he bought sweets, meats, cakes and string and cajoled shop-girls for credit. The marble slab and white wall-tiles of the butcher's shop window are still in situ although, according to a local resident, the display contained '… more flies than sausages'.

His castle, '… brown as owls', differs only in that its ivy cloak was cut back in the 1980s and it no longer functions as the garden for Castle House. He became a frequent guest of Richard Hughes and took advantage of the contents of Hughes's wine cellar in the castle ruins to fuel the re-writing of his adolescent memoirs – *Portrait of the Artist as a Young Dog* – in a converted sea-facing turret in the castle wall. He liked to have a view as he battled with old words and invented new ones. Richard Hughes later acknowledged that, while Dylan might have sponged off people financially, '… we sponged off him spiritually'.

And the Celtic Cross, prison cell, telegraph poles, old school, milk churn stand, iron boot-scrapers, up-street merchants' and sea captains' mansions, down-street cocklers' cottages, schoolroom, cobbles on Market Street (formerly Hangman's Lane … hangmen clearly much vaunted among early town-planners), town hall, and the Green Banks – the area below the castle where he said he wanted to be buried – would all resonate. As too would the garden door at Cliff House, the eerie 'Burnt House' up-river, the collapsing tombstones of St Martin's and the pared-down petrol pump outside the old bus garage. And strolling along The Lacques – Latin for lace – an area where Flemish weavers were imported to interbreed with the troublesome Welsh by Henry II – he would know the crow-cry of the hawk-scattering flock that blackens the sky as it protects its nests above the shaded cottages. And the estuary: he'd know that even more. No gentrification for herons, curlews, hawks and flounders; sewin, dabs, otters and seals; egrets, lapwings, cormorants and gulls and his own '… sea of scum': the slush-coloured bubble-bath slick that forms at mid-tide from the emissions of cockles and shellfish that were once the lifeblood of the town.

Phase out the twenty-first-century yellow lines, UPVC and satellite dishes and you not only see what he saw but hear what he heard – the cry of babies, bark of dogs, lap of the tide, squabble of drunks and the whistling wind; door slam, gate creak, gull caw, jackdaw chatter, bee buzz and the clip-clop of horses' hooves – not pulling a milk-float, dray, or rag'n'bone cart but pony-trekkers from the riding school. And the smells – clematis, apples, wild garlic, fried bacon, salt, freshly baked bread, honeysuckle, pickles, cockles, laverbread, fish, chips and rosebuds: sights, sounds and smells as pungent now as they ever were.

He'd recognize his former homes too: the fisherman's cottage on Gosport Street; Sea View, described by artist Augustus John as a 'dolls' house'; and most famous of all, the iconic Boat House. Two of them have signage to publicize their tourist ambitions. The third, halfway up the hill on the main road towards Broadway, bears a simple sign on its magnolia exterior: '22 Eros' – a humble cottage named after the Greek god of love. Then on to his fourth 'unofficial' home, the newly restored Brown's Hotel, where a skip and a jangle up the front steps takes afternoon revellers into the bar, as full of stories, banter and intrigues as it ever was. He would take in the hoppy smell of locally brewed ale (which he usually drank by the half-pint) but would baulk at the absence of smoke. Octogenarian Mae, formerly of Victoria Bakery, said he was '... a drinker, but never a drunkard, and generous too'. He sponsored her two shillings and sixpence for a ten-mile walk in 1952. Mae has been in Laugharne for sixty-six years and speaks with a broad Glaswegian accent. He was charmed by that too. Another local, Peggy, is ninety-two and said he was always smartly dressed and polite. He roared elsewhere. Here he wanted to fit in.

At the carnival last year he'd have enjoyed the fracking team outside the Mariners. Their publicity campaign advertising the search for shale gas on the estuary initially traumatized Laugharneys, but they chuckled as yellow smoke billowed from the frackers' 'truck' while water jets sprayed and sirens wailed. For one day, at least, fracking was fun. And there goes a Poet Laureate, a punk poet, a Kink, a Goodie, a Booker winner and a train-robber at the much-vaunted Laugharne Weekend. And here comes an American rock goddess, an heir to the throne, a Hollywood star and a thespian knight. Laugharne was known in the coffee houses of 1890s London and the great and the good are still drawn to a place which has managed to side-step change because it never had a railway, bypassed the industrial revolution and saw little tourism. Isolation kept the twentieth century at bay; even the main road out to St Clears was a dirt track until 1925. Laugharne offers sanctuary to those for whom the world is changing too fast; sanctuary that is largely down to some curious customs that date back to 1297.

The Laugharne Corporation is the last fully functioning corporation in the UK and has existed for over 800 years. Every other Monday the Portreeve, foreman and all-male jury hold court in the Town Hall to discuss the Corporation's burgeoning property portfolio. Every three years the community beats the twenty-odd-mile boundary to maintain the corporation's right to exist. At certain points known as 'hoisting places' the foreman asks a newcomer to name the location. If the answer isn't forthcoming the unfortunate individual is up-ended and given a light smack on the rump. The customs of the court keep Laugharne separate. It remains an insular place: many here don't drive, mobile phone reception is patchy at best and the sight of a traffic warden is met with indignation. One local, annoyed at getting a ticket, commented: 'If they told us they were coming I wouldn't have parked there'.

Apart from everything else he'd know the tales. He loved stories, sitting shyly in Brown's Hotel, pencil and dismantled cigarette packet at the ready. He happily reported that Laugharne had '... colossal liars to listen to'. If he were here, ears open, today, he'd garner enough material to write a sequel to

Under Milk Wood in a weekend. Maybe he'd record the morning men who have rarely known work shouting instructions to skilled tradesmen beavering away on the rooftop opposite, or mention the first police house-to-house enquiries for years when an investigation was launched into the broken window on King Street. This place is full of stories and story-tellers with their witty one-liners, half-heard fragments and dubious information which often verges on the scandalous. Salacious snippets are gathered, sculpted, embellished and inflated until a story fit for a bar-room performance emerges, whilst in another pub a different variation of the same source material might be heard. Indeed arguments can ensue as to whose unreliable narrative is the most reliable. Here is a tattooed pensioner reminiscing about his street-fighting days to German tourists – 'If I got off the bus and wasn't punched in the head, I'd wonder what was wrong!' There is a man hawking a picture of an old sailing boat for beer money. Here is a man who was once arrested at machine-gunpoint at a Turkish airport for being a terrorist. Some stories are reported as humorous yarns. Others have a meaner twist but all are equally compelling, such as the tale of the hard man who became trapped in the quicksand and chose his last moments to yell obscenities at his enemies. Or the woman arrested for impersonating a nun while collecting for charity on Swansea's streets while six months pregnant. Or the thwarted woman who had a compromising picture of her married lover printed on a tee-shirt. Or the man who paid a couple of cocklers fifty quid to torch his car, only to find his wife had forgotten to renew the insurance. Or the air–sea rescue mission launched after it was reported that a half-naked woman was attempting to drown herself on Ginst Point. It turned out to be a young mum, full of life, half-cut and skinny-dipping. Rumour becomes gospel in this place. A sozzled observer saw a lone police car make a routine left turn past the quarry towards the marsh road. One witness, one police car. Rumours ran around the streets like demented terriers. 'There was a raid tonight. Seven cop cars, armed police, two ambulances went down and when they got there they found drugs, machine guns, cash and Russian prostitutes. Turns out it's a front for London gangsters – money laundering, all sorts – I thought something funny was going on down there ...' And before dawn there were reports that the local piggery had been searched for bodies.

His body lies in the cemetery of St Martin's Church but his description rings as true today as the bell on the old town clock above the town hall – built by public subscription in 1853 – a bell that chimes just before the hour, or just after the hour, but never at the correct time. Once a year on Big Court Night, the Portreeve (the figurehead of the corporation), resplendent in chains of gold cockleshells, is carried by burly aldermen around the town hall three times in a sedan chair. A week later there is a breakfast of cold meats followed by a church service and an all-day booze-up around the bars of the town. These events have taken place on the first weekend of October for over 800 years. On 9 October 1953 Dylan wrote to the then Portreeve of Laugharne apologizing for not being able to attend the breakfast as he had to go to London and then on to America. It was the last letter he wrote.

He called Laugharne '… the strangest town in Wales'. It still is. He loved and loathed this place which is in equal measure disorienting and comforting, amusing and dark, quirky and deep, crude and crafty, wild and watchful, wicked, wet but warm-hearted. On the scrounge to a benefactor, he grumbled '… the weather gets me like poverty – shrouds me in my wet self, rains away the world'. But it was also '… this place I love' and it is clear this place, his adopted home, was an inspiration to the end. On 5 November 1953, four days before he died of pneumonia, high living, bad diet, gastric problems, asthma, diabetes (undiagnosed), exhaustion, depression, abandonment, morphine and medical negligence in a New York hospital, a BBC broadcast had him celebrating Laugharne as '… this timeless, beautiful, barmy (both spellings) town … a legendary lazy little black-magical bedlam by the sea … there is nowhere else quite like it at all'. His writings made his 'legendary' Laugharne famous across the world, but he would know this place if he were still with us.

Books

Ferris, P., *The Collected Letters of Dylan Thomas* (London: Dent, 1985).
Graves, R. P., *Richard Hughes* (London: Andre Deutsch, 1994).
Thomas, D., *The Collected Poems* (London: Dent, 1952).

Broadcasts

Thomas, D. 'Laugharne', BBC (1953).

Dylan the Eavesdrop

Roger McGough

Brown's Hotel in the pretty village of Laugharne in south-west Wales is where Dylan Thomas used to drink, and according to local legend, eavesdrop on bar-room conversations to provide lines and characters for *Under Milk Wood*. Let us imagine the snug on a cold winter's night as the landlord greets one of his regulars ...

'Well, if it isn't Dai the Fish. Had a good day, boyo?'

'Aye, I've been out on the sloeblack, slow, black, crow
black fishingboat-bobbing sea, and I've got a thirst like a
dredger so give me a pint of stout will you. Quiet in here tonight?'

'Aye, you can hear the houses sleeping in the streets,
in the slow deep salt and silent black, bandaged night.
That will be one shilling and fourpence.'

'I see Dylan the Eavesdrop is up to his old tricks,
pretending to be so busy writing poems he can't hear us.
Watch this. Good evening, Mr Thomas, Caitlin in London is she?'

'Yes, Dai, she'll be back home tomorrow.'

'I bet you can't wait, eh? Whacking-thighed and piping
hot, thunderbolt-brassed and barnacle-breasted,
flailing up the cockles with eyes like blowlamps
and scooping low over her lonely hotwaterbottled body.'

'That's right, Dai, yes.
Er... "barnacled-breasted" – that's one word, is it?'

Reading with Dad

Aeronwy Thomas

If I could catch my dad after his bath, he would read to me. Comfortably ensconced in a capacious armchair, on his lap, he would read me stories and rhymes of his choice. From my vantage point I could see the estuary through the slats of the balcony but shut out all distractions to listen to Dad. Was it going to be *Grimm's Fairy Tales* or *The Old Woman Who Lived In A Shoe* with all the children?

Heaven, it was going to be *Little Red Riding Hood*. 'Who would you like to be?' he asked. 'You're so good as the wolf,' I replied, 'so you can play him and the woodchopper.' Of course, I was left with the title role, if Dad agreed. Soon we were in the wood with the nasty wolf hiding behind trees and the poor girl in her red cape visible to all. Dad made me read all the dialogue which I pretended was a little difficult for my reading skills. 'I only know the easy words', I lied. I made myself easy in the armchair sitting on his lap as if I owned him.

Another session we read *Hansel and Gretel* and I was forced to run around looking for matches. 'This is the place the children slept when they first ran away from their nasty family', he said, pouring a mound of matches on the floor. I didn't think they looked like a leafy mound to serve as a bed but did not like to say so. He then made an outline with matches of the witch's cottage made from sweets to tempt Hansel and Gretel. What about the cauldron or oven to cook them, I demanded. He placed his beer glass in the house which didn't convince me. 'What about something smaller?' I asked. Finally, to my satisfaction, he poured out the dolly mixture he kept in his pocket into the sweet house and I fashioned an oven from a piece of plasticine. There followed a debate about who should play the witch and the less interesting characters of the children. In the end, Dad adopted a falsetto voice adding words that I knew were not on the page and made quite a convincing evil old lady. I might ask him to wear a hat from our dress-up box another time, I thought.

Dad could also make lots of other characters from fairytale and nursery rhyme come alive. There was the gruff Giant in *Jack and the Beanstalk* and the jumpy white rabbit from *Alice in Wonderland* read in a staccato, neurotic voice. Aladdin had a similar voice to the witch, one without the frightening tones. It was the best time of the week when Dad opened a book with me.

Always one to seize the moment, I would lurk outside the bathroom door where you could hear him try out different characters from *Under Milk Wood* such as Mrs Dai Bread One and Mrs Dai Bread Two. As the bath was newly installed thanks to a patron, both my parents spent a long time there topping up the hot water. We, the children, had to make do with the tin bath in front of the Aga. As he emerged, hot and steamy, I would pounce with my reading requests, nipping into the bathroom to see whether his detective novel had fallen into the bath water or mainly to fish out any sweets he might have left.

I can remember once Mother, who was impatient to get out for their every night pub session, walking in while we were reading from Struelpeter, waving a pair of scissors to cut Dad's toenails. We were delighted with the timing, and asked Mother to try and not cut off his toes as well.

Later Than Laugharne

Aeronwy Thomas

Herons, mussel pools, gulls and pipers,
encircle our 'house on stilts high among
beaks and palavers of birds'. Cormorants
scud and gulls glide in my memory.
The stones, washed by the tide, which I
would turn looking for blue and white,
or floral pieces of china for our crockery
houses ... And the fish my mother would
catch and I throw back into the swirling
waters of the estuary all around us ...
    I remember them well.
... And high tide covering our back garden
through a hole in the stone wall which
embraced our home. The tide carrying
our makeshift boats on its back, pieces of lumber,
an old zinc bath, and I can still recall
the envy I felt when they bought my brother
a boat called The Cuckoo ...
    The names come tumbling back –
... And I remember the hole in the wall was
Called grandly by all, The Harbour.
... And who could forget sliding down the
mudbanks at low tide into the rivulets
left by the receding water, or running along
the cliffwalk and stirring up a din outside
the shed that was my father's writing den.
    The memories race back –
... And the thrill of peeping through
the keyhole (I was always the most naughty)
to see my father writing his poems about
gulls, hills and cormorants on estuaries
which he saw through his wide-vista window,
as he sat, bent, writing in crabbed letters,

pressing against the hard surface of the
kitchen table that was his desk ...
    We were poor those days –
Though I can't remember being poor
in Laugharne, in those balmy,
never-to-be-forgotten days,
green and golden ....

Herons, gulls and pipers still encircle
our house on stilts,
and the cormorants still scud and glide
in my memory ....

Courtesy of Peter Ross

PART THREE

LEGACY

I hope to show in this final part of the book how my grandfather's short life has had a lasting influence on future generations. His work continues to inspire, and lives on through writers, musicians and artists.

I start this section with two letters that demonstrate the impact and shock of my grandfather's death, on 9 November 1953, at just thirty-nine years old. The first letter is an appeal from the Dylan Thomas Fund Committee. The reason I've included this letter is that I wanted to highlight the distress of my grandfather's friends. Their compassion is apparent when they comment that his death is an 'incalculable loss to literature' and they point out the personal tragedy is that 'he leaves a widow and three children'. I find this upsetting when I suddenly remember that those three children were my mum and her brothers.

The second letter is from Florence Hannah Thomas, my great-grandmother, Dylan's mother. I found this letter extremely difficult to read, especially the line: 'to think in one year I lost my whole family – one I'm afraid I shall never get over'. This sentence is incredibly powerful, as it is unbearable to imagine the suffering and anguish she feels.

My grandfather died of bronchopneumonia, aggravated by neglect of himself and negligence by others, in New York, following a gruelling performing tour. Daniel Williams's essay looks into the reasons why Dylan Thomas caught the cultural imagination of 1950s America. He compares Dylan with the saxophonist Charlie Parker and shows how they were both perceived as dedicating their lives to their craft, while living lives of excess. Daniel indicates that they 'became symbolic figures, removed from actual history and recreated'. From my recent visit to New York, I observed the respect and admiration many people in the city still feel towards my grandfather.

The essay written by Clive Woosnam tells a story of a thriving society that celebrates the life and work of Dylan Thomas in Australia. He points out that 'In Sydney, there is no society for such famous poets as Blake, Burns, Coleridge, Donne, Eliot, Hardy, Keats, Shelley, Tennyson or Yeats, while there is one for Dylan Thomas'. I thoroughly enjoyed reading about their biennial trip based on Dylan's short story, 'The Outing'. The group travel to the aptly name township of Swansea, 130 kilometres north of Sydney, and read Dylan's poetry and prose in a setting very reminiscent of Dylan's famous Boat House at Laugharne. Their 'Dylan's Mountain Christmas' trip sounds equally entertaining. I have included an extract of the play *Under Mulga Wood*, written by a member of the society, Will Christie, set in the outback of Australia, inspired by my grandfather's play.

In contrast to the international reaction, John Goodby's essay is strongly critical of how Dylan Thomas has been 'excluded, marginalized and patronized by English critics'. He thinks that the situation is so grave that 'for about forty years he has been more or less ignored by the canon-makers and historians, treated as a colourful minor poet at best, and at worst as a kind of poetic charlatan'. He tells the reader that Dylan Thomas's poetry suffered from the fact that it crossed borders. It has English, Welsh, Irish, American and European elements. It is considered too tough by the mainstream, too mainstream by the avant-garde, too Welsh by the English, too English by the Welsh, and too populist by cultural elitists. John says: 'He was left to drown in his legend, abandoned as a serious writer.'

Having drawn attention to the problem Dylan's poetry has faced, John then reinforces previous essays and demonstrates that Dylan Thomas had a profound influence on successful poets in the 1950s and 1960s across the world. This, he comments, 'is reflected in the extent to which he has been translated into major and minor European languages, Arabic, Korean, Japanese and Chinese. Forty languages in all, the most of any British poet of the period.'

The essays by Cerys Matthews, George Tremlett and Hilly Janes challenge the reader to question the 'legend' of Dylan Thomas. They put forward some different images of my grandfather based on interviews by Cerys's uncle Colin Edwards, stories from Hilly's father Fred Janes, and recordings of Dylan's wife, Caitlin.

Cerys explains that 'to Colin all went radio silent in Wales on Dylan in the years after his death, while in America, Canada, Germany and Australia his work outshone the headlines and myths ... so Colin determined to do something about it'. He wanted to try and share the lesser-known side of Dylan – his early years, the introspective, sensitive side of the poet, the things about him people loved. Cerys herself continues to try to bring the focus back to my grandfather's talents and is a wonderful ambassador of his work.

George expresses the alarm he felt as he 'became increasingly aware that something was wrong with the Dylan Thomas story ... Analysing *Dylan Thomas in America* [by John Malcolm Brinnin], I found Brinnin often exaggerated, describing events as if he had been there when he had not. Combine that with the negligence uncovered by Nashold and Jones's delusions – and you reveal a legend built on falsehood.'

Hilly talks about Dylan being 'a compassionate and generous man who abhorred authorianism', a man who 'experienced the world in terms of words and translated his experience directly into structures of words – into poetry'. She shows how her father, the artist Fred Janes, the musician Dan Jones and

Dylan complemented each other. Fred explains: 'Three arts – poetry, music, painting – but the overlap was exciting. Enthusiasm was infectious and I think we all learned from each other.'

Within this section, there are testimonies from people that have been influenced by Dylan Thomas. Here are some quotes to give you a taste of what is coming up.

The very first stage direction in Under Milk Wood is 'Silence' … In that silence I heard a community awakening from dreaming in Welsh; I heard a community suddenly stirred by its newfound ability to communicate in Welsh, to remember, love, laugh, chatter, sing, cry, to live life to the full in Welsh.

T. James Jones describing how he created and wrote his own play, *Dan y Wenallt*, inspired by *Under Milk Wood*

The authentic sound of a world I knew, but heightened and transfigured into word music.

Gillian Clarke, the Welsh poet laureate

Dylan Thomas has always been my favourite poet and I have a portrait of him that hangs in my private study at home.

Jimmy Carter, former president of the United States of America

The sheer joy of the words … I had fallen in love with words.

Terry Jones, actor, describing the first time he heard *Under Milk Wood*

It made my head swim and my skin prickle and my heart pound – and the true test of poetry is always physical.

Philip Pullman, author

Dylan Thomas is a unique, visceral and musical voice … truths about what it means to be human.

Owen Sheers, poet

The music is delivered by the words themselves … utterly backed up by the underlying tempo. As I read it I realized it was masterful. A bossa nova of a poem.

Griff Rhys Jones, actor and comedian, describing the poem 'Do Not Go Gentle Into That Good Night'.

In public Dylan Thomas celebrated Dionysus but in the still night, he laboured at his sullen art, it was Apollo who guided his hand.

Michael Sheen, actor

From the start of our marriage, Dylan Thomas was very much part of our lives.

Trefor Ellis, Dylan's son-in-law and my dad

They wanted me at the party ... Because I'm Dylan's Daughter.

Aeronwy Thomas, Dylan Thomas's daughter and my mum

I hope this section will demonstrate the admiration contemporary writers, actors and musicians continue to have for my grandfather's work, one hundred years since his birth, and over sixty years since his death.

THE DYLAN THOMAS FUND

c/o Philip Wittenberg, Treasurer
70 West 40th Street, New York, N. Y.

November 10, 1953

Dear Friend,

I am sure you have read in the press of the sudden and tragic death of the great poet Dylan Thomas. Thomas died of encephalopathy at St. Vincent's Hospital in New York on November 9th, after an illness of four days. He was only 39 years old. He was attended by one of the finest brain surgeons in New York and everything possible was done to save him.

Thomas' death is an incalculable loss to literature. His work was growing in stature with every year. But there is also a personal tragedy - he leaves a widow without means of support and three children - which gravely concerns his friends and admirers.

As spokesmen for a committee of his friends we are making this urgent appeal to you for a contribution to The Dylan Thomas Fund, which we have hastily organized, which will be used to meet his medical bills and funeral expenses and, if the response is as generous as we hope, to tide his family over the next difficult months.

Please send your check to The Dylan Thomas Fund, care of Philip Wittenberg, Treasurer, 70 West 40th Street, New York City. An accounting of disbursements from the Fund will be sent to the contributors at a later date.

For the DYLAN THOMAS FUND COMMITTEE

W. H. Auden	Marianne Moore
E. E. Cummings	Wallace Stevens
Arthur Miller	Tennessee Williams

Thornton Wilder

Pelican House
Laugharne.
Carms.

d march.
11

Dear Miss Ross.

Thanks so much for your very kind invitation for the "tribute to Dylan" at the Bishop's Gore School. I'm very sorry but I shant be able to come as I have been in bed for a month, suffering from nervous exhaustion & its now so the Doctors tell me that the troubles I had last year are telling on me. I still cant believe that I shant see my boy any more, how I miss him I can never tell, to think in one year I lost my whole family, it's been a very severe blow, one I'm afraid I shall never really get over.

Remember me to Fred & his wife

I am yours very Sincerely
Florence. H. Thomas.

P.S. Caitlin is in London at the moment so cant answer for her, as I dont know when she is returning.

Letter from Dylan's mother.
1954

Courtesy of Hilly Janes

THE
CARTER CENTER

4/18/2013

To Hannah Ellis

   I wish you well in the publication of the Centenary
Celebration book relating to your grandfather's birth. As you
already know, Dylan Thomas has always been my favorite poet
since I first became familiar with his work fifty years ago when
I read "A Refusal To Mourn the Death by Fire of a Child in
London." I have been to Laugharne several times, and worked to
have his great contributions commemorated in Westminster Abbey.
In fact, the people of Wales gave me a duplicate of the stone in
the Abbey, plus a portrait of him that hangs in my private study
at my home.

   I did write a poem about this experience a few years ago,
which is quoted on the attached page.

   Best wishes,

   Jimmy Carter

A President Expresses Concern
on a Visit To Westminster Abbey

Poet's Corner had no epitaph

to mark the Welshman's

sullen art or craft

because, they said,

his morals were below

the standards there.

I mentioned the ways of Poe

and Byron,

and the censored Joyce's works;

at least the newsmen listened,

noted my remarks,

and his wife Caitlin wrote.

We launched a clumsy, weak campaign,

the bishops met

and listened to the lilting lines again.

Later, some Welshmen brought to me

a copy of the stone

that honors now the beauty he set free

from a godhead of his own.

J. Carter

'Wales-Bird' – Dylan Thomas and Charlie Parker

Daniel G. Williams

I

In 'The Pursuer', a short story by the celebrated Argentine novelist Julio Cortázar, a ground-breaking jazz musician named Johnny Carter is pursued by Bruno, a critic who is increasingly anxious about his inability to capture the essence of jazz in prose. According to Doris Sommer, Cortázar's original Spanish conveys Bruno's uneasiness and self-doubt about his vocation as a critic, an anxiety intensified by the fact that 'Johnny's capacity for intellectual speculation' is 'more than equal to Bruno's'. Johnny quotes Dylan Thomas's 'O make me a mask' and proceeds to offer an interpretation of the poem which develops into a meditation on the arbitrariness of words and signs. The Argentinean Cortázar uses Thomas's words as the epigraph to his work, which is dedicated in memoriam to the musician on whom the story is so clearly based: alto saxophonist Charlie Parker. There's no evidence that Parker himself ever offered an interpretation of lines by Dylan Thomas, but Cortázar is drawing on the fact that many likened Parker to Thomas, not least in the fact that their remarkable creative exploits were seen to 'be matched by equally extraordinary acts of personal dissolution'. Parker died in New York, aged thirty-five, in 1955. Thomas had died two years earlier in the same city, aged thirty-nine. Both deaths offered themselves to romanticization and mythologization. Rather like Thomas's character Samuel Bennett, who was destined to shed 'seven skins' in the original plans for the short story 'Adventures in the Skin Trade', Cortázar's Carter performs many roles, wears many masks, and is continually eluding the pursuit of critics and coroners alike. The saxophonist and his artform elude the formal confinement required of prose. The problem for Carter is that Bruno's biography of his life contains the bare facts, 'but what you forgot to put in is me'.[2]

[2] Julio Cortázar, 'The Pursuer', in *Blow-Up and Other Stories*, trans. Paul Blackburn (New York: Pantheon, 1967), 182–247. Doris Sommer, 'Grammar Trouble for Cortázar', in *Proceed With Caution, When Engaged with Minority Writing in the Americas* (Cambridge, MA: Harvard University Press, 1999), 211–33.

The fictional saxophonist's critique of Bruno's work may be levelled, with some justification, at this essay. For I am less concerned with the actual, historical, figures of Charlie 'Bird' Parker and Dylan Thomas, than I am with what they came to represent in 1950s America. As will become clear, they were very widely compared, most influentially so in poet Kenneth Rexroth's celebrated essay 'Disengagement', which attempted to trace the roots of the 1950s 'Beat movement'.

> Like the pillars of Hercules, like two ruined Titans guarding the entrance to one of Dante's circles, stand two great juvenile delinquents – the heroes of the post-war generation: the saxophonist, Charlie Parker, and Dylan Thomas. If the word 'deliberate' means anything, both of them certainly deliberately destroyed themselves.
>
> Both of them were overcome by the horror of the world in which they found themselves, because at last they could no longer overcome that world with the weapon of a purely lyrical art ... Dylan Thomas's verse had to find endurance in a world of burning cities and burning Jews. He was able to find a meaning in his art as long as it was the answer to air raids and gas ovens ... I think all this could apply to Parker just as well, although, because of the nature of music, it is not demonstrable – at least not conclusively.[3]

Rexroth's placement of Dylan Thomas and Charlie 'Bird' Parker in the context of wartime atrocity and destruction implicitly raises the question of the function of art during, and following, a period of frightening barbarity. It is clear from the opening quotation that for Rexroth – who never developed his comparison beyond a few vague references to both artists' 'lucidity' and 'fluency' – Charlie Parker and Dylan Thomas were responding to a crisis in post-war culture; that of how, in the aftermath of the death camps and the atomic bomb, could art endure at all. There is evidence throughout Thomas's letters and poems that he was haunted by the atrocities of war, testifying to the truth of Rexroth's dramatic observation that his 'verse had to find endurance in a world of burning cities and burning Jews'. In a letter to an unknown woman written in May 1945, Thomas evokes 'the throbbing of tractors, the squealing of rats and rabbits in the traps, the surging of seagulls, thrushes, blackbirds, finches, cuckooing of cuckoos, cooing of doves, discussion of works, blinding of wives, sputtering of saucepans and kettles' outside his window in New Quay, before noting that it is an 'ordinary day, nature serene as Fats Waller in Belsen'.[4] The discrepancy, in this essentially humorous anti-pastoral scene, between the trivial everyday goings-on of a Welsh coastal town and the atrocities recently perpetuated and disclosed on mainland Europe is disconcerting, as is the way in which Thomas heightens that discrepancy by juxtaposing the Harlem stride-

---

[3] Kenneth Rexroth, 'Disengagement: The Art of the Beat Generation' (1959), in *The Alternative Society* (New York: Herder and Herder, 1970), 1.

[4] Dylan Thomas, *Collected Letters*, ed. Paul Ferris (New York: Palgrave Macmillan, 1985), 617.

pianist Fats Waller (who had died in 1943) with Belsen. Fats Waller is made to represent a natural life force that is seemingly unaffected and oblivious to the barbarism of war. This tendency to represent African-Americans as sources of natural primitivism in a hostile and alienating world has a long history, but was given a new lease of life in the writings of 1950s America, and is a characteristic of the racial thought of that period. The ubiquitous comparison made between Dylan Thomas and Charlie Parker was informed by this romanticizing and mythologizing primitivism.

II

In his study of jazz as myth and religion, Neil Leonard analyses the tendency to view Charlie Parker as a 'trickster', that 'complicated figure, part human, part animal' who

> is an ambivalent, ambiguous figure full of contradiction and irony – in one moment charming, altruistic, intelligent and creative, and in the next gross, stupid and deceptive, a liar, thief, or seducer. He may have uncertain sexual status or outlandish appetites symbolized sometimes by outsize genitals ... He may combine black and white symbolism in clever chicanery, marked by a childishness that can be his undoing.[5]

Leonard proceeds to discuss a whole range of outlandish stories concerning Parker, such as the following account by Ross Russell of a night in 1948 at the Argyle Lounge, an expensive Chicago club.

> Charlie finished a set and placed his horn on the top of the piano. Then he stepped off the bandstand, walked past the tables on the main floor, into the foyer, entered the pay telephone booth, closed the door and proceeded to urinate on the floor. The yellow stream gushing forth as from a stallion, its pool dark and foaming as it spread under the door of the telephone booth and into the foyer. He came from the booth laughing. There was no explanation or apology.[6]

There are stories of Parker's insatiable sexual appetite – such as Miles Davis's recollection of sitting in the back of a taxi while Bird, already 'shot up' on heroin, drinks whisky, eats chicken, and tells his female companion for that night 'to get down and suck his dick'.[7] Tales of Dylan Thomas's behaviour tend to be less explicit, but he is similarly represented as a figure who openly breaks the conventions of respectability. John Berryman recalled Thomas's 'social savagery' at a post-reading party in Seattle.

---

[5] Neil Leonard, *Jazz: Myth and Religion* (Oxford: Oxford University Press, 1987), 122–3.

[6] Ross Russell, *Bird Lives* (New York: Charterhouse, 1973), 257. Quoted in Leonard, 123.

[7] Miles Davis, *Miles: The Autobiography* (London: Palgrave Macmillan, 1989), 55–6.

We had about ninety seconds' talk when out hostess, an affected and imperious lady known locally as the Duchess of Utah, crashed into and between us with 'Well! Literary gossip, eh?' in a tone both injured and superior, meaning that we had no right (after thirteen years) to seclude ourselves from the avid professors and professors' wives for one minute, or rather two. Thomas had already greeted everyone, incidentally; I kept out of the way until his chores were done. He was still on his first drink. Now he looked at our short hostess with resentment and contempt, and said slowly, 'We were just discussing Hitler's methods of dealing with the Jews, and we have decided that he was quite right'.[8]

Berryman proceeds to defend Thomas as no anti-Semite, and is anxious to note that they had in fact been discussing the poems of Alun Lewis, whose work Thomas had just read. But the story is a particularly unpleasant example of Thomas's role as outrageous taboo breaker, and Berryman is deliberately reinforcing that dimension of his character. There are many stories of this kind in John Malcolm Brinnin's *Dylan Thomas in America*, where the Welsh poet's primitivism, childlike nature and subversive tendencies are consistently foregrounded.

The sexual life of Dylan Thomas was already as much a source of legend as was his fabulous capacity for alcohol. Reports from Boston to Los Angeles suggested he lived by lechery, fondling girl sophomores and the wives of deans with an obsessive disregard for anything but his own insatiable desires. The tumescence of his poems fed such rumours and supported them; uncovering sexual imagery in the poems of Dylan Thomas had already become a national undergraduate pastime. The precise, obscene references and the four-letter ejaculations of his drunken talk, his often lascivious retorts to civil questions, and his lewd attentions to details of the female anatomy were repeated and embellished. In California, it was reported, he had suffered through an intolerably long and dull dinner party with a group of male professors. When cigars were passed around, Dylan, refusing to sink into the general stupor, addressed the company: 'Gentleman, I wish we were all hermaphrodites!' 'Why,' said one of the professors politely, 'why do you wish that Mr. Thomas?' 'Because, gentlemen, then we could all **** ourselves'. Similar stories cropped up everywhere, along with rumours of a sexual prowess and a sexual preoccupation indicating satyriasis.[9]

Both Thomas and Parker were constructed in terms that correspond closely to the figure of the 'trickster', that 'liminal figure' in whom we see, according to Victor Turner, 'naked, unaccommodated man, whose nonlogical character

---

[8] John Berryman, 'After many a summer: Memories of Dylan Thomas', *Times Literary Supplement*, 3 September 1993, 13–14.

[9] John Malcolm Brinnin, *Dylan Thomas in America: An Intimate Journal* (1955. New York: Viking, 1959), 75–6.

issues in various modes of behavior: destructive, creative, farcical, ironic, energetic, suffering, lecherous, submissive, defiant, but always unpredictable'.[10] In the cultural imagination of 1950s America, Parker and Thomas embodied certain, perhaps necessary, ideals of the transgressive artist.

Thomas's four visits to the United States occurred when the Cold War was at its iciest, with McCarthyism at its height before the slow thaw that occurred following the death of Stalin, who, like Thomas, died in 1953. It was a period of American military dominance, consumer craving and political conservatism in which a new generation of American writers bared the dark side of national affluence. The post-war economic boom had supposedly landed Americans in a placid valley of consumer goods: pastel pedal-pushers, self-cleaning ovens and cheeseburgers delivered by waitresses on roller-skates. In this situation, literature had become merely one among numerous expressions of cultural activity in competition for people's time, attention and money. Literature had become bureaucratized, had lost its aura, and society seemed to be a massive supermarket designed to fulfil the needs of consumers. Randall Jarrell's witty essay 'A Sad Heart at the Super-market' offered a plangent diagnosis of the future of culture in a consumerist society, and the same note is echoed by Allen Ginsberg 'shopping for images' in his poem 'A Supermarket in California' and by Lawrence Ferlinghetti in 'The Pennycandystore beyond the El'.[11] Theodore Roethke captures the spirit of the age when he describes the 'frigidaires snoring the sleep of plenty' in 'Last Words', and the need to choose between newly available goods works through the poetry of the fifties as a diffuse but insistent voice.[12] Saul Bellow warns us in his novel of 1956 *Seize the Day*: 'You want to avoid catching the money fever. This type of activity is filled with hostile feeling and lust. You should see what it does to some of these fellows'. Unfortunately, Tommy Wilhelm, Bellow's main character, does catch the money fever, and the novel's final scene shows him weeping at a stranger's funeral, mourning the death of genuine human connections in a harsh and alienating world. Tommy's grief and isolation ennoble him, since fifties novelists agreed that those who succeeded in the mercenary culture were, in the words of *Catcher in the Rye*'s Holden Caulfield, 'phony bastards'.[13]

This was the context for the rise of the 'hipster', described by Norman Mailer in his essay of 1957, 'The White Negro':

A totalitarian society makes enormous demands on the courage of men, and a partially totalitarian society makes even greater demands, for the general

[10] Quoted in Leonard, 127.
[11] Randall Jarrell, *A Sad Heart at the Supermarket: Essays and Fables* (London: Eyre and Spottiswoode, 1965). Allen Ginsberg, *Collected Poems 1947–1980* (New York: Harper and Rowe, 1984). Lawrence Ferlinghetti, *These Are My Rivers: New and Selected Poems* (New York: New Directions, 1993).
[12] Theodore Roethke, *The Collected Poems* (New York: Anchor Books, 1975).
[13] Saul Bellow, *Seize the Day* (New York: Viking, 1956), 7. J. D. Salinger, *The Catcher in the Rye* (New York: Little, Brown, 1951).

anxiety is greater. Indeed if one is to be a man, almost any kind of unconventional action often takes disproportionate courage. So it is no accident
that the source of Hip is the Negro for he has been living on the margin
between totalitarianism and democracy for two centuries.[14]

The hipsters represented a counterculture in formation, and had their
worldview expressed and dissected by the writers of the 'Beat era' such as Jack
Kerouac, Allen Ginsberg and William Burroughs. If Norman Mailer suggests
that one source of 'the hip' was the Negro, then another source was Dylan
Thomas. Part of the appeal of Dylan Thomas to the writers of 1950s America
was that his early death and commitment to his art proved that he was no
'phony bastard'. He was perceived to be that which the Beats most admired
– a poet who dedicated his life to writing, and who was seen to live a life of
excess. Whereas Salinger's Holden Caulfield, like many other fifties misfits,
is ushered into the analyst's office, tranquillized and made to adapt, Dylan
Thomas avoided such enforced conformity by allegedly drinking himself to an
early death.

Thus, if a lascivious sexual appetite, outrageous behaviour and willingness
to break boundaries and taboos were elements of the primitivizing of Thomas
and Parker, another, not wholly unrelated, response was their mythicization.
During their lives, and particularly following their deaths, Thomas and Parker
became symbolic figures, removed from actual history and recreated as deified,
religious types representing broader spiritual and cultural forces. Karl Shapiro
was discomfited by the way in which Dylan Thomas's perceived 'childishness'
and 'innocence' caused him to be seen as a victim of capitalism and 'the signal
for a verbal massacre of the bourgeoisie, reminiscent of the early decades of
our century'.[15] Shapiro was responding to works such as Kenneth Rexroth's
lengthy poetic 'massacre of the bourgeoisie', 'Thou Shalt Not Kill' – a response
to Thomas's death on 9 November 1953.

> He is dead.
> The canary of Swansea.
> Who killed him?
> Who killed the bright-headed bird?
> You did, you son of a bitch.
> You drowned him in your cocktail brain.
> [...]
> You killed him,
> Benign Lady on the postage stamp.

---

[14] Norman Mailer, 'The White Negro', in *The Penguin Book of the Beats*, ed. Ann
      Charters (New York: Penguin, 1993), 585.
[15] Karl Shapiro, 'Dylan Thomas', in C. B. Cox, ed., *Dylan Thomas: A Collection of
      Critical Essays* (New Jersey: Prentice Hall, 1966), 273

[...]
In your lonely crowd you swept over him.
Your custom built brogans and your ballet slippers
Pummelled him to death in the gritty street.[16]

It was at Rexroth's weekly seminars in his apartment at 250 Scott Street, San Francisco, that Ginsberg heard him read his elegy to Dylan Thomas, and the poem's claim that the values of a capitalist society destroy human creativity would reverberate through Ginsberg's celebrated poem 'Howl' a few years later. If Ginsberg, in that poem, observed 'angel headed hipsters … contemplating jazz', Jack Kerouac attempted to fuse music with poetry in his recordings with pianist Steve Allen and saxophonists Al Cohn and Zoot Sims. In a letter to Ginsberg he boasted that his jazz-accompanied readings were the 'greatest poetry records since Dylan Thomas'.[17] In the '239th chorus' of his 'Mexico City Blues', featured on the first of his albums, Kerouac captured the process by which Charlie Parker became mythicized as a transcendent being lying beyond the realities of material life:

Charley [sic] Parker Looked like Buddha
Charley Parker, who recently died
Laughing at a juggler on the TV
after weeks of strain and sickness,
was called the Perfect Musician.
And his expression on his face
Was as calm, beautiful and profound
As the image of the Buddha
Represented in East, the lidded eyes,
The expression that 'All is Well.
You had the feeling of early-in-the-morning
Like a hermit's joy, or like
    the perfect cry
Of some wild gang at a jam session
'Wail, Wop' – Charley burst
His lungs to reach the speed
Of what the speedsters wanted
And what they wanted
Was his Eternal Slowdown.
A great musician and a great
    creator of forms

16 Kenneth Rexroth, 'Thou Shalt Not Kill', in Charters, ed., *The Penguin Book of the Beats*, 233–41.
17 Ginsberg, 'Howl', in Charters, ed., *The Penguin Book of the Beats*, 62. Jack Kerouac and Allen Ginsberg, *The Letters*, Bill Morgan and David Stanford (eds) (London: Penguin, 2011), 406.

That ultimately find expression
In mores and what have you.[18]

David Yaffe notes that as a good friend of Williams Burroughs ('Old Bull Lee' in
On the Road), Kerouac would recognize the lidded eyes 'not as mere Chinoiserie
but the nodding out of a junkie'.[19] But the painful reality lying behind Parker's
breakneck solos – fuelled as they were by heroin addiction – is of no real interest
to Kerouac, who sees in the founder of bebop the visage of the Buddha himself.

III

Despite the Beat borrowings from the clothing, lifestyles and attitudes of
jazz musicians generally, and black beboppers such as Charlie Parker specifically, African-American Beat writers, as A. Robert Lee noted, 'might well be
thought to have gone missing in action'.[20] The African-American novelist and
playwright James Baldwin criticized the famous scene from *On the Road* where
Sal Paradise walks 'At lilac evening ... among the lights of 27th and Welton in
the Denver colored section, wishing I were a Negro' as 'absolute nonsense and
offensive nonsense at that'.[21] The Black Nationalist Eldridge Cleaver, on the
other hand, defended the depiction of African-Americans by white Beat writers
because the Beats 'dared to do in the light of day what America had long been
doing in the sneak-thief anonymity of night – consorted on a human level
with blacks'.[22] Indeed, there were a few significant 'black Beats', most notably
Al Joans, who daubed Greenwich Village with 'Bird Lives' graffiti following
the saxophonist's death, and Bob Kaufman, whose poem to Bird, 'Walking
Parker Home', in his collection *Solitudes Crowded with Loneliness* is followed
by a poem entitled 'Afterwards they Shall Dance' that portrays some of the
key artists deemed to have influenced the Beat movement, ranging from Poe to
Baudelaire to Billie Holiday. A stanza is dedicated to Dylan Thomas:

> Dylan took the stone cat's nap at St. Vincent's, vaticaned beer, no defense;
> That poem shouted from his nun-filled room, an insult to the brain, nerves,
> Save now from Swansea, white horses, beer birds, snore poems,
>   Wales-Bird.[23]

[18] Kerouac, '239th Chorus', from *Mexico City Blues*, in Charters, ed., The Penguin
Book of the Beats 53–4.
[19] David Yaffe, *Fascinating Rhythm: Reading Jazz in American Writing* (Princeton:
Princeton University Press, 2006), 143.
[20] A. Robert Lee, 'Black Beats: The Signifying Poetry of LeRoi Jones/Amiri Baraka,
Ted Joans and Bob Kaufman', in Lee, ed., *Beat Generation Writers* (London: Pluto
Press, 1996), 159.
[21] James Baldwin, 'The Black Boy Looks at the White Boy', in *Nobody Knows My
Name, Collected Essays: Vol. 2* (New York: Library of America, 1998), 278.
[22] Eldridge Cleaver, *Soul on Ice* (New York: McGraw-Hill, 1968), 72.
[23] Bob Kaufman, 'Afterwards they Shall Dance', in *Solitudes Crowded With Loneliness*
(New York: New Directions, 1965), 6.

A great deal of biographical information is packed allusively into a stanza which follows the Beat tendency to celebrate Thomas as a romantic who dedicated himself to poetry and drink. St Vincent's is the Roman Catholic hospital in New York where Thomas died, the white horses invoke the waves off the Welsh coast while also referring to the poet's favourite bar in Greenwich Village, and the African-American poet's reference to Thomas as 'Wales-Bird' links Thomas with Charlie 'Bird' Parker while also invoking images of transcendence.

Charlie Parker and Dylan Thomas also appear in the writings of the most celebrated 'black Beat', LeRoi Jones. Jones is a particularly interesting figure as he began as a Beat poet in 1950s Greenwich Village, before abandoning his Beat bohemianism for black nationalism, his home downtown in Greenwich Village for an apartment uptown in Harlem, and his (partly Welsh) slave name LeRoi Jones for the African Imamu Amiri Baraka. Baraka's character Clay in the play *Dutchman* undergoes a similar conversion as the drama develops, and towards the end he seeks to destroy the white, Beat, image of black musicians:

> Charlie Parker? Charlie Parker. All the hip white boys scream for Bird. And Bird saying, 'Up your ass, feeble-minded ofay! Up your ass'. And they sit there talking about the tortured genius of Charlie Parker. Bird would've played not a note of music if he just walked up to East Sixty-seventh Street and killed the first ten white people he saw. Not a note![24]

The black Buddha of Kerouac's poem, who tells us that all's well with the world, becomes the vengeful militant of Baraka's play whose art is a sublimation of murder. Baraka traces the development of his thought, from Beat to Black Nationalist, in his autobiography of 1984, and includes a passage on his responses to Dylan Thomas.

> There were writers too in that circle. One I remember, Clyde Hamlet, who imitated Dylan Thomas. But many people did then. [Steve] Korret's work at this time was connected very consistently with Thomas, who was roaring around the Village, especially the White Horse Tavern ... Hamlet was suave and sophisticated, I thought, he was hip to me. That's why I couldn't understand his poetry sounding so exactly like Dylan Thomas's when it seemed to me, once I'd read Thomas, that anyone reading him would realize immediately that his poems were simply Thomas imitations and little else.
>
> What I'd said before about how my reading was taking me into something and away from something at the same time is relevant here. Because this circle of Korret's and indeed his influence, to a certain extent, was merely a continuation of the other 'whitening' influences I had been submitting to enthusiastically under the guise of information, education ... So that Europe as intellectual center was yet another stone to the weight of 'alienation' from black (if that is not too strong a word) that was building up in me.

[24] LeRoi Jones/Amiri Baraka, *Dutchman*, in Henry Louis Gates et al. (eds), *The Norton Anthology of African American Literature* (New York: Norton, 1997), 1897–8.

Exiting from one world and entering another. That's the way this learning
I'd committed myself to had taken shape ... And I learned quickly that the
Cages and Cunninghams were very highly esteemed in that circle. Almost
mythological beings, and ditto 'Dylan,' as Korrett called him, like they were
cutbuddies. So I was heavily into Dylan.[25]

The shift from 'Beat poet' LeRoi Jones to 'black nationalist' Amiri Baraka can
be traced in these responses to Charlie Parker and Dylan Thomas. Baraka's
autobiography testifies to the centrality of Thomas's work for the Beat writers
of 1950s Greenwich Village, but what is most noteworthy here is the way in which
Thomas is made to represent the domination of European literary models and
values on the black artist. Writing from the black nationalist standpoint that he
adopted in the 1960s, Baraka is dismissive of his own literary activities as a Beat
writer and considers his 1950s works as the products of a false consciousness in
which his primary literary influences were contributing to his alienation from
'blackness'. Far from being Shapiro's marginal Welsh writer whose surrealistic
and anarchic poems placed him at odds with American consumerist culture and
mainstream English poetic practices, Thomas, for Baraka, is a representative of
the 'intellectual worship of Europe' which is 'the remnant of colonialism, still
pushed by the rulers through their English Departments and concert halls!'.[26]

Notwithstanding the power of Baraka's nationalist rejection of Thomas,
there are other, alternative responses to the Welshman's work within the
African-American literary tradition. Richard Wright, for example, used lines
from 'Light Breaks Where No Sun Shines' as an epigraph to his controversial
'White Man Listen'. Wright drew on Thomas's

When logics die,
The secret of the soil grows through the eye
And blood jumps in the sun ...

to reinforce his rejection of 'blood and soil' as the basis for political action.
Wright called on 'the White man' to turn to the 'precious heritage – the freedom
of speech, the secular state, the independent personality, the autonomy of
science – which is not Western or Eastern, but human'.[27] In Wright's work (as in
that of Edward Said more recently), exilic outsiders are the vehicles for enacting
a humanist tradition that builds on the most valuable strains in Western and
Eastern thought, and Dylan Thomas seemed to embody a poetic expression of
this universalist belief. Similarly, black Californian poet Al Young views Dylan
Thomas as a figure who can testify to poetry's ability to speak across lines of
nationality and ethnicity, and to transcend the often highly charged debates on

[25] Amiri Baraka, *The Autobiography of LeRoi Jones* (Chicago: Lawrence Hill Books, 1984), 187–8.
[26] Baraka, 187.
[27] Richard Wright, 'White Man, Listen!' (1957), in *Black Power: Three Books From Exile* (New York: Harper Perennial, 2008), 643, 727.

culture, race and identity in which it occasionally becomes embroiled. When asked, in the late 1990s, to introduce his favourite poet for an anthology, Young chose Dylan Thomas. The editors asked him to reconsider – they wanted him, a contemporary African-American poet, to pick a black poet. He ended up introducing Langston Hughes, but in a gesture of protest at having been racially pigeonholed in this way, Young wrote his introduction to Thomas in any case, and printed it on the web.

> I had clipped this black and white publicity likeness of Welsh poet Dylan Thomas from a New Directions catalog and Scotch-taped it next to a cut-out from *Down Beat* of Bird: jazz genius Charlie Parker. One of my outspoken buddies who visited my attic digs would always stare at those two pictures and comment: 'Who did you say this poet dude was? He looks like he's more tore up than Bird'. ... The Dylan Thomas of whom I speak with such runaway affection was not only a poet; for a literate chunk of the English-speaking world, he seemed the epitome of a poet. That he died at 39 in 1953 was important to my generation. Parker, who died two years later, only made it to 35 ... The whole point, we thought, was to make a statement, make a splash, and then die early enough to let people know you really meant what you stood for ...
>
> It was love of Dylan Thomas' art that led me to learn about things Welsh just as my love of Charlie Parker's music led me back to Kansas City with its wide-open gambling, prostitution, political corruption and graft, and all that plentiful, beautiful music. Each of them keeps leading me back to my own origins and pre-natal origins through the light-years time takes to fill the sky of one mind, one heart. 'The common wages / Of their most secret heart,' was one way Dylan Thomas put it.[28]

Al Young's words reinforce a number of my arguments here: Thomas's significance in 1950s America and the widespread comparison with Charlie Parker in particular. More significantly, in a surprising and revisionist development of the primitivist terms in which Thomas was appropriated by the Beats, Al Young testifies to the way in which Dylan became a significant figure for African-American artists themselves. The African-American responses to Thomas's work underline the fact that 'Dylan' became more than the sum of his parts in the United States. 'Dylan' was, then, a culturally constructed figure of some significance as he got drawn into broader, and often highly charged, debates on the relationship between the cultures of black and white America, and between American and Europe. While for Amiri Baraka, Thomas represented the oppressive 'worship of Europe', Al Young in his 'Poem to Dylan Thomas' speaks of the Welshman's key role in encouraging a young black poet

[28] Al Young, 'The Dylan Thomas I Looked Up' (2002), *The Alsop Review*, ed. Jack Foley. http://www.alsopreview.com/foley/jfdthomas.html [accessed 18 June 2002].

to voice 'all I'd heard and seen and breathed / down there inside your dream, and mixed it well / with wishes and bewitchments of my own'.[29]

IV

When Dylan Thomas died in New York in November 1953 he was, according to Igor Stravinsky, 'on the first leg of his journey to my home in California, and we were both looking forward to getting better acquainted personally and working on the idea of an opera'.[30] Thomas had met Stravinsky in Boston the previous May, and following that meeting discussed his ideas for a libretto with the organizer of his US tours, the poet John Malcolm Brinnin:

> They would do a 'recreation of the world' – an opera about the only man and woman alive on earth. These creatures might be visitors from outer space who, by some cosmic mischance, find themselves on an earth recently devastated and silenced by global warfare; or they might be earthlings who somehow have survived an atomic miscalculation. In either case, they would re-experience the whole awakening life of aboriginal man. They would make a new cosmogony. Confronted with a tree pushing its way upward out of radio-active dust, they would have to name it, and learn its uses, and then proceed to find names and a definition for everything in earth. The landscape would be fantastic – everything shaped and colored by the dreams of primitive man – and even the rocks and trees would sing.[31]

It is by now a commonplace to describe Modernism as a response to a crisis of representation or a crisis of language – a crisis that took on a revived immediacy following the atrocities of the Second World War.[32] Thomas's libretto seems to enact a scene where language is reconstructed anew, with a direct connection being re-established between word and referent, signifier and signified. The apocalypse gives rise, dialectically, to a utopia where language can be freed from corrupted social conventions and stifling historical associations. In 'From Love's First Fever' Thomas speaks of learning

> man's tongue, to twist the shapes of thoughts
> Into the stony idiom of the brain,
> To shade and knit anew the patch of words
> Left by the dead ...[33]

[29] Al Young, 'A Poem for Dylan Thomas', *Heaven: Collected Poems 1956–1990* (New York: Creative Arts Books Company, 1992).

[30] Igor Stravinsky, 'The Opera That Might Have Been', *Adam: International Review*, No. 238 (1953), 8.

[31] Brinnin, *Dylan Thomas in America*, 216.

[32] See, for example, Astradur Eysteinsson, *The Concept of Modernism* (Ithaca: Cornell University Press, 1990), 73–6.

[33] Dylan Thomas, *Collected Poems 1934–1953*, Walford Davies and Ralph Maud (eds) (London: Everyman, 1988), 22.

It is precisely his attempts at knitting language anew, at revivifying both poetic language and poetic forms, that mark the late-modernist impulse in Thomas's works.

Charlie Parker was also engaged in revivifying the vocabulary of jazz, and in doing so had turned to Stravinsky for inspiration. Parker's admiration for his classical contemporaries has been widely noted. Bill Coss observed in the fifties that Parker 'seldom listened to jazz anywhere unless he happened to be on a job. His main interest was in classical music, mostly the moderns', and Ted Gioia has noted the 'strange and subtle ways' in which this interest manifested itself; he would often call his band up to the stage with a few lines of Hindemith's 'Kleine Klammermusik', he asked that Bartok be played at his daughter's funeral and towards the end of his life he approached Edgard Varèse asking for composition lessons.[34] In a Leonard Feather 'Blindfold Test' of 1948, Parker correctly identified Stravinsky's 'The Song of the Nightingale' and commented: 'Is that Stravinsky? That's music at its best. I like all of Stravinsky.'[35] Recalling his time in Parker's band, trumpeter Howard McGhee noted that Parker

> knew everything, and he hipped me to, like, Stravinsky and all those guys. I didn't know nothin' about Stravinsky. So Bird was the first one to tell me about it. So like, *The Rite of Spring*, he brought it over to the house and let me hear it. And I said, 'Yeah, this cat, he's kind of cool, you know; he knows what he's doing.'[36]

Alfred Appel Jr. recalls an evening 'in the winter of 1951, at New York's premier modern jazz club Birdland':

> As Parker's quintet walked onto the bandstand, trumpeter Red Rodney recognized Stravinsky, front and almost centre. Rodney leaned over and told Parker, who did not look at Stravinsky. Parker immediately called the first number for his band, and, forgoing the customary greeting to the crowd, was off like a shot ... At the beginning of his second chorus he interpolated the opening of Stravinsky's *Firebird Suite* as though it had always been there, a perfect fit, and then sailed on with the rest of the number. Stravinsky roared with delight, pounding his glass on the table, the upward arc of the glass sending its liquor and ice cubes onto the people behind him.[37]

It is a telling moment, for it was partly the assimilation of harmonic and rhythmic devices from contemporary classical music that led, in Martin

---

[34] Carl Woideck, ed., *The Charlie Parker Companion: Six Decades of Commentary* (New York: Schirmer Books, 1998), 51. Ted Gioia, *The Imperfect Art* (Oxford: Oxford University Press, 1988), 72.

[35] Woideck, 68

[36] Woideck, 152.

[37] Alfred Appel, Jr., *Jazz Modernism: From Ellington and Armstrong to Matisse and Joyce* (New York: Alfred A. Knopf, 2002), 60.

Williams's words, to bebop's 'renewed musical language, with which the old practices could be replenished and continued'.[38]

The juxtaposition of tradition and renewal, of the modern and the primitive, characterizes Stravinsky's composition 'In Memoriam Dylan Thomas'. The piece was completed a year after Thomas's death, is scored for four trombones, string quartet and tenor, and is written in the serial style which Stravinsky began to experiment with in later life. The opening and closing instrumental passages were described as 'dirge-canons' and they frame the central portion in which the tenor sings Thomas's poem 'Do Not Go Gentle Into That Good Night', accompanied by just the strings. The trombone is perhaps the most basic of brass instruments due to its reliance on varying the length of the tubing rather than on valves to achieve different pitches, and may thus be seen to represent the primitivist dimension in the works of both Thomas and Stravinsky. The string quartet on the other hand, associated in particular with Haydn and Beethoven, represents the Western classical tradition. Stravinsky's composition may in this sense be considered a meditation on Thomas's reception in the United States; the writer of taut, complex lyrics of formal and psychological complexity represented in the strings is informed by the brooding, disturbing presence of the subversive, primitivist, Celtic, druidic Thomas in the trombones. This essay concludes with this fitting musical juxtaposition.

---

[38] Martin Williams, 'Charlie Parker: The Burden of Innovation' (1970), in Woideck, ed., *The Charlie Parker Companion*, 13.

Dylan Downunder

Clive Woosnam

The wonderful sunlight there, the hills, the great bridges, the Pacific at your shoes. Beautiful Chinatown. Every race in the world. The lobsters, clams & crabs. Oh Cat, what food for you. Every kind of seafood there is. And all the people are open and friendly.

Substitute prawns and oysters for clams and this could be a visitor writing about Sydney today. Instead, it's Dylan Thomas writing to Caitlin in 1950, describing the delights of San Francisco – a city often compared with Sydney. Dylan never had the chance to visit Sydney; the closest he came was Iran on one side and Los Angeles on the other.

If he had made the journey, would he have enjoyed what he found? Today, almost certainly, the answer would be yes, but he might have had some misgivings in 1950, given Sydney's licensing laws at that time. Strong British links coupled with limited pub opening times did not appeal to him. On his 1950 North American tour he described Vancouver as 'a quite handsome hellhole...more British than Cheltenham', and complained bitterly about the licensing restrictions which made him 'thank God to be out of British Canada & back in the terrible United States of America'. Sydney's licensing laws were repressive, but less severe than Vancouver's and, with the sunshine more consistent than in San Francisco, he might well have found the city to his liking.

Certainly, both his sons liked Sydney well enough to live here for some years, and his granddaughter Jemima and daughter-in-law Louise still live here. The Dylan Thomas Society of Australia, based in Sydney, was the first such group formed outside Britain, while mention of the poet in the media occurs on a regular basis. Dylan's works have frequently found their way into school and university English Literature syllabuses, and *Under Milk Wood* is often performed in theatres across Australia.

Poetry lovers around the world may be surprised to learn that Dylan Thomas was the subject of a spirited debate in one of Australia's main daily newspapers at the beginning of 1937, when he was just twenty two years and two months old. The debate, on the merits of modern poetry in general and Dylan's poetry in particular, continued in the Adelaide Advertiser for six weeks in feature articles and the letters columns.

Here are three brief excerpts:

WHAT is this modern verse? The question is prompted by the discussion which has arisen following publication in "The Advertiser" of a notice of Dylan Thomas's "Twenty-five Poems" (Dent). The reviewer dismissed this slender book of poems with the critical observation:— "A book of advanced modern verse for those who profess to understand it." The notice moved Professor J. I. M. Stewart, of the Adelaide University, to write in a letter which was published in "The Advertiser":— "Mr. Thomas is recognised by many people as among the writers of good verse today. Some of his work first appear in the *Criterion* and some in a popular newspaper. Where there is a public for poetry it is discussed." This letter in turn was followed by others less appreciative of modern verse. As to Mr. Thomas's ideas, his publishers say that this collection of his poems has been "carefully chosen to represent his distinctive personal voice". "This young Welsh poet," they add, "has, during the last two years, attracted an unusual amount of attention with his Dionysian verse. His name has appeared in several journals which take poetry seriously." Whether the generality of readers will take Mr. Thomas's poetry seriously is another matter.

Later, one writer put forward an authentic stanza from a Dylan Thomas poem then added a stanza of his own as an imitation, then wrote:

Mr. Thomas is an acknowledged Neo-Georgian poet; and it is doubtless an impertinence in me thus to mingle his verses with mine: for I am not an acknowledged Neo-Georgian poet, nor, indeed, a poet of any other kind. But. if it comes to a test of intelligibility, I shall not decline the encounter, in a mere panic induced by my own presumption. I feel that my stanza, although I own it to be perfectly fog-bound and unintelligible to me, and confidently assume that it will convey no more to anyone else, is just as clear as Mr. Thomas's stanza...

Amid the many letters questioning Dylan's motives or, indeed, whether his work could be considered poetry at all, there were some brave defenders of his work, who argued that he was simply following the same experimental path of earlier poets who had become less controversial over time.

It is lazy minded, if not brutal of us to dismiss carelessly the earnest and skilful verses of such men as Gerard Manley Hopkins, that father of modern verse, and those of his followers who have had the "courage to experiment and the conviction that there were ways of expression more direct than the ordinary syntactical one." With the consciousness of the problems of our time there is an even greater need for the recourse to the spiritual beauty of poetry. Harsh is the voice of the poet who cries aloud in the wilderness, and it is a wilderness indeed when his poetry falls on deaf ears.

It is unlikely that Dylan's work ever again stimulated so many letters and articles over so short a time in a daily newspaper. His death was portrayed in Australia as elsewhere in such a lurid way that it overshadowed his life and work. John Malcolm Brinnin's book, *Dylan Thomas in America*, and Sidney Michael's play *Dylan* both helped to popularise his legend as a hell-raiser over his achievements as a writer. *Under Milk Wood* and 'Do Not Go Gentle…' would be the only works of Dylan's widely known by today's Australian public, but wider still would be the awareness that Dylan came to a bad end at an early age.

Yet, as we know, some of Dylan's work attracts devotees from many backgrounds. In Sydney there is no society for such famous poets as Blake, Burns, Coleridge, Donne, Eliot, Hardy, Keats, Shelley, Tennyson, Wordsworth or Yeats, while there is one for Dylan Thomas. How could Dylan get a level of support not available to so many other writers? It is worth looking at the Dylan Thomas Society of Australia more closely to see how it arose and how it has managed to continue its active life.

Prior to 1994 Sydney knew Dylan Thomas through poetry anthologies, productions of *Under Milk Wood*, isolated performances of shows such as Ray Henwood's *No Good Boyo*, Bob Kingdom's *Return Journey* or Sidney Michael's *Dylan*, and occasional study topics in school or university English courses. The only regular readings or recitations of Dylan's work took place at the twenty or thirty Sydney Welsh Choir concerts each year, where I had the privilege of familiarising audiences with some of Dylan's lighter works.

Then, just before the 80th anniversary of Dylan's birth, in October 1994, a previously unknown fan of Dylan's came up with a bright idea: an 80th birthday party for Dylan held in the Southern Highlands resort town of Bowral. Robert Jones, the man in question, was a hotel manager there. He staged a weekend residential mini-festival at his Links Hotel and enough supporters arrived to make a success of the initiative. This is where the seeds of the Dylan Thomas Society of Australia were sown.

One month later, Jones had a very short book on Dylan published. Titled *Time Passes*, and subtitled, *Dylan Thomas's journey to Under Milk Wood*, the book was a series of samples of Dylan's poetry and prose to entice the unfamiliar reader to discover more of his work. The one key point in the book that stands out in retrospect is that Robert Jones insisted that Dylan was suffering from asthma and pneumonia and died from 'a fatal mistake in treatment' (an injection of half a grain of morphine sulphate) at a time when most writers were happy to trot out the story of the eighteen whiskies.

The Dylan Thomas Society of Australia was eventually created on 12 March 1995, in what might seem the somewhat inappropriate surroundings of a Thai restaurant in Sydney. The winds of change at the Thai Phoon restaurant blew in along with the clouds of coincidence, in that the inaugural meeting took place on the same day that a choir from Dylan's home town of Swansea appeared in Sydney for the first time.

The DTSA's first meeting was attended by only around a dozen people, with Robert Jones, naturally enough, elected president. I was given the chance to recite a story and a poem or two of Dylan's, before rushing off to our choir's reception for the visiting Morriston Orpheus Choir from Swansea, where I recited Dylan's much-loved story, *The Outing*. It was wonderful to think that such a famous choir had arrived in Sydney on the perfect day to celebrate their home city.

From the outset, it was decided that the Dylan Thomas Society of Australia should aim at gaining popular support in the community, and should avoid becoming either a predominantly Welsh society or a predominantly academic society. I think we managed to do this quite successfully, and Robert Jones was the ideal president to follow such a path. Despite his name, he had no known Welsh blood and, though University educated, had not followed an academic career.

Robert and Jan Jones hosting an early event

The society determined that there should be a few regular events throughout the year. The first, in early February, was to be the Annual General Meeting, which we decided should be as much a social celebration as an administrative necessity, while in April we planned a *Legend & Poet* evening of readings. Later regular events were to include a Dylan Thomas lecture and a birthday celebration in late October.

The first birthday celebration, in 1995, involved a feature story in the Sydney Morning Herald and an overnight stay in the aptly named township of Swansea, 130 km North of Sydney, attended by around thirty members of the new society, with a video on Dylan's life, a dinner in his honour, a speech about the poet and various readings of his work. As Swansea has sea, sand, estuary and water birds, we were able to spend the morning reading more of Dylan's poetry and prose in a setting very reminiscent of Dylan's famous Boat House at Laugharne.

Reading Dylan's words at the Legend & Poet event

We tried and failed to get the local authority at Swansea to make the Dylan Thomas birthday weekend a regular event on its calendar, but the increased publicity of the centenary may help to sway a future decision. We now use Swansea as the destination for our biennial Outing, a day trip from Sydney and back paying homage to Dylan's famous story, in which a small boy is forced to go on a charabanc outing with a group of elderly and increasingly inebriated men. Currently we stop at *Doylo's* (Doyalson RSL Club) only an 'oo' away from being *Dylan's*, where I get the chance to recite *The Outing* to the chara-bancers, then we have lunch in the dining room of Swansea RSL Club, looking out at the 'fishing-boat-bobbing' sea, and read aloud some of Dylan's lyrical works set along his home coastline.

Three photos to show some of the group in and around the caves

From there we move to the magic world of Caves Beach and into the caves themselves. They produce an atmosphere that never fails to impress our members, while the acoustics lend themselves to our joint rendition of stories such as *Who do you wish was with us?* – a story set among the cliffs and rock platforms of the Gower. At the beach we hear again the multi-layered humour of *Holiday Memory* before we make the short journey to Catherine Hill Bay, a coal-mining town with a white sand beach and a pub dating from the 1870s.

The pub's name is officially The Wallarah, but it is known universally as *Catho's*. I'm sure Caitlin would have claimed it as her own and Dylan would have loved it. It's a somewhat tawdry place where squalor passes for atmosphere and loud electronic noise passes for music, but it has a clientele of elderly bikies and general eccentrics that could easily inspire another play for voices, while the wall is adorned with old photos and samples of primitive poetry. The charabanc then takes us back to Sydney, regaling us en route with DVDs of Dylan's life and works. We manage to keep up to date with new TV presentations, usually from Wales, and link them in with the material to be used at each of our stops along the way.

Our outing is, of course, very different from Dylan's, usually with a majority of women and quite devoid of small boys. We always reach our destinations, break no glasses and do not allow primus stoves aboard. And, if any travellers have forgotten their false teeth, they are sensible enough to keep quiet about it.

On our first outings we stopped at the Swansea Hotel for a drink. The attraction there was a photo circa 1920 of a genuine all-male group in a real charabanc which we regarded as an icon, until it disappeared in the refurbishment of the hotel. The dining room was also of great interest to us, as it served Thai food (reminding us of our society's birthplace) and had the Thai national flag – just like the flag of Siam in Dylan's story. And the menu had a meal that would most certainly have appealed to him. It was called *pad khi mow*, which was translated as *stir-fry meal for intoxicated person*. Dylan may not have liked the food, but he would certainly have respected the economy of language that could transmit so much information in just nine letters.

We alternate *The Outing* in odd years with *Dylan's Mountain Christmas* in even years. Both events are held in winter, to allow us to enjoy *A Child's Christmas in Wales* and other stories where there is snow and everyone is clad in winter woollies. Dylan's Christmas stories seem out of place in late December in Sydney, where the sun is burning down from a cloudless sky on a mid-summer scene. So we go to the Blue Mountains or Southern Highlands in winter and have a genuine Christmas menu of turkey, ham and blazing pudding. In 2004 we managed to time our journey perfectly and have a day amid real snow, not too far from Sydney, with snowmen outside the pub keeping guard on our festivities.

Robert Jones resigned as president at the end of 1997, but has remained a loyal member of the society with his wife Jan in the years since then. Dr (later Professor) William Christie of Sydney University's English Department took over the position and in October 1998 began the DTSA newsletter *Down Under Milk Wood*, with three issues each year. Interestingly enough, the very first edition featured *Musings and Memories* by Dylan's daughter, Aeron.

Real snow and snowman for a Dylan Christmas

The three DTSA presidents together in 2012

Will Christie is a talented writer, and was awarded the New South Wales (NSW) Premier's Biennial Prize for Literary Scholarship in 2008. He has long had a passion for the works of Dylan Thomas, and has written a number of performance pieces for our society as well as many important articles for the newsletter. He wrote an Australian outback version of Dylan's play-for-voices in 2003, to be first performed as part of our festival commemorating the 50th anniversary of Dylan's death. As *Under Mulga Wood*, it has been published in hard and soft-back editions, has been broadcast on national radio and performed widely in the professional theatre.

Will Christie explained the impact of Dylan in the following words:

> I stopped going to school very early during my last year of high school and spent my days in what we then called the Mitchell Library, now of course the older part of the NSW Public Library. This was a new and exciting world for me, the collective and creative aspirations of humanity – an emporium (to use Dylan's image) of dreams – and while I was lurking with intensity, if not intent, amongst its stacks and corridors, skimming or as we now say surfing text after text, dream after dream, I came across this volume by a poet I'd heard of but never read before – Poet in the Making: The Notebooks of Dylan Thomas. I began my arbitrary and shiftless search through the treasures of the Mitchell Library with a sense of enchantment, but when I found this book I was enthralled.

Other members of our society felt the impact of Dylan's words in a similarly forceful way, while there are some people linked to the society with personal memories of Dylan or his family. John Notary, the public officer of the DTSA, explained how he kept meeting Dylan by chance in London's Fitzroy Tavern, a favourite haunt of Dylan and other writers such as George Orwell. John knew Dylan was a poet and that he was going to America, and was saddened to hear of his death in New York. But John wasn't familiar with Dylan's work until...

> On the 25th of January 1954, I was just leaving home for a dinner date when I heard on the radio the latter part of the prologue to what I now know as Under Milk Wood. Entranced, I listened...Time stood still as this incredible drama for voices and radio unfurled. Finally, it finished, and to my utter astonishment the author was announced as the late Dylan Thomas. Dinner was memorable because my friend had also met Dylan at the pub and we just couldn't believe that he had written this masterpiece. I regret never ever being able to thank him for it.

Probably the most interesting personal link with Dylan's writings was provided by a doctor's wife I met in the Hunter Valley. She told me she came from Laugharne, and when I mentioned Dylan she replied, *He would come past regularly. I was 17 years old and lived in a house called Rose Cottage. I would say "Good Morning, Mr Thomas, and he would doff his hat. He was always very polite."*

Other DTSA members were friends or acquaintances of Dylan's sons Llewelyn or Colm when they lived in Sydney. We managed to get Colm and his Sydney wife Louise to attend a special gathering of our society and he impressed everyone with his unassuming nature. It's sad to think that all three of Dylan and Caitlin's children are now dead. One of our members worked with Llewelyn for years in advertising, and wrote an article on how he, son of the chain-smoking poet, was chosen to be the man to try to minimise the effects of cigarette packet health warnings when they were introduced in the 1970s.

While the DTSA was finding its feet in its early years the Sydney Welsh Choir continued to spread Dylan's words around Australia and many other parts of the world. In the sixteen years from 1990 the choir made five concert tours back to Wales incorporating performances in the USA, Canada and many European countries. The choir visited Dylan's birth-city of Swansea and his final home village of Laugharne several times and in 2002 gave a concert in the Dylan Thomas Centre in Swansea with a program centred on Dylan's writings.

The formation of the DTSA in 1995 had inspired the creation of a similar organisation, the Dylan Thomas Circle, in Vancouver, Canada. We have maintained fairly regular contact with this society over the years. Neville Thomas from Vancouver was our guest speaker at a Dylan Thomas celebration lunch a few years ago. Jeff Towns, currently chairman of the original Dylan Thomas Society in Britain, also came out briefly to Sydney when his son Joseph was a DTSA member.

Neville Thomas speaking at a DTSA lunch

Will Christie had major plans to put on an international symposium on Dylan in Sydney. With the initial support of the Historic Houses Trust, he contacted many of the world's foremost experts on Dylan's work and received favourable replies. Unfortunately, sponsorship proved more elusive and the scheme had to be abandoned.

In 2003 Will Christie had to spend much of the year carrying out literary research in Edinburgh, so I took over as president of the DTSA for that important year – the 50th anniversary of Dylan's death. We arranged a festival in late October and early November incorporating three main events: a production of *Under Milk Wood*, the first performance of *Under Mulga Wood* which has already been outlined, and a concert featuring the Sydney Welsh Choir scripted to link all the items to Dylan's life and work.

Our *Under Milk Wood* performance followed the original concept of Dylan, but with a substantially larger cast. The emphasis was squarely on the words and, though the cast drawn from the DTSA and the Sydney Welsh Choir was not generally experienced in live theatre work, the accents were authentic and the quality of the acting and singing first rate. *Under Mulga Wood* was performed by a professional cast and was an immediate hit. It is sad to think it has never been staged in Wales.

A later DTSA performance with a smaller cast

The concert commemorating Dylan's life and death was the third of its type we had staged and the most ambitious. It involved numerous recitations of poems and prose excerpts along with two excerpts from *Under Milk Wood* set to music: *Eli Jenkins' evening prayer* sung to *Troyte's Chant* and *Rosie Probert's poem* made even more dramatic by its musical setting. Along with the Sydney Welsh Choir we had the Newington College Chamber Choir singing the setting by William Matthias of Dylan's poem, *A Refusal to Mourn...* and the first performance in Australia of Stravinsky's *In Memoriam Dylan Thomas*, with string quartet, trombone quartet and tenor soloist.

Will Christie agreed to come back as president of the DTSA for a final year in 2004; since then, he has happily served as vice-president while I have continued as president of the society. Will was able to maintain his role as editor or co-editor of our newsletter, despite his heavy commitments at University, right up to the end of 2008, when he finished with a bumper edition. Since then, Helen Woosnam has been editor of the magazine which has been standardised to sixteen pages and now includes many colour pictures and is issued in March, July and November each year. We occasionally have pieces involving original research, some new explications of Dylan poems, and lots of up-to-date news.

Among the many events that the society has staged over the years, there have been several memorable Dylan Thomas lectures. Probably the three most popular were by iconic Australian writer and presenter Phillip Adams, European Union Ambassador Aneurin Rhys Hughes (educated at Dylan's old school), and Geraint Evans, a Welsh academic then teaching at Sydney University.

We have also held two receptions at the British Consulate-General in Sydney, with its magnificent views over the Opera House, Harbour Bridge and Circular Quay. When the first reception took place we were impressed to discover that the Consul-General, Peter Beckingham, had his own Dylan Thomas link. On leaving school he found employment with a record company and the first recording he had to work on was the original 1954 Richard Burton production of *Under Milk Wood*.

The second consulate reception was important in that we invited representatives from all the literary societies in Sydney, and even attracted some from Melbourne. This led to the creation of LitSocSyd, an umbrella organisation guiding literary searchers to their correct destinations. The community of literary groups in Sydney is now much more close-knit as a result.

Over the years I have been intrigued to see the fluctuations in attitude of the Wales Tourist Board/VisitWales and BBC Wales towards Dylan Thomas and Welsh choral music. As president of both the DTSA and the Sydney Welsh Choir I had a good deal of communication with Welsh tourism authorities and found them generally uninterested in Welsh choral music in Australia, which they considered to be 'old' Wales, lacking the *wow factor* of such esoteric events as coasteering and bog-snorkelling. Dylan Thomas was considered marketable, and I was often invited to recite his poems or short stories at special events advertising Wales. Yet, strangely, the BBC Wales TV team that came out to film *The Welsh in Australia* in 2013 were far more interested in the choir than Dylan, despite the impending centenary.

The DT100 Festival is certainly an attraction as far as the DTSA is concerned. The Sydney Welsh Choir and DTSA have joined forces to mount a tour of Wales, Ireland and England in September/October 2014. There will be four concerts in Wales (in Tenby, Swansea, Caerphilly and Aberystwyth),

The British Consul with Helen & Clive Woosnam

two in Ireland and two in England, with seven of the eight concerts featuring host choirs as well as ours. We visit all manner of places associated with Dylan in Wales, Ireland and England, from his father-in-law's ancestral home in Ireland to the plaque commemorating Dylan in Westminster Abbey, and will perform spoken word passages from Dylan's works as well as music that can be linked to him. Apart from concerts, we will give short recitals in such well-known Dylan locations as Laugharne and places with an important but less obvious link such as St Asaph's Cathedral where Dylan made his only solo TV performance.

The touring party returns to Sydney in time for the actual centenary in late October, allowing us to put on two significant events: a performance of Will Christie's *The Road to Milk Wood*, which has been given two public airings in the last decade or so, and the second ever performance of my play-for-voices, *Good Night, Dylan*. I wrote this piece to increase public awareness of the true causes of Dylan's death, while highlighting the broad sweep of Dylan's talent as a writer, and the humour and insight of his work. It was performed once only, in September 2012, so its second performance is long overdue.

It is good to see the acceleration of interest and organisation of the centenary festival, with the consolidation of planned events and the establishment of patrons and ambassadors. I was interested to see Rhodri Morgan, the Chancellor of Swansea University and former First Minister of Wales,

The cast of Good Night, Dylan

on the ambassadors' list. He came out to Sydney several times following the memorandum of understanding with the state government of NSW. Our choir sang to him on more than one occasion, and I was asked to recite something appropriately Welsh at one of his conferences. I had arranged to perform my version of Richard Burton's *A Welcome in the Valleys* but, just as I was about to begin, Rhodri asked me what I was about to recite. I told him, and he was horrified. "It has to be Dylan Thomas", he said. I was impressed. Richard Burton was out, Dylan Thomas was in and, as president of the Dylan Thomas Society of Australia, I was only too happy to oblige.

Patrick Milligan, brother of Spike Milligan, and one of the DTSA's oldest and most charismatic members, on his 87th birthday

The legacy of Thomas's work: *Under Milk Wood* and William Christie's version, set in the Australian outback, *Under Mulga Wood*.

UNDER MILK WOOD

[Silence]

FIRST VOICE (*Very softly*)

To begin at the beginning:

It is spring, moonless night in the small town, starless and bible-black, the cobblestreets silent and the hunched, courters'-and-rabbits' wood limping invisible down to the sloeblack, slow, black, crowblack, fishingboat-bobbing sea. The houses are blind as moles (though moles see fine to-night in the snouting, velvet dingles) or blind as Captain Cat there in the muffled middle by the pump and the town clock, the shops in mourning, the Welfare Hall in widows' weeds. And all the people of the lulled and dumbfound town are sleeping now.

Hush, the babies are sleeping, the farmers, the fishers, the tradesmen and pensioners, cobbler, schoolteacher, postman and publican, the undertaker and the fancy woman, drunkard, dressmaker, preacher, policeman, the webfoot cocklewomen and the tidy wives. Young girls lie bedded soft or glide in their dreams, with rings and trousseaux, bridesmaided by glow worms down the aisles of the organplaying wood. The boys are dreaming wicked or of the bucking ranches of the night and the jolly, rodgered sea. And the anthracite statues of the horses sleep in the fields, and the cows in the byres, and the dogs in the wetnosed yards; and the cats nap in the slant corners or lope sly, streaking and needling, on the one cloud of the roofs.

You can hear the dew falling, and the hushed town breathing. Only your eyes are unclosed, to see the black and folded town fast, and slow, asleep. And you alone can hear the invisible starfall, the darkest-before-dawn minutely dewgrazed stir of the black, dab-filled sea where the Arethusa, the Curlew and the Skylark, Zanzibar, Rhiannon, the Rover, the Cormorant, and the Star of Wales tilt and ride.

Listen. It is night moving in the streets, the processional salt slow musical wind in Coronation Street and Cockle Row, it is the grass growing on Llareggub Hill, dewfall, starfall, the sleep of birds in Milk Wood.

Listen. It is night in the chill, squat chapel, hymning in bonnet and brooch and bombazine black, butterfly choker and bootlace bow, coughing like nanny-goats, suckling mintoes, fortywinking hallelujah; night in the four-ale, quiet as a domino; in Ocky Milkman's lofts like a mouse with gloves; in Dai Bread's bakery flying like black flour. It is to-night in Donkey Street, trotting silent, with seaweed on its hooves, along the cockled cobbles, past curtained fernpot, text and trinket, harmonium, holy dresser, watercolours done by hand, china dog and rosy tin teacaddy. It is night neddying among the snuggeries of babies.

Look. It is night, dumbly, royally winding though the Coronation cherry trees; going through the graveyard of Bethesda with winds gloved and folded, and dew doffed; tumbling by the Sailors Arms.

Time passes. Listen. Time passes.

Come closer now.

Only you can hear the houses sleeping in the streets in the slow deep salt and silent black, bandaged night. Only you can see in the blinded bedrooms, the combs and petticoats over the chairs, the jugs and basins, the glasses of teeth, Thou Shalt Not on the wall, and the yellowing, dickybird-watching pictures of the dead. Only you can hear and see, behind the eyes of the sleepers, the movements and countries and mazes and colours and dismays and rainbows and tunes and wishes and flight and fall and despairs and big seas of their dreams.

From where you are, you can hear their dreams.

Captain Cat, the retired, blind seacaptain, asleep in his bunk in the seashelled, ship-in-bottled, shipshape best cabin of Schooner House dreams of never such seas as any that swamped the decks of his S.S. Kidwelly bellying over the bedclothes and jellyfish slippery sucking him down salt deep into the Davy dark where the fish come biting out and nibble him down to his wishbone, and the long drowned nuzzle up to him.

UNDER MULGA WOOD

A Play for Australian Voices, First Movement

FIRST VOICE [*rising softly out of the silence*]

Let's start from scratch.

It's a dead still, dry season, never-never night in the small town of Goadabuggerai; not a star for the askin', it's tarblack as far back as the blind eye can't see and dark as a blackfella's navel. The dirt roads are dead silent, now, as the bush hard by holds its harsh breath and slumps down past hushed mudflats, small-pocked by the black eyes of yabbie pools, to the dream-haunted shores of the Mulga Lagoon, where dunnarts and wattled-bats, wallaroos and water rats fumble and forage for their wide-eyed lives.

Unleering, now, are the long windows on the second storey of Goadabuggerai's one, proud pub; the brick bungalows, baked fibro, and weatherbeaten weatherboards of the back country town are blind as bats — or pie-eyed as Snakebite Dave, dead to the world in his three-legged dining chair on the pub's verandah. The tides of silence surge through the shadowed air, and all the people round the dumb and blinds-down town are sleeping now.

Shoosh. The milk-pukers and the toddler-warriors are asleep at last, spread-eagled on their mothers in the sticky midnight. The cockies are sleeping, the stockmen and shearers, punters and pensioners, garbo, grease monkey, copper and cook, teacher, tennis coach, postie and publican, the stock and station agent and the surly wives. Young girls lie webbed in their sweaty hair and grope down the crowded aisles of their strobe-lit dreams after lead singers on a country tour of their bodies, while the boys are dreaming thump and tackle, try and triumph in the ruck and tumble of the rugby dark. And in the paddocks, the black silhouettes of horses asleep on their legs cut sharp against the star-less bruise black of the night sky. The feral cats slink and fossick among half-empty tins in the town dump, while the mange-mottled, three-legged guard dog, Rascal, keeps his proud distance and his snout intact. In the yards of the houses, night lets sleeping dogs lie whimpering in their makeshift corners, and sleeping cats practise for the sleeping they'll do all day.

Only you can hear the seeds bursting in the dry quiet, the houses shrinking and settling, and the snuffed town snoring.

Only your eyes are unclosed — yours and the eyes of that moonstruck army of mammals and birds mobilised by the dark; only your eyes, and the eyes of the bronze digger on the Anzac memorial in Federation Park, vigilant in the eternal dark.

And you alone can trace the fine, faint whistle and metallic gallop of the still far away first Western mail train from the hub of Dubbo, on its ritual round of Narromine to Trangie, Nevertire and Nyngan, Mullengudgery, Girilambone, Coolabah and Byrock, slowing down to Goadabuggerai, then Bourke and back.

SECOND VOICE
Listen. It is the ghost gums mourning the dying fall of a lost breeze in the drought-and-out paddocks all around, the sleep of silent laughter in the kookaburra bush. It is night, turning in its sleepy streets; night, lost in the wide emptiness of Cook Drive and Centennial Parade, where the one set of traffic lights in the slow down town acts as referee.

Listen. It is night in the town's one weatherboard Presbyterian church, squat and cubic like an overgrown letterbox; night in Ben Peters' pub, like an empty glass; in Trim Rowlands' barber shop, like a bald head; in Doc Bradshaw's surgery, like a black stump; in Johnno Johnston's general store, like a ratsak custard. It is tonight in Macquarie Street, drifting up the asphalt like a barge; in Gungun Street, goosestepping in bare feet along the troughs of pale sand.

Look. It is night, celebrating its reign over the talismanic skulls of dead sheep on the banks of the Mulga Lagoon, over rust and woodpile in the dark yards, over time and tedium, good and bad; night, glorious in obscure pomp and circumstantial emptiness. But still ...

FIRST VOICE
Time passes.

SECOND VOICE
Listen.

FIRST VOICE
Life passes.

SECOND VOICE
Come closer now.

FIRST VOICE
Come with us to the back blocks, up the concrete jigsaw-puzzle strips of driveway fighting back the buffalo grass, past the Holdens with furry, stuffed dice unrolling in their windscreens and blunt threats on their bumper bars. Be careful of the bindi-eyes, slide behind the dehydrangeas and camellias, browned and withered in the flower, and come quietly onto the patterned

split and warp of wide verandahs where you alone can see the blind venetians behind bare glass, the blank backs of Christmas cards slotted in rows and the black and white photos curling on the sill. Come to the flyscreens, fraying along the slits of kitchen knives and cats' claws, through the scuffed and smudged front doors with bells for belly buttons and curtained portholes, and into the dead still, dead quiet of the living rooms that only you can see.

SECOND VOICE
And what you see are the pastel-coloured walls, flecked with constellations of swatted flies, where porcelain ducks yearn on the wing past faded Namatjira calendars. On tiny bookcases, the Reader's Digests and ageing, urine-coloured paperbacks collapse like dominoes, while on matching tables, still, silent dregs of Coke and beer keep watch from stolen Leagues Club coasters. In the kitchens, hidden in the plastic filagree folds of café curtains on the sills, the chipped mugs and ashtrays from Port Macquarie or Ulladulla house a treasure trove of chewed biros and pencil stubs, matchsticks, twisted ties, pins, paper-clips, dead keys and currency no longer current.

The smell of fried onions, chops and mystery bags is thick in the warm air and, over the patchwork fridges, [the loud ticking of a clock is heard] wall clocks pick at the seconds in the silence, measuring out the long watch of a world bound for the pandemonium of morning.

FIRST VOICE
But stay with us yet [the ticking stops]. Stand still awhile, and let time pass.

Only you can see — above the beds and kennels, baskets and cushions, sofas and folding chairs, utes and panel vans, haystacks and hammocks, floors and gutters where the entire cast of Goadabuggerai sleep out the one play of their lives — the light, fantastic circus of their dreams.

SECOND VOICE
From where you are, the curtain rises on their dreams.

FIRST VOICE
Snakebite Dave, a drover who crossed as many women as deserts in his walkabout life before being retired by a dingo and a dark night, lies straight and stiff as a magician's sidekick on the two back balanced legs of his three-legged chair and dreams of

SECOND VOICE
purple evenings gully-raking up the Cuttaburra Channels against a breeze as tender as the touch of love, the sun kept lively by the long shadows beyond its reach, and the sky a canopy of forever, wider even than the luminous and saffron earth.

And out of the galloping twilight drift all his mates — the lost and lame whom life has since put down.

Dylan, Colin and Me

Cerys Matthews

Cerys Matthews on her uncle, Colin Edwards, who conducted and collected key interviews on Dylan Thomas during the 1960s.

Colin Edwards's visits to our home are now synonymous in my mind with a long-dead hamster called Dolig, who disappeared as a fat, golden hamster up our chimney one day and reappeared a week later as a skinny, black rodent. It was the early 1980s – era of that washable 1970s pattern wallpaper, jewel-coloured acrylic carpets and velour three-piece suites – and my uncle Colin would each year be found resplendent on the sofa, waxing lyrical about the Middle East, Yehudi Menuhin, the last royal family of China (Colin's wife was a blue-blood Chinese exile whose hands had been broken to stop her from playing piano during the Cultural Revolution) and Dylan Thomas.

Normal bedtimes were ignored and we would hang on to every word. The evening would swirl by with this journalist and broadcaster, haloed with his New World vigour, so happy at the helm of our ship.

He was a small, passionate Welshman whose work in the Royal Air Force, then as a reporter (including with the UN), led him to live far from his homeland all his adult life, but like many expats, Colin loved his old country more than that country could ever begin to love itself. This is the key to what became his lifelong obsession: collating and chronicling information about another small, passionate Welshman – Dylan Thomas.

Colin's global perspective allowed him to see the need for more research to be done on Dylan Thomas before too much time elapsed after his death in 1953. He saw that Dylan was far more revered and popular outside of Wales, and that Wales's rather conformist nature had meant that many tended to want to turn their back on their errant son – this man who had caused scandal by his drunken, buffoonish behaviour.

Few Welsh Baptists of the 1950s and 1960s would have appreciated the more bohemian games of 'cat and dog' which Dylan would play – by going round on all fours, biting the ankles of the artists and liberal thinkers drinking in pubs like the Fitzrovia in London – and then to go off and die like that in New York in a whisky-fuelled orgy! ('What will the neighbours say, what will the neighbours ... ???')

You can all but imagine Wales's old provincial folk declaring Dylan's work 'not our cup of tea at all' lest it cast shame on them in some way! It seemed to Colin that all went radio silent in Wales on Dylan in the years after his death, while in America, Canada, Germany and Australia his work outshone the headlines and myths he had largely built around himself, so Colin determined to do something about it.

Colin already had close contact with the Thomas family, as he explains in this letter dated 29 October 1965:

> To date I have recorded more than seventy interviews, starting with Dylan's mother, who was an old friend of my family in Swansea …

It wasn't long till he and Florence, Dylan's mother, hatched up a plan to try and share the lesser-known side of Dylan – his early years, the introspective, sensitive side of the poet, the things about him people loved – and Colin started on this mission to interview all the people he could possibly find who had come into contact with him: friends, family members, work associates, sponsors, fellow amateur dramatics. A few years later he wrote:

> I have interviewed 122 other relations, close friends and literary colleagues of Dylan during extended visits home to Britain, three trips to Czechoslovakia and two to Italy.

By the mid-seventies this had risen to over 150 people and France, Switzerland and Iran were added to the countries visited.

On top of all this travelling and interviewing, and in addition to his full-time work as a journalist and author, Colin also made three documentaries for the Canadian Broadcasting Company: *The Real Dylan*, *Dylan as a Youth* and *My Son Dylan*. Moreover he began writing the ultimate biography, but died on 11 July 1994, and it was never finished. His life's work, however, continues to throw light on this great poet who walked among us too short a time. It informed Constantine Fitzgibbon's biography, the respected *The Life and Times of Dylan Thomas* (though Colin's input went uncredited, which was an upset) and it will inform the drama currently [at time of writing] being made by the BBC on the lead-up to Dylan's death in America, Andrew Davies's *A Poet in New York*.

Until recently, I was under the impression that most of Colin's tapes were destroyed once they had been transcribed, but with great relief not only do some copies survive from the ones he thoughtfully gave his interviewees, but all are still kept safe and sound in the National Library of Wales. I look forward to sharing these interviews with listeners as part of a radio documentary I'm making for broadcast during the centenary year. The interviews themselves make interesting reading; two books, published by Seren, are based entirely on these transcriptions: Dylan Remembered Vols 1 and 2 – all finely edited by D. N. Thomas, whose book *A Farm, Two Mansions and a Bungalow* was made into the rather skewed Hollywood blockbuster film on Dylan, *The Edge of Love*.

But there is 'hot off the press' news too … Jeff Towns has been successful in finding the first and only known surviving film footage of Dylan Thomas – and guess what? He was led to it through my uncle's work. Jeff explains:

Colin Edwards figures in no small way because it was reading page 181 of Vol. 2 of the D. N. Thomas edition of the tapes that prompted me to look again at *Pandora and the Flying Dutchman* (a 1951 film infused with surrealism, which Dylan loved, directed by Albert Lewin, with James Mason and Ava Gardner, and based on the legend of 'The Flying Dutchman').

Jeff continues:

I had recently acquired an original of the photo printed on page 180 of Dylan on set with one of the actors and this got me looking again [at the film], and this time I discovered just nano-seconds of film of Dylan Thomas walking across the beach.

It's an astonishing find and one which raises hope that more film of Dylan Thomas exists somewhere in the world … and our search will continue.

That these two small and passionate Welshmen from the last century fill my thoughts so often tickles me, but I am touched so by Dylan's work: his poetry – like 'Being But Men', 'Should Lanterns Shine', 'The Hand that Signed the Paper', or his essays on poets like Wilfred Owen and Edward Thomas, his stories about Laugharne, America, Swansea and oh! his 'A Child's Christmas in Wales', and all this before I even mention his glorious celebration of human life, *Under Milk Wood* … Well, being such a fan of Dylan Thomas, I am naturally very proud of my family's connection with him.

I share my uncle's opinion, too, that the boy who wrote such intense and searing poetry in his box room in Swansea and the man who spent hours obsessing over words in his shed overlooking the estuary and that lover of melody and rhythm and flow who found something to love even in people's flaws, and who has given so many people all over the world such comfort – it is this side of Dylan Thomas which is far more interesting than any screaming (but ultimately unfulfilling) headline.

Finally, there's one more thing that connects me with these two men – broadcasting. I joined the BBC in 2008; I make documentaries and have my own radio show that I programme and present, celebrating music alongside poetry, and each week as I walk to work I pass the Stag where Dylan drank. Sometimes, I'll have a drink myself, and I'll lift my pint and toast the poet and my journalist uncle, and drift back to those far-off '80s evenings with their terrible wallpaper, escaping hamster and wonderful stories …

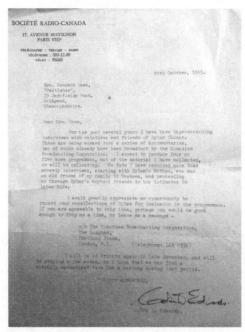

'To date I have recorded more than seventy interviews, starting with Dylan's mother ... through Dylan's boyhood friends to his intimates in later life'

Colin and Me

The Kind of Man He Was

George Tremlett

My English teacher introduced me to Dylan Thomas. This was at King Edward VI Grammar School, Stratford-upon-Avon, where Shakespeare learned to write in the very same room that we did. The school had links with the Shakespeare Memorial Theatre, with free tickets for dress rehearsals and the run of its wardrobe for school plays.

The teacher, Wood, clearly thought I spent too much time alone with Shakespeare, for my idea of a good night out was paying 2s 6d for a balcony ticket and 3d on binoculars to look Olivier in the eye. I never missed a production.

'Try the modern writers', said Wood, mentioning Dylan Thomas. So I listened to his radio talks, watched him reading 'A Story' (now known as 'The Outing') live on BBC TV on 10 August 1953 and read Mimi Josephson's interview 'Poet In The Boat House' published that same week in *John O'London's Weekly*. Thus began my lifelong interest in the poems of his maturity, mostly those in *Deaths and Entrances* or written towards the end of his life, which reach that level of uniqueness that makes works of art complete in themselves, be they a Giacometti, a Modigliani or 'Poem in October'.

The controversy surrounding the poet began with John Malcolm Brinnin and *Dylan Thomas in America*, published eighteen months after Thomas died. I remember those months well. We lived fourteen miles from Stratford. With an hour to kill before catching the bus, I dropped into the town library nearly every afternoon. The magazines gave me a broad awareness of a world way beyond my teenage boundaries.

What I particularly recall was the growing respect for Dylan Thomas: *Under Milk Wood* published in book and recorded form, new editions of *Deaths and Entrances*, *The Collected Poems*, *The Doctor and the Devils* and *Portrait of the Artist as a Young Dog*, and the previously unknown *Adventures in the Skin Trade*.

Between school and bus, I discovered perspectives that are no more and was totally unprepared for Brinnin's bombshell, described by Kenneth Tynan as 'that terrible footnote to literary history'. My library hours told me his story of Dylan's life didn't tally. This impression was strengthened by Caitlin's prefatory statement:

> There is no such thing as the one true Dylan Thomas, nor anybody else ... It is impossible to hit back at a man who does not know that he is hitting you, and who is far too cautious of the laws of libel to say plainly what can only be read between the lines ...

And she wrote of her desire to write 'a better truth than Brinnin's'. The thought never occurred to me that I might help her write that better truth ...

I would also join Eric Barton, the bookseller, and friends for quaintly surreal evenings at the Sesame Club in the room where Dame Edith Sitwell once held court, with its slightly shabby décor, listening to Dylan's contemporaries. This further suggested to me that there was something wrong with the Dylan story.

One day the Dean of Westminster told Aeronwy, Dylan's daughter, he would love to see a plaque installed in Poet's Corner but this had to meet the Abbey's design standards, with a £3,000 'dowry' for its future upkeep. Aeronwy told us this after a meeting of the Dylan Thomas Society. I suggested raising the money through a concert. My colleagues at the Greater London Council let me have the Queen Elizabeth Hall on a Sunday night, rent-free, but that raised another problem. None of us knew how to plan a concert. It was agreed I should write to Lord Harlech, Chairman of HTV (a Welsh television service), seeking help – and, as if on cue, US President Jimmy Carter expressed surprise that there was no Dylan Thomas plaque in Poet's Corner. Thereafter it was plain sailing. Aeronwy and I sat on committees to plan the concert and ceremony, HTV suggested the Duke of York's Theatre would be cosier, and Jonah Jones was invited to carve the plaque.

When Richard Burton heard the concert would be held on 28 February 1982, he offered to be our compere. Elizabeth Taylor was appearing in the West End and joined him on stage for a gently emotional Welsh evening of poems, memories and readings from *Under Milk Wood*, rounded off with supper at the Garrick.

The following day's service at Westminster Abbey, on St David's Day, was open to anyone and over three thousand people turned up, some from across the world. After the service, there was a reception at the House of Lords. A chance meeting there led to my trying to solve the Thomas Enigma. The room was packed. We found ourselves squeezed into a corner with Ted Hughes, barely able to move our elbows. Hughes had not been invited either, but had travelled up from North Tawton, anxious to share in what became a spontaneous tribute to Dylan. My wife and I had once lived in Devon and knew North Tawton well. We talked about many things, until Hughes asked: 'Have you read the biographies?' I said I had. 'Aren't they dreadful?' he added, 'Dylan can't have been the kind of man they say he was or he'd never have pulled it off – and none of us would be here today.'

Hughes knew I had written books on rock'n'roll, and said: 'You're just the man to write about Dylan. He'd have loved rock'n'roll ... Dylan would have known what all that was about ... Why don't you do it? A book needs to be written by someone who cares – and you obviously care or you wouldn't be here today.'

We continued chatting for over an hour, pinned shoulder to shoulder, fresh drinks and occasional trays of food travelling hand to hand above our heads, until our conversation veered back to Thomas. 'Where would you start?' he asked. 'With Caitlin', I replied. Aeronwy introduced me to her mother when Caitlin was visiting London. We lunched together but then Caitlin decided to go to Ireland and work instead on a book with Theodora Fitzgibbon, the wife of Dylan's friend and first biographer. This all came to an embarrassing end when Theodora announced over her dinner table that she slept with Dylan during the war. Caitlin cut short her trip, never spoke to Theodora again, flew back home and phoned to see if I was still interested.

* * *

John Ackerman once told me he thought he knew why the Thomases married. 'Dylan needed someone stronger than he was', said Ackerman. I believe that was right; but it was a rare strength that made Caitlin one of the great literary wives. Believing totally in his 'gift', she was willing to endure any hardship, provided his work came first, bringing routine and an artist's discipline to his life.

In journalism and work for radio, words came easily, but Caitlin understood why poems were different, structured, their purpose defined, each line honed down to essentials, not a word wasted or a comma out of place; for this is the frame of mind with which artists approach a blank canvas ... and if you study the poems Dylan wrote after they met, a pattern emerges. Each became complete in itself, without repetition – the principle taught by Henry Tonks, Professor of Fine Art at the Slade.

Caitlin was as strict with me and I found that an enlivening experience. After hearing her divide her rivals into 'bed and breakfast women' and 'the blue stockings' I knew exactly where 'bible-black' and 'fishingboatbobbing sea' came from, but her hardness ran deeper, for Thomas was inclined to whimsy; she was not. 'Keep it simple, keep it simple', she would say as he wandered in and out of her kitchen, sounding out words. It is no coincidence, in my view, that the truly great Dylan Thomas poems were mostly written after they met.

Young Thomas, provincial reporter, small-town actor and aspiring socialist, was somewhat overblown. Few major poems came out of his Swansea years. I realized Caitlin spotted weaknesses like that when I heard her describe Augustus John ('always one more brush stroke than he needed') and Matthew Smith ('too much red on his palette'). When I mentioned how long Thomas took to write a particular poem, she sharply rebuked me. 'Words don't come easily; it sometimes takes a long time to find them', she said.

Caitlin understood.

* * *

What kind of a man was he? That became more clear after I chanced upon *Conversations with Capote* by Lawrence Grobel and read how Capote doubted Brinnin's accuracy. Analysing *Dylan Thomas in America*, I found Brinnin often exaggerated, describing events as if he had been there when he had not. Combine that with the negligence uncovered by Nashold and Daniel Jones's delusions – and you reveal a legend built on falsehood.

What kind of a man was Dylan Thomas? He certainly wasn't the man the public think they know in this, his Centenary year. Thomas was far more reliable, rarely missing a performance or deadline, keeping to daily routines. In Laugharne he is remembered as shy and humble; attending christenings or funerals, dances at the Memorial Hall, drinking Buckley's beer in half-pints, following cricket, rugby and boxing, betting on horses, playing cards, bar billiards or dominoes, enjoying the town's life, as we all do, each in our way, for we all have our moment.

Dylan Thomas was not an alcoholic, but his knees wobbled, he sometimes blacked out and he tended to fall asleep when his body could not cope with more than a couple of pints of beer to end his day, probably because he was suffering from the diabetes which was only discovered as he lay in a coma – and which remained unknown until Nashold gathered the evidence for our book *The Death of Dylan Thomas*.

Meanwhile Caitlin, ever the true Bohemian, drank her bottle dry, while Thomas leased the Pelican for his parents, saw them daily and became a gentle if somewhat distant father, enjoying family highs, especially Christmas, but leaving her to discipline the children when they were naughty.

And as for all the women? Well, there weren't any illegitimate children, no paternity suits, no petitions from angry husbands and no convincing evidence so far as I can tell that he ever truly loved another woman. He dallied here and there, but Caitlin got it about right, dubbing them 'bed and breakfast women' – for that was what he needed, even from the 'blue stockings' who frightened her.

It was all very rock'n'roll, really.

A Most Lovable Fellow

Hilly Janes

Dylan Thomas had many friends. His charm, wit and natural ability as a mimic and storyteller won him affection and admiration from countless people, and, as his career took off, he became what we would now call a brilliant networker. That was essential. A teenage poet who was determined to earn his living by writing had very few opportunities or outlets in south Wales in the 1930s. That is why Dylan spent almost as much of his life in London as he did in Swansea and Laugharne, hobnobbing with the literati who could publish his poems in literary magazines and commission book reviews. And in the pubs and clubs of Soho he made contacts in the BBC and the film world who were vital in getting him work as a broadcaster and scriptwriter – crafts at which he also excelled.

Many of these professional associates became close friends, but it was in his home town of Swansea that Dylan formed important relationships that lasted a lifetime – and beyond, for those he left behind when he died, aged 39. Among these was a remarkable collection of creative young men that included the poet Vernon Watkins; Charles Fisher, another poet, author and journalist; the composer and conductor Daniel Jones; and the artist, writer and broadcaster Mervyn Levy. Another was my father, Alfred Janes – Fred to family and friends – also an artist, who made three portraits of Dylan, two during the poet's lifetime and one posthumously. While Dylan became more famous than any of them, the achievements of this group reached far beyond the industrial Welsh town where they were brought up, and were due in some part to the support and stimulation they offered each other, not just in their formative years but throughout their lives.

All of these friends, with the exception of Vernon, went to Swansea Grammar School where Dylan's father, D. J. Thomas, was the senior English master. He was a formidable teacher with a first-class honours degree from Aberystwyth University, whose passion Fred witnessed at first hand. 'He relished language as Dylan relished it. His father savoured words and poetry as other people savour food and drink and from his earliest childhood Dylan was totally immersed in a sea of language', Fred recalled. The bookshelves of D. J.'s 'den' at home were lined with English classics which Dylan read voraciously, and which were read to him from an early age. The young poet had little inclination to study anything else and left school at sixteen with only one basic qualification, in English. But in this, Fred knew, he was a true scholar.

Fred was three years older than Dylan and they did not meet until 1931, when they had both left school. The place was 'Warmley', the home of their mutual schoolfriend, Daniel Jones, who lived not far from Dylan's house in Cwmdonkin Drive. Dylan's first encounter with Dan was a schoolboy scrap, which he described in 'The Fight', one of his many vivid autobiographical short stories. By this time Fred was a scholarship student in portraiture at the Royal Academy Schools in London. Dan, a precociously gifted musician and composer, was studying English at Swansea University and Dylan was filling notebooks with poems, having left his first job as a trainee reporter on the *South Wales Daily Post*. Dan and Dylan were by then already close friends and deeply interested in each other's work. Fred could only meet them when he was back in Swansea on holiday, but he found the time they spent together at Warmley – as welcoming a household as its name suggests – just as stimulating as his exciting student life in London. Fred explained:

Dan, Dylan and I thought of ourselves loosely as a group and spent many happy hours together whenever the opportunity arose, discussing our work and thrashing out our ideas. It was already clear that Dylan, as it were, actually experienced the world in terms of words. Just as a computer accounts for the world in terms of numbers, Dylan Thomas translated his experience directly into structures of words – into poetry.

We all played together on the piano, on any available instruments, on the plates, pots, pans and washboards. I think we felt, Dylan especially, that a certain element of pandemonium was an essential ingredient of civilised behaviour. There is no doubt that the counterpoint as he practised it with fire irons and coal scuttle takes on a forcefulness not easily forgotten. It was fun but it was also one of the most important influences on one's work, which far from being of a temporary nature, continued to develop.

Three arts – poetry, music, painting – but the overlap was exciting. Enthusiasm was infectious and I think we all learned from each other. The strength of that overlap was the strength of that bond. One kind of artist understands another because he understands some of the possibilities and the potential, the problems and limitations of the medium in which he works, and he understands these because they parallel the characteristics of his own medium. We talked and argued endlessly about these notions. It seemed to me that Dylan divined that the meaning of a word changed – be it infinitely subtly – on every occasion of its use and that everyone who used it changed it according to the evolution of his own perception.

Their get-togethers would also take place at Dylan's house in Cwmdonkin Drive, where his mother, Florence, a deeply maternal and sociable woman who adored her son, would sustain the young men with piles of sandwiches. If they were all a bit the worse for wear after a visit to the pub, they might stop off at Fred's sister's house just down the steep hill from Cwmdonkin Drive to sober up. Dylan, with his slight, girlish frame, never held his drink as well as the others.

The young poet was already visiting London in search of work. His sister Nancy, who had married and lived on the outskirts, could put him up, and he had started to correspond with another aspiring poet, Pamela Hansford Johnson, who became his first girlfriend. They were both winners of a poetry competition in the *Sunday Referee*, the prize for which was the publication of a book of poems. Dylan's first volume appeared at the end of 1934, soon after he celebrated his 20th birthday. The moment had come to make a more permanent move to the big city – and it was reassuring for his parents to know that their somewhat wayward son would be staying with his older friend Fred, whom they knew well.

Mr Janes drove the pair up to their digs at Redcliffe Street in Earl's Court, Dylan wearing a huge check overcoat, pork pie hat and bearing an enormous suitcase. Fred, despite being a prizewinning student, had left the RA Schools by then, bored by its stuffy traditional approach but galvanized by the possibilities of a new kind of art on show in the commercial galleries just behind the Royal Academy, where modern painters like Picasso, Braque, Miró and Kandinsky were on show. But he stayed on in London, taking the rooms in Redcliffe Street unfurnished but managing somehow with the £1 weekly allowance given him by his parents (Dylan got the same) to acquire a few odds and ends of furniture, although the only chair became a makeshift easel.

Mervyn Levy, who, like Fred, had studied at Swansea School of Art but was now at the Royal College of Art in Kensington, lived upstairs and the three young men settled into what Fred described as a 'happy shambles', the floor strewn with beer and milk bottles and fag ends. If a parental visit was imminent, there would be a massive tidy-up, but tea could only be taken one at a time from the sole cup. Once, to Fred's horror, one of the camp beds they slept and sat on collapsed under Dylan's father.

Fred was the chef but Dylan seldom seemed to eat. 'Perhaps it was because my favourite dish was a huge pancake of boiled onion and potatoes fried afterwards to a golden brown – the colour, I think, meant less to him than it did to me!' The company made up for the discomfort. Both Dylan and Mervyn could be enormously funny. 'We had some wonderful times together', Fred said, 'that have merged into a sort of kaleidoscopic image of laughter, arguments, experiments, quarrels and more laughter.' They all took each other's work completely for granted.

Despite the squalor, Fred saw how hard Dylan worked, often sitting up in bed in his pork pie hat and overcoat to keep warm. 'He would revise tirelessly and the room could be inundated with papers, gradually to be organized and collated and resulting frequently in a poem appearing complete and written out in his inimitable hand on a large sheet of card to be "seen" as well as read'. As an artist Fred was keenly aware of Dylan's highly developed visual sense – obvious in poems like 'Vision and Prayer' in which each verse forms an identical lozenge shape. He also speculated that Dylan's playful mixing of sound patterns with verbal clues was akin to Picasso's device of placing an eye here and a nose there and forcing the looker to complete the face.

Barely house-trained artists and poets were not the most popular tenants with landladies, however, and no one stayed in their digs for long. 'Swansea's bohemians in exile', as Dylan described the ménage, soon moved to another flat in nearby Coleherne Road. It was here that Fred painted his first portrait of Dylan, now in the National Gallery of Wales in Cardiff. Despite his angelic looks, he was by no means a perfect sitter – he never stayed anywhere for long and was 'in and out like a cat in a tripe shop'. Fred's working methods were equally meticulous as Dylan's but he stood day after day at his easel, painting still lifes of fruit, fish and flowers, in which the background incorporated details from the subject matter in repeated geometric motifs. In a technique that he invented himself, he overlaid the finished work with a grid-like pattern that he incised with a penknife, gently softening the lines with a rag soaked in turps to produce a jewel-like quality. This painstaking approach became a running joke with Dylan, who often asked after Fred in the many letters he wrote later to Vernon and others. 'How is that blizzardly painter, that lightning artist, that prodigal canvas stacker? Has he reached the next finbone of the fish he was dashing off before the war? Please give him my love.'

Sometimes Dylan would turn up with a new friend – a down-and-out from the embankment, a broken-down American boxer, a communist in hiding from the fascist Sir Oswald Mosley's 'blackshirts', who attended mass rallies and made trouble on the streets for anyone whose beliefs did not conform to their own. Dylan was a compassionate and generous man who abhorred authoritarianism, and his waifs and strays would stay for a while, maybe hours, days or weeks, then disappear for good. His empathy for and ability to get on with people from extremely diverse backgrounds often won him a reputation as a poseur, especially in more snobbish intellectual circles, but to Fred it was the sign of a complex character with a gift for putting all sorts of different people at ease. 'The intelligentsia, the bartenders and even the herons could easily take him as one of themselves!', Fred remarked.

In 1935 the flatmates went their separate ways, but Fred saw as much, if not more, of Dylan back in Swansea. Dan's family had moved to Harrow and, after studying at the Royal Academy of Music, he travelled around Europe on a prestigious Mendelssohn scholarship. Fred was more likely to see Dylan at 5 Cwmdonkin Drive, where the Grammar School friends still in Swansea would gather for more banter, argument and to listen to Dylan read his works-in-progress. 'We were spellbound with the richness of his voice and his quite uncanny power of bringing clarity to verse that seemed so obscure in print', Fred recalled. Dylan loved acting and many of his Swansea friendships were made or cemented at the town's thriving Little Theatre, where he appeared in several productions. These readings and performances nurtured his talent as a BBC broadcaster and highly sought-after reader of poetry, particularly in the USA.

Dylan soon introduced Fred to another Swansea poet, Vernon Watkins, a slightly older man who worked as a cashier in Lloyd's bank by day and wrote poetry by night. Vernon's parents, like Dylan's mother, both worshipped at Paraclete chapel in the Mumbles, the pretty seaside village at the western end of the great expanse of Swansea Bay. Florence's brother-in-law was the minister there and he suggested to Vernon that he look up his nephew. Not that Dylan got on with the Reverend Rees, whose brand of Welsh Nonconformist Bible-thumping religion he detested. 'I hate you from your dandruff to your corns', Dylan once scribbled in a notebook. Fortunately the two young poets felt differently about each other and, in a town where poetry mattered very little to most people, became close friends and collaborators.

Vernon's parents lived in a large family house along the cliffs at Pennard on the Gower peninsula, half an hour's bus journey from the town. Fred, Vernon and Dylan spent many Sundays together at Vernon's home, where Dylan was always impeccably behaved and much loved by the Watkins family. The three enjoyed walking along this part of the coast, with its wonderful views across Three Cliffs Bay to Oxwich Point. Sometimes they would venture further afield to spectacular Rhossili, the village at Gower's western tip, where the tide cuts off towering Worm's Head from the mainland, trapping hikers with only sheep for company – an adventure that Dylan recorded in another autobiographical short story, 'Who do you wish was with us?'. On one memorable Sunday at Pennard they read a laudatory review in the *Sunday Times* of Dylan's next volume, *Twenty-Five Poems,* by the influential literary patron Edith Sitwell. He was just twenty-two years old. 'It was quite a day', Fred noted.

Both Fred and Dylan spent time in Cornwall around that time, Fred to rub shoulders with the artistic colony around St Ives and Dylan to recuperate from the excesses of London life. The following year he married his girlfriend Caitlin Macnamara there, but she and Dylan's Swansea friends would never become close. Their main meeting point by now, if and when they were all in Swansea, was the Kardomah cafe, where they exchanged news and views over cheap, chicory-based Camp coffee – they couldn't afford anything else. Dylan recalled these gatherings in his play for voices, *Return Journey,* surely one of his most accomplished works. Written for the BBC in 1947, its narrator revisits the town of his youth and asks after 'Young Thomas'.

Passer By:
Oh, him! He owes me half a crown. I haven't seen him since the old Kardomah days. He wasn't a reporter then. He'd just left the grammar school. Him and Charlie Fisher – Charlie's got whiskers now – and Tom Warner and Fred Janes, drinking coffee dashes and arguing the toss.

Narrator:
What about?

Passer By:
Music and poetry and painting and politics. Einstein and Epstein, Stravinsky and Garbo, death and religion, Picasso and girls ...

Narrator:
And then?

Passer By:
Communism, symbolism, Bradman, Braque, the Watch Committee, free love, free beer, murder, Michelangelo, ping-pong, ambition, Sibelius and girls …

Narrator:
Is that all?

Passer By:
How Dan Jones was going to compose the most prodigious symphony, Fred Janes paint the most miraculously meticulous picture, Charlie Fisher catch the poshest trout, Vernon Watkins and Young Thomas write the most boiling poems, how they would ring the bells of London and paint it like a tart.

Passer By:
And after that?

Narrator:
Oh the hissing of the butt ends in the drains of the coffee-dashes and the tinkle and gibble gabble of the morning young lounge lizards as they talked about Augustus John, Emil Jannings, Carnera, Dracula, Amy Johnson, trial marriage, pocket money, the Welsh sea, the London stars, King Kong, anarchy, darts, T. S. Eliot, and girls …

Thanks partly to *Return Journey*, the group were christened the 'Kardomah Gang', but, as Fred pointed out, it was a somewhat romanticized label. Dan Jones and Vernon were never in the cafe at the same time and did not meet until the 1940s. And the fiercely independent Fred didn't want to be part of anyone's gang. The Kardomah was still a bombsite when Dylan wrote the play, as the centre of Swansea had been destroyed by a ferocious three-night blitz during the war which reduced many of Dylan's old haunts to rubble. The lounge lizards had been scattered across the world as they volunteered or were called up, but Dan and Vernon met each other at Bletchley Park, where many of the country's brightest minds were put to the task of breaking enemy codes (Dan from Japanese). Dylan spent much of the time in London writing scripts for the government's morale-raising propaganda and recruitment films. The opportunities for meeting were few and far between, especially after Fred was posted to the Middle East for almost three years without returning to the UK.

They regrouped in 1949, when Dylan, Fred, Dan, Vernon and an aspiring writer called John Prichard, who had won a coveted US *Atlantic Magazine* prize for one of his stories, gathered in the BBC's Swansea studio for a broadcast called *Swansea and the Arts*. They were all trying to settle back into normal life in Wales and by now they were achieving the recognition that had been delayed by the war – although in Dylan's case it had offered some great opportunities.

His readings on the radio of funny, affectionate pieces like 'Reminiscences of Childhood', which evoked the Swansea of his boyhood so colourfully, had been a tonic for listeners ground down by austerity. A third volume of poetry, *Deaths and Entrances*, which included deeply moving work inspired by the horrific scenes he had witnessed in London during bombing raids, was published just after the war and became one of his best-selling collections.

It took the others a little longer to get back into their creative strides. Fred had only been able to produce a few drawings during the conflict, but by 1949 had painted enough new pictures to hold a one-man show at the town's elegant civic Glynn Vivian gallery. They included portraits of Dan and Vernon that capture their true likeness, but also something of their very different personalities – Dan forthright and quizzical, Vernon a gentler, more ethereal soul. As well as chamber and orchestral works, Dan had already completed the first of thirteen symphonies he was to compose during his lifetime, which was premiered by the Royal Philharmonic in Swansea that year. Vernon had seen several volumes of his poetry published. The broadcast was considered important enough for the group to be pictured on the front cover of *Radio Times*.

Dylan was the narrator, introducing them all in turn. He recalled jokingly the rooms he shared in London with Fred and 'his apples carved in oil, his sulphurously glowing lemons, his infernal kippers'. The group explained in turn why Swansea was attractive as a town to artists, writers and musicians, citing the extraordinary contrast between its industrial base and docks to the east and the staggering beauty of the Gower peninsular to the west – Dylan's 'ugly lovely town' – as well as the friendliness of the people and their lack of pretension.

This was the year, too, that Dylan moved to the Boat House in Laugharne with Caitlin. They had settled happily but all too briefly in the 'strangest town in Wales' before the outbreak of war put everyone's dreams on hold. Like all his friends, Dylan was now a family man with a wife and children to support. There was no time to while away arguing the toss over coffee dashes, although Dylan frequently stopped off in Swansea on his work trips to London or the BBC studios in Cardiff. From 1950 onwards he embarked on a series of poetry reading tours that criss-crossed the US with schedules so punishing – not to mention irresistible temptations to stray off the straight and narrow – that he was away for months on end, with little time for letter-writing.

But if the opportunity arose, Fred, who unlike most of the others could drive and owned a car, visited Laugharne with his wife Mary and their son, who played with Dylan's children on the shoreline below the Boat House,

> ... my seashaken house
> On a breakneck of rocks
> Tangled with chirrup and fruit ...

'Chirrup and fruit' became the title of a later painting by Fred that celebrated in a welter of motifs and glowing colours the natural world at which both he and Dylan marvelled. It is now owned by the in the Glynn Vivian in Swansea.

Fred's portraits of Dylan, Dan and Vernon were the focus of a 1953 BBC TV programme *Home Town – Swansea*, broadcast from Cardiff. Sadly this and the one other TV recording of Dylan, in which he read a short story, have been lost, but thanks to Vernon an account of the recording and Dylan's words were preserved in an article he wrote for the *Texas Quarterly*, a US arts journal. The TV set was a mock artist's studio, and each member of the group talked about their portrait – 'that dewy goblin portrait frog-goggling at me out of the past', as Dylan described his. The linkman was Wynford Vaughan-Thomas, another former Swansea Grammar School boy and Little Theatre member, now a senior BBC journalist who had distinguished himself as a war reporter.

Dylan laid on some classic Thomas nostalgia for the viewers, talking to Fred about 'the Golden Days in London, when we were exiled Bohemian boily boys. There were three of us then, you and me and Mervyn Levy, three very young monsters green and brimming from Swansea, stiff with lyrics and ambitions and still lifes, all living together in one big bare barmy beautiful room kept by a Mrs Parsnip, as far as I can remember.'

It was the last time they were together. Shortly afterwards Dylan set off on his final tour of the US, from which he returned in a coffin after a bout of undiagnosed and mistreated bronchial pneumonia, his health further compromised by smoking, heavy drinking, poor diet and record levels of smog in New York that autumn. Fred had been in the process of painting a second portrait of Dylan in 1953, but he had to finish it from memory and photographs. It was bought a few years later by the University of Texas at Austin, which owns a large archive of material relating to the poet.

The next time Dylan's old schoolfriends met was at his funeral in Laugharne in November. They were all devastated by his death and Dylan's ghost both haunted and inspired them for years to come. Strangers would arrive at their homes or workplaces, sometimes unannounced, wanting to talk about their famous friend. There were arguments over Dan's editing of the final versions of Dylan's work, especially *Under Milk Wood*, which was performed and published posthumously in the UK. Accounts of Dylan's behaviour, such as John Malcolm Brinnin's *Dylan Thomas in America,* that emphasized his weaknesses, were greeted with dismay by those who knew him well, and both Dan and Vernon's wife, Gwen, published their own memoirs to try and set the record straight. Fred kept his counsel but the family ties were still strong. He welcomed Dylan's mother, Florence, who had lost her husband, daughter and son in less than a year, as a guest at the Janes family home in Gower. Later, when we moved to London, Dylan's daughter Aeron often visited our house in Dulwich Village.

But Dylan inspired them creatively in equal measure. Dan composed his fourth symphony in memory of him. Vernon wrote several moving elegies and published an edited collection of the many letters Dylan had written to him. Fred made a third portrait of his friend that also hangs in the Glynn Vivian in Swansea. He usually declined requests for interviews or to write articles about him, but five years after his death he had this to say about Dylan Thomas:

He was a most lovable fellow and I shall always count the hours spent in his company as the most precious gift from the gods, when one's sense of being alive was increased tenfold. I am profoundly grateful for having been one of his countless friends

Dylan Thomas by Alfred Janes, 1964, pen and ink, Glynn Vivian Art Gallery, © Estate of the artist

Self-portrait in uniform by Alfred Janes, pencil, 1942, private collection, © Estate of the artist

Encounters with Dylan Thomas

Michael Sheen

My first encounter with Dylan Thomas I suppose must have been, as it was for so many Welsh children, listening to the delirious dream of *Under Milk Wood*. The mountain-forged, liquid growl of Richard Burton's First Voice synonymous with the mythic and myth-making 'play for voices'. Eventually I came to play the part myself in a school production. (I remember lots of teenagers in black shirts, strewn busily around multi-levelled rostra, like a slightly disorganized fascist youth rally.) Those lines stuffed to the brim with sounds and ideas, so full and fecund and sensual, it felt like there must be juices dribbling down my chin from the speaking of it, from the colour of its saying. A few years later I tried to write a piece in the style of it for a devised youth theatre production based on his life and work. Its mixture of sly parochialism and exotic sensuality underpinned by a roiling pagan intelligence is an enticing and utterly elusive seam to mine. You can parody it, but to emulate its dark magic you would have to drink from the same enchanted waters that Dylan himself did, strike the same infernal pact with whatever Welsh devil he met at the crossed paths of Cwmdonkin Park.

A swirling life he had. The stories and the legends are legion of course, but the truth has many sides and that side of the truth is too easily romanticized and simplified. This side, the side revealed in the work, speaks to me of a man living at once in both the warmth and disturbance of memory and the past, able to conjure its familiarity and its safety as well as its strangeness and mystery, and at the same time living in the cold outposts of the cosmos, isolated out at the edges of human existence, looking into the void and shapeless dark and wrestling with its forms and meanings.

His hunger for the world of corporeality can be frightening at times and surely emanates from a mind haunted by the uncouplings that a fractured world can induce. In public he celebrated Dionysus, but in the still night, as he laboured at his sullen art, it was Apollo who guided his hand. He may have worshipped at a wild and unfettered altar, wreathed in vines and wetted moss, but discipline and control were in his compass too. The magic circle he stood within was conjured not out of an electric spontaneity alone but cold, hard crafting, also.

It is at times when the authority of the life force is visited upon us that we feel the need for a deeper expression than our everyday language can provide.

We yearn to speak truths both alien and familiar, and in a tongue not always bound by reason. We often look to religious tracts or the dark pathways of myth. Dylan Thomas was fluent in this 'other' tongue. When I returned to my training after a breakdown of sorts, it was 'Poem in October' that I brought with me as ballast. When I was asked to perform for Russian families grieving their husbands and fathers and sons, dead in the mines, it was 'And Death Shall Have No Dominion' that provided the only adequate words I could muster. Likewise, when my father asked me to speak at his own father's funeral, it was those same words, defiant and exhilarating and accepting all at once, both apocalyptic with 'break in the sun till the sun breaks down' and heartbreakingly simple and observational with 'no more may gulls cry at their ears', that helped make the impossibility of death tolerable. I read recently that a police commander at the head of a task force charged with the capture of a man responsible for the deaths of countless women came across the Thomas poem, 'Refusal To Mourn The Death By Fire Of A Child In London', and found in its sharp humanity and revelatory vision a meaning and resonance that inspired him – 'After the first Death, there is no other'.

Dylan Thomas navigated dangerous waters and flowed with deep primal currents. It may have taken a heavy toll on him in his life but it gives his work the vitality and the immediacy that can hit you like a slap on a cold day.

There is no other writer whose work exhilarates me like his can. No one whose vision of this life can fill me with the same sense of awe and appetite. No one whose words can make my mouth water as much, or whose images demand such mouthing.

For the rest of my life, when those times are upon me that demand a song in that other tongue, words that can hold their value on the darkest of river crossings, a telling to say what cannot be framed but must be lived, then it's at those times that I will be most grateful for the work that he has given us and the all-too-short life that it burst from.

'The liquid choirs of his tribes': The Influence of Dylan Thomas

John Goodby

I

Dylan Thomas presents a problem for chroniclers and critics of twentieth-century English language poetry, particularly its Welsh and English strands, which has yet to be fully acknowledged. So great is this problem that for about forty years he has been more or less ignored by the canon-makers and historians, treated as a colourful minor poet at best, and at worst as a kind of poetic charlatan. Thus, from *The Auden Generation* (1976), *British Writers of the Thirties* (1988) and *English Poetry Since 1940* (1993) to the present, Thomas has been excluded, marginalized or patronized by English critics. In Wales his cause was championed, soberly and intelligently, by John Ackerman, Walford Davies, Ralph Maud and James A. Davies, between the 1960s and the 1990s. But in Tony Conran's *Frontiers in Anglo-Welsh Poetry* (1997) and M. Wyn Thomas's *Corresponding Cultures* (1999), and in more recent work by Welsh critics, there is a marked unwillingness to tackle Thomas's poetry except in a very limited way. This suggests that the problem he poses stems not so much from his notorious 'obscurity' – as William Empson said, once you know that the early poetry is based on a few basic ideas, it becomes fairly easy to decipher, and there are many glosses of Thomas's difficulties anyway – but rather from a perennial problem in deciding what kind of writer he is, and how to place him.

Up to the mid-1970s Thomas was a favourite not only with the general reading public, as remains the case, but with critics too. This was because he could be labelled a 'Romantic' poet, and critical discourse about poetry was capable of including such a figure, albeit with some protests from the likes of David Holbrook, the Movement writers and followers of F. R. Leavis. But the little-England backlash which began around 1976 broke this consensus – just as other aspects of the post-war consensus were then being broken – and the new order had no place for such an overtly 'poetic' poet as Thomas. He was ruthlessly excluded in the new Oxbridge-generated, Audenary narrative of twentieth-century English poetry, and sidelined by cymrocentric accounts of Anglo-Welsh poetry. Thomas's poetry suffered from the fact that it crossed borders, wove together English and Welsh elements (and Irish, American and

European ones, for that matter). In the new era of identity politics he fell between several stools; considered too tough by the mainstream (beyond an unrepresentative handful of anthology pieces), too mainstream by the avant-garde, too Welsh by the English, too English by the Welsh, and too populist (not to say popular) by cultural elitists, he was left to drown in his legend, abandoned as a serious writer.

Yet even when his critical reputation had been at its height, in the 1950s and 1960s, the 'Romantic' tag attached to him had never been right for Thomas. Nor had his supporters ever really grasped this fact. Thus, R. B. Kershner in 1976 had claimed, wrongly but revealingly, that his poetry was 'itself a kind of endpoint in its own direction, like *Finnegans Wake*, rather than a stimulus to further exploration'.[1] Not only has *Finnegans Wake* actually had many outcomes, but the bracketing of Thomas with Joyce alerts us to his modernist provenance.[2] In this regard, the observation about being an 'endpoint' is crucial. For, as I hope to show, Thomas actually has been a powerful leaven in British poetry since his death. As a contribution to reinstating him as a central figure in twentieth-century *British* poetry, I shall show in what follows that Thomas had a profound influence on successor poets in the 1950s and 1960s. What is unique about this, I shall argue, is that it affected both sides of the bifurcated British poetry scene, the so-called 'mainstream' and 'alternative' (or 'experimental', 'neomodernist' or 'linguistically innovative') streams. This breadth of influence, paradoxically, indicates the reason for his later critical erasure; because he straddles both sides of the divide he unsettles the attempts of each to define itself against the other, just as he problematizes the attempt to define essential 'English' or 'Welsh' poetries. In this sense he is trapped between the post-1970s divisions of British poetry and culture, haunting the zone between them. Occasional attempts to come to terms with him by mainstream poets and critics reflect a nagging sense that he is important, but inevitably fail to incorporate him because to do so would require recognition of the suppressed modernist strand of British post-*Waste Land* poetry which Thomas, to some extent, embodies.[3]

II

Over the last two decades, it has become increasingly apparent that Thomas's poetry was not some one-off aberration, however brilliant, which simply

[1] R. B. Kershner Jnr., *Dylan Thomas: The Poet and His Critics* (Chicago: American Library Association, 1976), 128.

[2] In the same spirit, David Daiches noted '[he] had no lessons to teach others as Pound and Eliot had'. See Kershner, *Poet and His Critics*, 128.

[3] Of 'British' poetries, I only have space for a discussion of English and Anglo-Welsh and the Scottish W. S. Graham. Work in this area has only begun; for one recent case study, see my '"Bulbous Taliesin": MacNeice and Dylan Thomas', in Fran Brearton and Edna Longley (eds), *Incorrigibly Plural: Louis MacNeice and his Legacy* (Manchester: Carcanet, 2012), 204–23.

appeared according to its own rules. A greater understanding of the variousness of Modernism now offers explanations for the origin of the 'process style' of *18 Poems* (1934), which so startled and impressed his contemporaries. It is increasingly apparent that this style was the result of an inspired fusion of the principles of Eliotic Modernism, the wordplay of Joyce and the sexual vitalism of Lawrence, within the traditional forms revived by Auden and his followers, C. Day Lewis, Stephen Spender and Louis MacNeice. Between summer 1933 and spring 1934 Thomas subjected Modernism's collage-based image sequences to the constraints of standard syntax and inherited stanza forms, metre and end-rhyme. The result was an unprecedented and unsettlingly mongrel style, with a foot in both modernist and traditionalist camps, of immense rhetorical power.

This blend of seemingly incompatible elements is matched in the manner and matter of *18 Poems* and *Twenty-Five Poems* (1936). A line such as 'O see the poles are kissing as they cross', in 'I see the boys of summer', is blatantly *un*clear about whether the 'poles' are lovingly or masochistically kissing, and whether 'cross' is crucifixion, resolution, sexual breeding or anger. Thomas, that is, is not interested in taming modernist energies as part of a liberal humanist project of recuperation and symbolic closure, as most British poetry is. On the contrary, he tries to ramp up antinomies as part of an existential-expressionist, Gothic-grotesque modernism, behind which lies also the sonorousness of Shakespearean blank verse, the conceitedness of the Metaphysical poets and, above all, the visionary and antinomian poetics of William Blake. His subjects are the basics ones of the lyric tradition: love, death, birth, sex, faith, with particular emphasis on the theme of (im) mortality. And despite their concern with visionary and dreamlike states, his poems embody the lacerating paradoxes of the historical crisis of the early 1930s at mythic, biological and cosmic levels, by contrast with the purely sociological surfaces of more overtly 'political' poetry of the time. His hyphenated, ambivalent Anglo-Welsh condition was what made Thomas a poet who could achieve unignorable successes in seemingly incompatible modes. Reading 'Fern Hill' and 'Altarwise by owl-light', we might feel entitled to ask just how such different poems could have been written by the same poet.

III

Perhaps the most striking example of the dual aspect of Thomas's influence was in the USA (where it has proved, however, shortest-lived). As Eric Homberger once noted, 'no British poet since Dylan Thomas has made a significant impact on American taste'.[4] Thomas gave a revivifying jolt to the schizophrenically sedate American poetry culture of the early 1950s, when the liberal intelligentsia were still cowed by McCarthyism. Thomas's eagerness for America, and

---

[4] Eric Homberger, *The Art of the Real: Poetry in England and America Since 1939* (London and Totowa, NJ: Dent and Rowman and Littlefield, 1977), 180.

it for him, stemmed from his non-English in-betweenness, and it helped that he was fascinated by American poetry, and that his own work was indebted to Walt Whitman and could sound like Hart Crane. An American edition of his work had appeared as early as 1940, and American critics such as Marshall W. Stearns and David Aivaz pioneered Thomas criticism. For his part, Thomas acted as a transatlantic conduit, introducing 'budding [English] poets' at Oxford in the mid-1940s to the then little-known work of Richard Wilbur, Allen Tate, Robert Penn Warren, John Crowe Ransom and Wallace Stevens.[5] Touring in America in the early 1950s, he met and befriended numerous other poets (it is particularly notable that several young African-American poets – Bob Kaufman, Clyde Hamlet, Steve Korrett and Al Young – felt that Thomas, through his outsiderness, spoke to them).[6] At the minor cost of being typecast as a Celtic *primitif*, he had come close to being an honorary American poet by the time of his death.

The chief point about Thomas's influence was that it extended to practitioners of both 'cooked' and 'raw' poetry. His muscular lyricism informs Robert Lowell's 'The Quaker Graveyard in Nantucket' (1945) and John Berryman's *Homage to Mistress Bradstreet* (1953), while the vegetable vein of 'The force that through the green fuse drives the flower' helped Theodore Roethke break with Auden and Yeats to achieve the Freudian and plant-life imaginings of his major achievement, the 'greenhouse poems'. Less obviously, the surrealism of the early 1950s New York School poets treads a path Thomas took nearly twenty years before.[7] While Frank O'Hara reportedly excused himself from hearing Thomas read in order to avoid 'all that Welsh spit', he was an admirer nevertheless; as John Ashbery has noted, 'the more abandoned side of Dylan Thomas' was one of the very select number of bases for O'Hara's freedom of expression.[8] And in less urbane mode, Kenneth Rexroth's angry elegy

---

[5] John Wain, *Sprightly Running: Part of an Autobiography* (London: Macmillan, 1962), cited in James Keery, 'Menacing Works in My Isolation: Early Pieces', in *The Thing About Roy Fisher*, John Kerrigan and Peter Robinson (eds) (Liverpool: Liverpool University Press, 2000), 79.

[6] Among those Thomas met in the USA were Richard Wilbur, Robert Lowell, Elizabeth Bishop, Delmore Schwartz, Theodor Roethke and W. S. Merwin; away from the academic circuit he met authors as various as Kenneth Rexroth, Robinson Jeffers, William Faulkner, Kenneth Patchen, Ray Bradbury and Henry Miller, as well as non-literary artists such as Max Ernst, John Cage, Charlie Chaplin and Andy Warhol.

[7] John Berryman, *Collected Poems 1937-1971* (London: Faber, 1991), 138, 146, 147. See Philip Coleman, '"An unclassified strange flower": Towards an Analysis of John Berryman's Contact with Dylan Thomas', in Glyn Pursglove, John Goodby and Chris Wigginton (eds), *The Swansea Review*, 22–33. Louis Simpson, *A Revolution in Taste* (New York: Macmillan, 1978), 38.

[8] O'Hara's dismissal is reported in James Schuyler's 'The Morning of the Poem'. See James Schuyler, *Collected Poems* (New York: Farrar, Strauss and Giroux, 1998), 286. For Ashbery, see *The Collected Poems of Frank O'Hara*, ed. Donald Allen (Berkeley: University of California Press, 1995), viii.

for Thomas, 'Thou Shalt Not Kill' (1954), became the chief model for Allen Ginsberg's 'Howl'. In the late 1950s, his private travails, as described by John Malcolm Brinnin in *Dylan Thomas in America*, served as a model for the Confessionals' self-wounding honesty, just as Thomas's exemplary bohemian commitment was taken to endorse Beat self-exposure.[9]

This aspect of Thomas's impact allows other, more tentative parallels to be drawn with regard to his amenability to avant-garde practices. His 'hewn' forms seem far removed from the 'composition by field' of Charles Olson's 'Projective Verse' (1950), but more than a shared *zeitgeist* links Thomas with Olson's claim that 'not the eye but the ear' should be the 'measurer' of poetry, that poets should 'take speech up in all its fullness', and go 'down through the workings of his throat to that place where breath comes from, where breath has its beginnings, where drama has to come from, where, the coincidence is, all act springs'.[10] While Thomas was no proto-Projectivist, he shares with Olson a concern with the materiality of language, and valorizes 'voice' to a near-mystic degree. The stress of both on utterance, physiology, flux and linguistic materiality suggests other parallels, based on a shared rejection of plain styles. Similarly, Robert Duncan, who wrote an admiring review of *A Portrait of the Artist as a Young Dog*, sounds very much like Thomas describing how poems should work 'from', not 'towards', words in his essay 'Equilibrations':

> The poem is not a stream of consciousness, but an area of composition in which I work with whatever comes into it. Only words come into it. Sounds and ideas. The tone leading of vowels, the various percussions of consonants. The play of numbers in stresses and syllables ... Rimes, the reiteration of formations in the design, even puns, lead into complexities of the field ... A word has the weight of an actual stone in his hand. The tone of a vowel has the colour of a wing.[11]

It is as if Duncan recalls 'Once it was the colour of saying' here, and its 'stone[s] [wound] off like a reel'. In his odder manner, John Cage, too, echoes

---

9 It was in 1954, at one of Rexroth's weekly seminars, that Ginsberg first heard the poem, which claimed, as 'Howl' would in 1956, that bourgeois attitudes and capitalist values were responsible for murdering artists. For a tribute to Thomas by one of the leading Beat poets, see 'Palinode for Dylan Thomas' by Lawrence Ferlinghetti in *These Are My Rivers: New & Selected Poems 1955–1993* (San Francisco: New Directions Books, 1994), 42–3.

10 Charles Olson, 'Projective Verse', in Paul Hoover, ed., *Postmodern American Poetry: A Norton Anthology* (New York: Norton, 1994), 613–21. From the mid-1930s on, Thomas had emphasized poetry's roots in the physiology of sound production, insisting on 'poetry that ... comes to life out of the red heart through the brain', attacking casual reading styles; 'this lack of aural value and ... debasing of an art that is primarily dependent on the musical mingling of vowels and consonants'. See Dylan Thomas, *Early Prose Writing*, ed. Walford Davies (London: Dent, 1971), 166.

11 Paul Hoover, *Postmodern American Poetry*, 621–6, 626–8.

the spirit of Thomas: 'Coexistence of dissimilars; multiplicity; plurality of centers; "Split the stick, and there is Jesus"'; 'Unimpededness and interpenetration; no cause and effect' – such aphorisms thematically remind us of the process poetic, but also that Thomas's craftedness was merely, as with Cage, the means to an arbitrary grace, to a verbal entity 'so constructed that it is wide open at any second to receive the accidental miracle which makes a work of craftsmanship a work of art'.[12] While some might demur at the association, these poets all share Thomas's resistance to 'realist & mimetic ideas about poetry', his attack on what the Canadian poet Steve McCaffrey calls the 'referential fallacy', and attempts at 'let[ting] the direct, empirical experience of a grapheme replace what the signifier in a word will always try to discharge: its signifier and referent'.[13] Their common aim, as Aivaz said of Thomas's work in 1945, is 'to free poetry from the strictures of paternity, from religion and from death' and to 'establish the unique individual not merely as the victim, but as the agent of choice; not alone *created by history* but *creative in history*'.[14]

IV

In the more conservative British poetry cultures, Thomas's impact has been less obviously apparent than in the USA, but more deep-rooted and durable. In Wales his influence on the early work of a slew of young poets in the 1940s and 1950s, including Leslie Norris, John Ormond and Dannie Abse, is clear; and the first major anthology of Anglo-Welsh poetry was titled *The Lilting House*. In general, however, Welsh poets soon came to treat Thomas warily. Some, like the Welsh language poet Pennar Davies, were openly hostile ('a gifted entertainer, a phenomenon in the history of twentieth-century publicity, and ... an interesting minor poet'); most gradually recognized the impossibility of creating an original style within the shadow Thomas cast. As Peter Finch put it in 1967, 'To live in Wales, // Is to be mumbled at / by re-incarnations of Dylan Thomas / in numerous diverse disguises'. Yet ironically the balefulness of Thomas's impact on poetry in Wales has turned out to reside not in direct influence, but in its opposite – the embrace, in reaction against him, of a post-Movement plain style, reinforced by the example of R. S. Thomas, leading to a poetry in which statement triumphed over style, or which was obsessed with roots, land, religion and family, forgetful of the ambitious modernist-tinged

---

[12] Dylan Thomas, *Quite Early One Morning* (New York: New Directions Press, 1954), 152.

[13] Steve McCaffrey, 'Diminished Reference and the Model Reader', *North of Intention: Critical Writings 1973–1986* (New York: Roof Books, 2000), 13–29. The point is not, of course, to deny that signification matters, but rather to interfere with the ideology by which the signifying process, and language itself, is rendered invisible.

[14] Robert Horan, 'In Defense of Dylan Thomas', *The Kenyon Review*, VII:2 (Spring, 1945), 305.

origins Thomas represented.[15] Only recently, in the 2000s, in work by Robert Minhinnick which unashamedly adopts a bardic-prophetic voice, has something of the Thomas inheritance been returned to and taken up.

To some extent, this was initially offset by the broadly positive British reception of Thomas. Al Alvarez's *The New Poetry* (1962), which countered Movement narrowness and defined the poetry-reading audience for over a decade, singled out Ted Hughes for praise, and Thomas for acting as a link between him and D. H. Lawrence.[16] This underplayed Thomas's own significance, but, as James Keery has argued, it is undeniable that 'much of [Hughes's] rewiring of English nature poetry is implicit in a single electrifying line', 'The force that through the green fuse drives the flower'.[17] Although a critical orthodoxy which sees the 1940s as 'the dire decade' has made it difficult to trace this continuity, Hughes himself had no qualms about flaunting it: 'Over Sir John's Hill' alone supplies 'The lark sizzles in my ear / Like a fuse' for *Gaudete*, 'down the drills of his eyes' for 'Jaguar' and the 'black- / back gull' of 'Wind'. As Keery drolly notes, the Thomas line 'To the hawk on fire ... In a whack of wind' sounds more like Hughes than Thomas himself.[18] More generally, many of Hughes's poems share Thomas's existential concerns, and often unravel inner and outer worlds as Thomas does, intrigued by, but critical of, the self-consciousness which separates man from the natural world.

Predictably, Hughes's critics have had problems with this. Keith Sagar claims Hughes in 1954 was 'too much under the influence of Dylan Thomas', although without saying how, eliding Hughes's deep indebtedness to the apocalyptic and neo-Romantic 1940s.[19] Sagar, that is, wishes to dissent from the Movement's drabness, without breaking with its basic aesthetic tenets: that poetry should be discursive, empirical and expressive of a stable self. However much he can be said to observe these himself, Hughes was shaped by Thomas and 1940s poetry in his formative years. As Keery observes, the point is 'both made and missed' by Hughes's biographer, Elaine Feinstein, when she observes, without registering the significance of the fact, that '[Hughes's] supervisor [at Cambridge] ... confessed that she had learned more from him about Dylan Thomas than he had learned from her about John Donne'.[20]

One poet Hughes would have introduced to Thomas's poetry, of course – had she not already known it as well as he did himself – was Sylvia Plath. In high school Plath had 'imitated and idolized' Thomas; at college she wrote a paper on him and won an honourable mention in a writing contest named

---

[15] Pennar Davies, 'Sober Reflections on Dylan Thomas', *Dock Leaves*, 5:15 (1954), 13–17.

[16] A. Alvarez, *The New Poetry* (London: Penguin, 1962; repr. 1966), 23.

[17] James Keery, 'The Burning Baby and the Bathwater', *P. N. Review* 171, 33:1 (September–October 2006), 59.

[18] *Ibid.*

[19] *Ibid.*

[20] *Ibid.*

after him. If *The Bell Jar* is any indication, she also spent much of her free time reading his work. Indeed, she 'loved Dylan Thomas ... almost more than life itself', and put an end to her engagement to a long-term boyfriend because of 'a knock-down-drag-out argument ... over whether Thomas's death had been the fault of [Brinnin]' or not.[21] Commentators have made the point that Plath saw Ted Hughes as 'a second Dylan Thomas', and that this constituted not a little of his appeal. One game the couple played involved Hughes calling out 'a line of Thomas or Shakespeare', and Plath completing the passage. As in Hughes's case, the fascination was non-intimidating and highly productive. Plath's poems are densely intertextual with Thomas's; in fact, according to Gary Lane, 'Dylan Thomas is the vocal colossus of Plath's *The Colossus*'. In one extreme case, 'The Snowman on the Moor', Thomas's style breaks in at the poem's mid-point to correct the 'pretty poeticisms' of its first part, dubiously representing the female speaker's desire for a more masculine power via a welter of allusions to 'A Winter's Tale', 'In the White Giant's Thigh' and 'Into her lying down head'.[22] The very title of 'All the Dead Dears' adopts *Under Milk Wood*'s 'all my dead dears', and exemplifies Thomas's process philosophy in its interinvolvement of the living and the dead and the usurping of one generation by the next. Its undersea details derive from Captain Cat's undersea interlocutors: 'How they grip us through thick and thin / The barnacle dead! ... until we go, / Each skulled-and-crossboned Gulliver / Riddled with ghosts, to lie / Deadlocked with them, taking root as the cradles rock'.[23] More important still is Plath's development of Thomas's poems of gestation, birth and dialogues with embryos, such as 'If my head hurt a hair's foot', in her pregnancy poems 'The Manor Garden', 'You're' and 'Nick and the Candlestick'.

Plath, like Thomas, is also a rare case of the 'serious' mid-century poet who engaged with mass culture. A publisher of chick-lit fictions in *Mademoiselle* and *Seventeen* as well as poems in the *TLS*, Plath, like Thomas, was not embarrassed by the market, and in her relation to the institutions of culture she was, like him, a hybrid, 'crossing over the boundaries of cultural difference with an extraordinary and almost transgressive ease'.[24] It is noteworthy that critics at the time routinely gendered mass culture as female in order to dismiss it; this sheds light on the treatment of Plath's and Thomas's legends by critics.

---

[21] John Gordon, 'Being Sylvia Being Ted Being Dylan: Plath's "The Snowman on the Moor"', *Journal of Modern Literature*, 27:1/2 (Fall 2003), 188.

[22] As John Gordon notes, in this poem 'Plath's relation to Thomas goes beyond the usual questions of poetic influence. It is rather a matter of willed identification, a subsuming of self into other, of the "I am Heathcliff" stamp, effected through the appearance of a Thomas surrogate's surrogate and authenticated with an act of ventriloquy'. *Ibid.* 191.

[23] Sylvia Plath, 'All the Dead Dears', *Collected Poems*, edited with an Introduction by Ted Hughes (London: Faber, 1991), 70–1. For the other three poems, see Plath, *Poems*, 125, 141, 240–2.

[24] Jacqueline Rose, *The Haunting of Sylvia Plath*, 167.

The fact that both were savaged by David Holbrook on similar grounds (too 'hysterical', destructive of qualitative distinctions, etc.) is thus more than mere coincidence; it underlines the fact that both chose to write at a point of tension between high and popular culture, albeit Plath offers less 'resolution or dissipation of what produces the clash between the two' than the more genial Thomas.[25]

The nexus of Thomas and 1940s New Apocalyptic and neo-Romantic modernist-existentialist poetry has been a disguised, but highly significant one for other British poets of the last half-century. Geoffrey Hill's earliest poems were written at Oxford, where Thomas lived until May 1949, and, in their more intellectual vein, both 'Genesis' and 'God's Little Mountain' take their cue from him: 'By blood we live, the hot, the cold, / To ravage and redeem the world: / There is no bloodless myth will hold'.[26] Edwin Morgan, too, has claimed '[the Anglo-Welsh / New Apocalypse] interested me when I was starting off to write, people like Dylan Thomas and David Gascoyne'.[27] The indebtedness of the most important pioneer of post-war British neo-modernist poetry, Roy Fisher, goes deeper still:

> What is interesting … is that it was reading Dylan Thomas that enabled me to start [writing poems]. It was like one of those astronomical events where a body is struck by another and kicked out of its familiar orbit into a new one … I came across *The Burning Baby*, then read, along with the gang of surrealist and neo-romantic things I was hunting out, the first two collections of poems and *The Map of Love*. It was simply the spectacle of something quite primal … a sort of linguistic/imaginative magma, unsuspected innards, the breaking of taboos one hadn't known existed, that shook up my innocence. That was all. I've not returned to those Thomas texts for years, but they remain an extraordinary phenomenon, which won't quite factorize out into the visible elements − Welsh, the Bible, drink, testosterone and so forth − there's still something that resists explanation, however difficult it might be to find a place for it.[28]

The most powerful of Fisher's early poems, 'The Lemon Bride' (1954), owes much to the Thomas short story, 'The Lemon' (1934), which supplies it with 'lemon', wax, frost, tree, acid, knives, and the Thomas phrase 'outside weather'. Thomas's story involves a mad scientist, a boy, a girl, and a lemon containing an acid which kills and resurrects, while Fisher's poem presents the 'rage' and intactness of a violated girl who is a figure for the poet beset by 1950s culture; but both are mythopoeic constructs, with Fisher indebted to Thomas's

---

[25] *Ibid.*, 169, 10.
[26] Geoffrey Hill, *Collected Poems* (Harmondsworth: Penguin, 1985), 16.
[27] Interview with Edwin Morgan, *Angel Exhaust*, 10 (Spring 1994), 53.
[28] James Keery, '"Menacing Works in my Isolation": Early Pieces', in *The Thing About Roy Fisher: Critical Studies*, John Kerrigan and Peter Robinson (eds) (Liverpool: Liverpool University Press, 2000), 51.

figuring of sexual anxiety and gothic-grotesque menace in the poem which was his 'authentic point of departure'.[29]

Yet the most important impact Thomas has had on later British poetry is not Fisher, and perhaps not even Hughes and Plath. The Greenock-born, Cornish-domiciled W. S. Graham is an exemplary figure for late modernist poets such as Tony Lopez and Denise Riley, as he has been also for mainstream critics concerned to salvage a poet from what they view as the shambles of the 1940s.[30] To do so, however, the latter have had to write off Graham's links to Thomas and his membership of the 1940s New Apocalypse grouping, and dispute the continuity between his 1940s poetry and later, more widely admired work. Graham himself opposed this manoeuvre, insisting all his life that his early poetry was not qualitatively inferior to the later work. As he warned Michael Schmidt in 1977:

> It is not like that [growing out of the Thomas influence]. I was disappointed you writing the old cliché about me … I am getting better I hope. But it is not like a graph saying 'he started out not knowing what he was doing and then went through his Dylan Thomas phase (Which I got a great deal out of) and now he [is] refining himself … It was you belittling, too much, for the sake of the last books, the early poetry. Of course I think there is an advance, but if I put out 'Here Next the Chair I Was' [*Cage Without Grievance*, 1942], now, I would be proud and 'THEY' would like it well.

Lopez has convincingly argued that the even earlier poem, *The Seven Journeys*, 'contains in embryo almost all the subjects of his major works' and that 'Graham's development … was prefigured at the outset of his writing … [it was] not something that occurred to him after getting clear of youthful influence'.[31] Graham's personal bond with Thomas, who encouraged and promoted his work, visited him in Glasgow and socialized with him in Fitzrovia (he was the first fellow-poet to whom Thomas read 'Fern Hill'), was strong enough; but it is the poetic similarities which impress most.[32] In *Poetry Scotland* in 1946, we

---

[29] *Ibid.*, 50–1.
[30] Thus, for Neil Corcoran, although at first 'helplessly parasitic on Thomas', Graham's is 'arguably the finest contribution to post-war [British] poetry by a poet who began publishing in the 1940s'. Neil Corcoran, *English Poetry Since 1940* (London: Macmillan, 1993), 47.
[31] See 'His Perfect Hunger's Daily Changing Bread', review by James Keery of *The Nightfisherman: Selected Letters of W. S. Graham*, in *P.N. Review*, 27:1 (September–October 2000), 35–8.
[32] This event was commemorated by David Wright in his poem 'Incident in Soho', which describes this 'unlike making of history' at a time when 'History – big word – [was] being made … in Normandy'. Wright saw, but could not (being deaf) hear, Thomas reading a poem to Graham in a Soho pub, and asked him afterwards if he could see it: 'He gave it me, then turning to the other: / "Well Sydney?" The first reading of "Fern Hill"'. See Tony Lopez, *Meaning Performance* (Cambridge: Salt, 2006), 92.

find Graham fully endorsing the archetypal Thomasian claim that poetry must work 'from' rather than 'towards' words, to be 'made out of words' first and foremost, rather than subserve an expressivist or sociological poetic.[33] In *The Seven Journeys*, Graham, it seems, systematically externalized and extended those aspects of Thomas to do with linguistic play, textualized landscapes and verbal embodiments of the erotic and the unconscious, pushing towards a more explicit questioning of the relationship between language and the self, or being. He discovered the tropes he needed for this in Thomas; so, 'Ballad of the Long-legged Bait' is reworked in less frenzied spirit in *The Nightfishing* (1955), and the explorers and polar white-out of *Malcolm Mooney's Land* (1970) are cued up by Thomas's 'Cold Nansen's beak on a boat full of gongs' and the snowscape-text of 'A Winter's Tale' (*CP*, 110). But while these verbal and thematic similarities could be multiplied, they are rarely a weakness; Graham, like Hughes and Plath, actively incorporates Thomas, even as he acknowledges a debt.

At one point in Graham's late poem 'What is language using us for?' (1977), the speaker tells of an encounter on the ice-pack with 'The King of Whales', who 'dearly wanted / To have a word with me about how / I had been trying to crash / The Great Barrier'. The 'barrier' is, of course, language, and the King of Whales is described as 'A kind of old uncle of mine / And yours mushing across the blind / Ice-cap between us ... Shouting at his delinquent dogs'. His purpose is enigmatic, but Graham's speaker tells us that his aim is 'to find // Whatever it is he wanted by going / Out of my habits which is my name / To ask him how I can do better'.[34] He is, in other words, a poetic mentor; and there cannot be much doubt that Thomas is intended, given Graham's use of Thomas's favourite Wales / whales pun.[35] The apparatus to the *New Collected Poems*, predictably, makes no mention of the link, eliding one of the most creative relationships in mid-twentieth-century British poetry.[36]

Such misreadings have their equivalents on the other side of the poetic fence. In 1994, Nigel Wheale damned Thomas's 'hopelessly private obscurity', accusing him of 'writing with no recoverable patterns of any interest' – an odd position, perhaps, in an essay trying to rehabilitate Lynette

---

[33] Graham wrote, as if reiterating a lesson imparted by Thomas: 'The most difficult thing for me to remember is that a poem is made out of words and not of the expanding heart, the overflowing soul, or the sensitive observer. A poem is made of words. It is words in a certain order, good or bad by the significance of its addition to life and not to be judged by any other value put upon it by imagining how or why or by what kind of man it was made'. See *The Nightfisherman: Selected Letters of W. S. Graham*, Michael and Margaret Snow (eds) (Manchester: Carcanet, 1999), 379–83. See W. S. Graham, *New Collected Poems*, ed. Matthew Francis (London: Faber, 2004), xvi, xviii.

[34] *Ibid.*, 202.

[35] *Ibid.*, 127.

[36] *Ibid.*, 202–3.

Roberts.[37] Yet understanding has increased recently. Tony Lopez's 1991 study of W. S. Graham strove rather desperately to distance Graham from Thomas; however, his *Meaning Performance* (2006) offers redress, and usefully rebuts a few Thomas stereotypes.[38] In fact, most recent attempts to rehabilitate the 1940s and Thomas have been made by critics who are also neo-modernist poets, like Lopez and Keery, and British avant-garde *poetry* probably owes more to Thomas than it knows, as the work of Drew Milne, Geraldine Monk, Maggie O'Sullivan, David Annwn and Giles Goodland shows. Thomas's presence within this kind of writing may go back a long way; the Acknowledgements to *Poet in the Making* (1968) fascinatingly include Ralph Maud's thanks to one 'Jeremy Prynne, whose eyes I have used on the manuscript ... at various times'.[39]

V

Finally, we might consider Thomas's presence and influence in the non-anglophone world. The Welsh poet Euros Bowen once made the point that Thomas was not a Welsh poet writing in an English tradition, but rather a Welsh poet whose work was European in character, and although this makes too light of his confounding of English and Anglo-Welsh canons, it is revealing that Thomas was the object of tributes from poets as different as Johannes Bobrowski and Tristan Tzara, and that commentators on Russian poetry should observe that the closest English equivalent to the Mandelstam of such poems as 'The Slate Ode' is early Dylan Thomas.[40] Thomas, despite the disclaimers, was well aware of European poetry, from his own reading of the surrealists encountered in the journal *transition*, his involvement with the surrealists (he gave a poetry reading with Paul Éluard after the International Surrealist Exhibition in London, in June 1936), and from the translations of Rilke, Holderlin, Lorca and others passed on to him by Vernon Watkins. By contrast with the insular English tradition, Thomas's sense of poetry as the

---

[37] Nigel Wheale, 'Lynette Roberts: legend and form in the 1940s', *Critical Quarterly*, 36:3 (Autumn 1994), 13. Roberts's own poetry, of course, is hardly noted for its lack of 'private obscurity'.

[38] Tony Lopez, *Meaning Performance* (Cambridge: Salt, 2006), 92–4. Citing Philip Larkin's enthusiastic description of Dylan Thomas and his reading at the Oxford English Club in November 1941, Lopez adds: 'Notice that Thomas is portrayed ... as an ordinary "bloke" and also as a very worldly poet who is, as we learn from the jokes he makes and the parodies he reads, keenly aware of the dangers involved in the public role of the poet. He is in Larkin's sketch really the opposite of the bardic poet that the Movement writers later made him out to be.'

[39] Ralph Maud, *Poetry in the Making: The Notebooks of Dylan Thomas* (London: Dent, 1968), 43.

[40] Cited in Nathalie Wourm, 'Dylan Thomas and the French Symbolists', in Tony Brown, ed., *Welsh Writing in English: A Yearbook of Critical Essays*, vol. 5 (1999), 27.

art in which language was tested and re-forged makes him recognizable as a significant writer to non-anglophones in a way that, say, Larkin's empirical annotations on daily existence, plus apothegm, do not. This is reflected in the extent to which he has been translated – several times into the major European languages, for example, and into almost all of the minor ones, as well as partially into Arabic, Korean, Japanese and Chinese; forty-three languages in all, the most of any British poet of the period (Auden, by way of comparison, manages thirty-two). Indeed, his difficulty may paradoxically have added to his appeal, for, like Joyce, Thomas appeals as a test case of the translatable.

One example – that of the Romanian-Jewish Paul Celan – deserves particular mention in this regard. As James Keery has argued, Celan, Thomas and the New Apocalypse poets arose from the same matrix of European visionary modernism, and the frequency with which they arrive at similar verbal formulations is striking. Poems such as Celan's 'Epitaph for Francois' – although examples could be multiplied – uncannily echo such Thomas lyrics as 'The force that through the green fuse' and 'Twenty-four years' ('The two doors of the world / stand open ... We hear them slam and slam / and carry ... the green thing into your Ever').[41] This is more than coincidence, for as Amy Colin has noted, Celan read about and was influenced by 'Thomas's idea of poetic images as bearing the seed of their own destruction', and certainly read his poems.[42] Keery notes 'an intimate link between Thomas's "seedy shifting" and "gold tithings"' and a 'Celanian chain of metaphors derived from alchemy: gold-seed / semen-grain, etc. ... Celan pursued the quintessentially Apocalyptic theme of (im)mortality by means of the same blasphemous image-complex ("the exultant psalmist's sexual member bears the mark of God")'. Quoting Celan's 'Spasms', Keery adds: 'The last line ["I sing the scarscore of the bone-staff"] sounds like an out-take from "I dreamed my genesis"!'[43]

Such marked similarities shed an ironic light, of course, because the virtual unanimity of agreement in English critical circles on Celan's status as the greatest post-war European poet is often maintained by precisely those who have ignored, denigrated or patronized Thomas, from George Steiner onwards.

VI

An echo of the bad faith revealed by comparing the critical reception of Celan and Thomas – poems that 'work from words' are fine as long as they aren't in English – is evident in the way British poets, as well as critics, still tiptoe so gingerly around Thomas, as if recognizing that the ambitiousness of his work, the large claims it implicitly makes for poetry as an art, throw their

---

[41]   Paul Celan, *Selected Poems*, trans. Michael Hamburger (London: Penguin, 1990), 79.

[42]   Amy Colin, *Paul Celan: Holograms of Darkness* (Indiana: Indiana University Press, 1991), 99. As noted by Keery (see fn 43).

[43]   James Keery, 'The Burning Baby and the Bathwater', *P.N. Review*, 31:6 (July–August 2005), 59.

own self-denying ordinances into unflattering relief. This is Thomas as the absent presence in contemporary British poetry, respected abroad, still popular because his poetry is unafraid of being 'poetic', but treated as unsound by the professionals: he is what the French critic Pierre Macherey would call 'a silence which speaks'. A few poets – John Hartley Williams and Derek Mahon among them – have called for reinstatement, but apart from claiming that he is 'the real thing', they are vague as to how this might be done. Many more concede, as Michael Donaghy did in the late 1990s, that they were 'intoxicated' by Thomas as adolescents, but conclude that his 'failure to develop' makes him unsuitable as an example for the poet who wants to get on.[44] (This raises, of course, the need to distinguish between 'adolescent poet' in the merely derogatory sense, and 'poet of adolescence', which would include Rimbaud and Keats, as well as the issue of just why Thomas's many poems of marriage, war and fatherhood, written in 1938–53, are being ignored.)

Much of the problem remains a resistance to the implications of Thomas's language use. These are best articulated by Seamus Heaney, probably the best-known poet in these islands since Larkin. Thomas was the fly in the ointment of the upgraded Movement poetic Heaney inherited from Philip Hobsbaum, his earliest mentor, and this is reflected in a characteristic poetic and critical strategy in Heaney, whereby it is conceded that poetry 'cannot afford to lose its … joy in being a process of language as well as a representation of things in the world', but the extent of that 'process' is then reined in, well below any measure of it Thomas would have recognized.[45] Thomas was a favourite poet of the Belfast Group in the early 1960s, and he has a conflicted meaning for Heaney; the struggle with his example is arguably encoded in *Death of a Naturalist* (1966), which can be read as an extended reaction against 'Fern Hill' (this is how *real* farms work!) and a grudging tribute to the mimetic power and the pastoral vision of Thomas's late poetry more generally. What is noticeable in Heaney's 1989 essay *Dylan the Durable* is the way that, like so many other British poet-critics, he refers to just a tiny number of poems ('Before I Knocked' and 'Do Not Go Gentle Into That Good Night'). They are taken from either end of Thomas's writing life to give an illusion of career coverage, but no major poem written between 1933 and 1949 is mentioned, 'A Winter's Tale' excepted. Poems like 'A Grief Ago', 'Once It Was The Colour of Saying' or 'This Side of the Truth' would shatter the image of a poetic Peter Pan which Heaney wishes to create; they make clear the complex, protean, Joyce- and Blake-inspired nature of the mature poetry. Thomas has to be kept inside the 'adolescent' box, on pain of falling into Heaney's other, more dismissive category, that of 'tourist-board cliché', because the alternative raises difficult

---

44 For Donaghy, John Stammers, 'The Unconscious Power of Form', *Magma*, 8 (Winter 1996), pp. 39–44, see http://www.poetrymagazines.org.uk/magazine/record. asp?id=3297 (Accessed 1 March 2014).
45 Jeffrey Side, 'The Influence of Wordsworth's Empiricist Aesthetic on Seamus Heaney's Criticism and Poetry', *English*, 59:225 (Summer 2010), 157.

questions about what happened in mid-twentieth-century poetry. 'Tourist-board cliché', which Heaney applies to 'A Winter's Tale', actually works less well as a critique of the poem than as an example of how uncannily Thomas outs his attackers' blind spots – that is, there is a distinct sense of stones being thrown in glass houses by the author of sepia-tinted works such as 'The Wool Trade', 'Thatcher' and 'The Forge' when Thomas is slated for colluding with the heritage industries.[46] Amusing though this is, however, it reveals the size of the obstacles to reassessment.

By 'obstacles' I mean that, first of all, to properly reassess Thomas's influence, and hence his significance, it needs to be understood that the 1930s were not wholly dominated by Auden and social realist styles, and that the second half of the decade was shared between them both. There are many vested interests bound up in the concept of 'the Auden decade', however, and they remain powerfully entrenched in the English literary-critical world. In addition, to grant this much would mean that Thomas could not, therefore, be 'a forties poet' (he had, in any case, published two-thirds of all his poems by 1939). A revision of the forties, equally necessary, is the second obstacle; the standard account of the decade's 'dire'-ness is utterly inadequate to a period which produced not only *Four Quartets* and *Deaths and Entrances*, but David Jones's *The Anathemata*, Lynette Roberts's *Gods with Stainless Ears*, W. S. Graham's *The Nightfishing* and the masterpieces of H. D. and Edith Sitwell.[47] Again, defences are deeply entrenched; these works are all modernist, and the mainstream narrative requires that Modernism was dead by 1930, or 1939 at the very latest. Finally, and most difficult to surmount, there is the obstacle that reassessing Thomas's influence demands a rethinking of contemporary poetry.

[46] Perhaps the most piquant example of this is Don Paterson's 2004 review of W. S. Graham's *New Collected Poems*, which claims that the 1940s were a bad time for new poets because 'the high camp of Dylan Thomas and Wallace Stevens left almost a whole generation mincing in their wake, all with that mangled syntax and hysterical rhetoric that made the modernist drag-artist only too easy to spot'. In a marvellously unwitting self-revelation, Paterson's Dundonian macho fear of effeminacy and queerness blurts itself out. See 'Prism Visitor', *The Observer Review*, 2004.

[47] The works by Jones, Roberts and Graham were published in the 1950s, but written in the 1940s. The reason why the 1940s is so derided is because the existential-expressionistic mode forged by Thomas in 1933–4 was dominant then, and its unashamed linguistic excess offends supporters of 'the English tradition', as Donald Davies defined it in 1958: namely, the realist-discursive plain-style speaking voice poetic mode running from Thomas Hardy through Edward Thomas, 'the English Auden', Larkin, the Martians and the New Gen poets, with input from non-English and maverick figures such as Geoffrey Hill, Hughes, Plath and the Northern Irish poets. The chief stylistic trait of the 1940s, under the period sign of apocalypse, was a populist modernism evident in all the arts (as in the work of Henry Moore, Graham Sutherland and Michael Tippett). The poetic achievements of the decade bear favourable comparison with those of any other of the century.

This means confronting the 'faultline' mentioned earlier, because Thomas did not flirt with Modernism and then abandon it (as did Auden in 1932), but fused traditional form and modernist content and practices for a decade. Exploring Gabriel Pearson's notion that Auden and Thomas were the two halves of the great British modernist poet which English poetry failed to produce after *The Waste Land* would be one way of staging such a confrontation, but it has not yet happened.[48] Yet so great is Thomas's radical hybridity that he continues to persist as the ghost at the banquet of today's self-proclaimed 'pluralist' poetry culture. The point, to be clear here, is not that poets today *dislike* Thomas's work – they may, but they tend to be more receptive than the critics – but that the dominant critical narratives and their own conception of poetry (much narrowed since Thomas's time) prevents this. The 'pluralism' which emerged in the 1990s is not truly inclusive, because it is based on a consumerist definition of choice. Niche markets include everything except a questioning of the market itself. As John Matthias noted in 2000, such inclusivity extended 'to race, religion, class, language, gender, sexual preference – to everything, in fact, except [modernist-derived] poetics'.[49]

Accurate as this is, however, one major development whose effects Matthias could not have assessed in 2000, the 1997 devolutions, seems to promise the possibility of finding a way out of the maze of vested interests which stand in the way of a reassessment of Thomas, as outlined above. In general, the Welsh Assembly fosters a policy of linguistic culturalism, which imposes the Welsh language from above and makes it the (often unspoken) heart of cultural policy, thwarting a rethink of hybrid, in-between entities such as the work of Dylan Thomas. On the other hand, the very existence of the Assembly has had a countervailing effect; by making Welsh political identity more secure, it has inevitably legitimized thinking about Welsh cultural spaces in less either/or ways than in the past. This makes possible non-identitarian notions of identity, for Thomas to be conceptualized as 'Anglo-Welsh' without this hyphenation necessarily connoting self-division or psychic wounding. One of the most important aspects of Thomas's influence was as what Ortega y Gasset calls the 'vertical invader', the provincial who conquers the metropolis on his or her own terms through sheer force of will and originality (Lloyd George is

[48] Gabriel Pearson, *The Spectator Review of Books*, *The Spectator*, 20 November 1970, 731, 732. Pearson notes shrewdly: 'each over-developed what the other neglects; crudely, thought as against feeling. Auden handles language from the outside, like a craftsman or sportsman, while Thomas burrows into the body of the language itself from which he delivers oracles from the heat of its decomposition'. He concluded: 'Of the two, I believe, against the grain of current prejudice, Thomas denied less of himself than Auden and emerges from a reading of his poetry and prose as the richer, more humanly grounded artist'. One might demur at this, but still feel that the Auden–Thomas weighting needs revision.
[49] John Matthias, 'British Poetry at Y2K', http://www.electronicbookreview.com/ p. 30 (Accessed 20th January 2014).

the obvious Welsh counterpart in the political sphere). Well before the 1944 Education Act, Thomas established a pattern for the margin to write back to the centre, heralding the 'provincial' poets from all over the United Kingdom who would be its beneficiaries, from Douglas Dunn to Hughes and Heaney. He did so without their advantages because the sheer size of his talent enabled him to turn what would have been weakness in lesser writers into positives; very few writers have been so gifted. Nevertheless, it has become possible since 1997, it seems to me, to see in Dylan Thomas not only an enduring literary influence, or leaven, in English-language poetry, but the prophet of a more capacious, non-anglocentric, twenty-first-century sense of *British* poetry; one which is not only at ease with its different geographical identities, but with its different traditions and modes too.

Dylan Thomas

Philip Pullman

When I was sixteen or so, intoxicated by the poetry I found for myself as well as the official stuff doled out to us in school like the old naval rum-ration, one of the poets who made my head swim and my skin prickle and my heart pound (and the true test of poetry is always physical) was Dylan Thomas.

My enthusiasm for him was sudden and intense. With saved-up pocket money I bought a *Collected Poems* for eighteen shillings, and pored over it like an alchemist trying to extract the secret of the philosopher's stone. What I really wanted to do, of course, was write poetry myself. No: I'll be more exact; writing poetry was what I already did, but what I wanted to do was write good poetry. I thought the way to begin was by imitation. In Dylan Thomas I found a treasury of marvellous things to imitate, and for a time I wrote nothing but mock-Thomas.

And he's not hard to imitate badly, because at his worst (and who is always at their best?) he intones with a windy portentousness that doesn't, if you look at it closely, mean very much at all, but sounds terrific. I think that was what I was imitating most of the time. Well, it got it out of my system.

But scrutinizing verse with a hard mean eye, looking only for the flaws and giving a satisfied little nod when you find them, was never an activity that I found rewarding in myself or admirable in others. Nor do I like the cast of mind that scoffs at the things we loved when we were young. If we once loved them, they deserve honour and gratitude for the education they gave our feelings.

And I loved Dylan Thomas, and I read him by the hour. The method I used was one I still employ, and I recommend it: be solitary, and whisper the words. I found it was essential to get them in my mouth, to get my lips and my tongue around them, to involve my muscles and my nerves in the process. By themselves, my eyes didn't let enough in.

So it was, whispering in my bedroom by lamplight, that I thrilled at the poem that begins 'In my craft or sullen art'. I too was a lover, my arms around the griefs of the ages, and I too was the poet, exercising my craft or sullen art in the still night when only the moon rages. When I read it now I remember those feelings, and they rise up undimmed and undiminished.

And so it is now when I read 'Fern Hill', where I think all his gifts came together most richly and successfully. The evocation of childhood is both ecstatic and under perfect control, two things which are usually opposites, and the incantatory quality is firmly at the service of a meditation on time that is complex and penetrating – or is the meditating at the service of the incantation? Both are true, and the final lines remain unanswerable and unforgettable:

> Oh as I was young and easy in the mercy of his means
>> Time held me green and dying
> Though I sang in my chains like the sea.

Fashions in poetry, as in music and the visual arts, come and go, and they don't matter very much. What matters is the poetry, and what matters in poetry are the words. Dylan Thomas loved words, relished them, used them to bewitch. There is a sort of magic, enchantment, sorcery – something of that sort – in his best work. It seized me by the senses when I was young, and I loved it at once. I honour it still.

Life with Aeronwy

Trefor Ellis

I met Aeronwy Thomas (Aeron for short), Dylan and Caitlin's only daughter, in 1971, on a tour of Canada and the States with the Pendyrus male voice choir. At the time, I was living in Pontypridd, South Wales, and was working in a coal mine in the Rhondda valley as a measuring boy. I remember Aeron's first words to me: 'What is your star sign?', she asked.

'Aries,' I responded, 'what's yours?'
'Pisces', she replied.
'Oh! Water and fire. That makes steam!' I replied cheekily.

Our relationship continued after we returned home. After commuting to London most weekends, we got engaged at Christmas 1972 when on holiday in Penmachno, near Betws y Coed, North Wales. There was much resistance to this decision, with many negative and hurtful comments from Aeron's friends, such as 'Don't marry him he's from the valleys' or 'He's only marrying you for money'. Despite this, we got married on Sunday 29 April 1973 at St Jude's Church, Kensington. When we arrived back from our honeymoon we moved to New Malden in Surrey, the place we lived all our married life, and where I still live today.

From the start, Dylan Thomas was very much part of our lives. Aeron performed her father's work, and later her own, all over the world and I often joined her, singing one or two Welsh songs or acting out extracts from *Under Milk Wood*.

I have to admit I have always found Dylan's poetry difficult to understand, but I love his prose works, especially 'The Outing', 'A Child's Christmas in Wales' and *Under Milk Wood*. I really enjoy the humour and strange behaviour of the different characters. For this reason, when people just refer to Dylan as a poet, I think this is a big mistake. He has a wealth of wonderful prose work as well.

Going to various events and meeting distinguished people was daunting for me at first – from being invited to a party by the stage director Malcolm Taylor and his wife Annie, where we met quite a few of the actors in his stage version of *Under Milk Wood*, such as Philip and Ruth Madoc, Richard Davies, David Jason, Jenny Hill and Windsor Davies, to being at the premiere of the film of *Under Milk Wood* starring Richard Burton and Elizabeth Taylor. I have also had the privilege of meeting many of Dylan Thomas's more famous fans, including members of the Royal Family, actors Richard Burton, Anthony Hopkins, Catherine Zeta Jones, President Jimmy Carter, the former Archbishop of Canterbury, Dr Rowan Williams, the poets Ted Hughes and John Betjeman. It has taken me a long time to get used to it, and I still find it very overwhelming.

It was also such an honour to get to know Dylan's talented Swansea friends including the artist, Mervyn Levy. I have very fond memories of going on holiday with him and his family to north Wales. Early in the morning, when it was very cold, yet gloriously sunny, we would go for long walks. Mervyn admired the clear water of the river and we all observed him having a conversation with it. It was an amazing sight. Fred Janes, the artist who painted some iconic portraits of Dylan, was always incredibly caring towards Aeron and he became a family friend. We had a great day at his son's wedding in Clevedon. Daniel Jones, the composer, mentioned in Dylan's prose piece 'The Fight', was a lovely character. I remember that he used to go to the Newton Arms in the Swansea area on most days and would order himself a drink sitting in front of an open fire. I also met Wynford Vaughan Thomas, the BBC broadcaster and a friend of Dylan. He once told me that when Dylan was in London he only drank beer in half-pint measures and he would go home to sleep quite early.

I got to meet many biographers and scholars studying Dylan's life and work. Many I struggled to gel with, but not John Ackerman, the author of *Welsh Dylan*. He was not only a brilliant academic but an excellent poet; he was also very kind, gentle and would find the time to speak with fans and students, with a real knack to make them feel at ease.

My wife Aeronwy Thomas died in 2009. We had been together for nearly forty years, had two children, Huw and Hannah, and two grandchildren, Oscar and Charlie. During that time, Dylan Thomas played a major role in our lives, from the pictures on the walls to the books on the shelves and Aeron's strong desire to promote her father's work.

Dylan's Daughter

Aeronwy Thomas

They want me at the party
I don't know them
they don't know me
strangers
they want me
because I'm Dylan's daughter

Why can't my husband go
alone
they're his friends
his party
but no
they want me there too.

Can't you ring
I'm indisposed, awful cold
a bug
a severe allergy
to their kind invite.

No hope
no good prevaricating
got to bathe
prink and pother
choose an outfit
and worse
be ready on time.

'By six, did you say?'
'The earlier we get there the earlier we can leave'
he lies
knowing the return trek will be cold, late
lengthy

While I'm celebrated with
Prosecco and delicious food

he'll be singing his heart out
with his Welsh friends
last to go
befuddled and sung out
with me in tow

Ah, well
better get ready
Pronto
Because I'm Dylan's daughter.

Various Versions

T. James Jones

When I first read *Under Milk Wood* in 1954, I remember being struck by the Welshness both of the location and of most of the characters. I do not recall hearing the Dylan Thomas broadcast of *Quite Early One Morning* a year earlier (the initial broadcast was in 1944 – which even I would have been too young to appreciate!) but upon reading it in the late 1950s, I recall discovering the embryos, as it were, of a number of the *Under Milk Wood* characters: Captain Tiny Evans (Captain Cat), Parchedig Thomas Evans (The Reverend Eli Jenkins), the schoolteacher, Mr Griffiths (Mr Pugh), and the maid, Phoebe (Lilly Smalls). Moreover, both the name of and the obsessive houseproud utterance by Mrs Ogmore-Pritchard – 'And before you let the sun in, mind it wipes its shoes' – are recycled in *Under Milk Wood*.

Quite Early One Morning was written when Dylan Thomas lived in the village of Cei Newydd (New Quay) in Ceredigion, which was, in 1944, inhabited by a majority of Welsh-speakers. But it is common knowledge that Dylan's acquaintance with Talacharn (Laugharne), from 1938 onwards, was the catalyst for writing the play for voices, and that the bulk of the script was eventually completed after Dylan had finally settled in the Boat House in 1949.

It is often rumoured that if one had happened to be taking an afternoon walk on the footpath between Brown's Hotel and the Boat House at that time, one would possibly have overheard the very first renderings of the words of *Under Milk Wood* from beyond the door of the writing shed. That experience would have mirrored the device used in *Under Milk Wood*, namely having the audience overhearing conversations and monologues of its characters.

The writing shed overlooks the estuary which separated a predominantly English Laugharne from the Welsh-speaking villagers of Llansteffan and Llangain, who were familiar with Dylan's maternal Welsh-speaking family connections. His mother's sister, Annie, had provided him with countless summer holidays at Fernhill near Llangain, a farm whose small stock of horses, cows, pigs and dogs would not have heard much English. During those school holidays Dylan would have overheard a constant stream of Welsh on the Fernhill farmyard, on neighbouring farms belonging to Annie's family, in Carmarthen market and at the Sunday services in the Welsh Congregational Smyrna Chapel, Llangain.

During his nine months' stay at Cei Newydd in 1944, Dylan, on his daily walks to the shops and pubs from a rented bungalow on the outskirts of the village, would have encountered a constant hubbub of Welsh. The coastal village would have been home to a good number of Welsh-speaking sea captains. And to quote from the prologue to *Under Milk Wood*, 'the farmers, the fishers, the tradesmen and pensioners, cobbler, schoolteacher, postman and publican, the undertaker and the fancy woman, drunkard, dressmaker, preacher, policeman ...' would probably have been, in the 1944 Cei Newydd, Welsh-speakers.

Geraint Bowen, the chaired bard at the 1946 Mountain Ash National Eisteddfod, recounts in his autobiography, *O Groth y Ddaear*, how his father, Orchwy Bowen, minister of the Welsh Congregational Chapel at Cei Newydd, spent the best part of 1944 confined to the manse, due to ill health. It is conceivable that the Reverend Bowen would have been seen at regular intervals opening the front door to stand in the manse doorway, and, to quote the narrator of *Under Milk Wood* regarding the Reverend Eli Jenkins, 'looking out at the day and up at the eternal hill, and hearing the sea break and the gab of birds ...'. The obsessive preoccupation of Eli Jenkins in Bethesda House with *eisteddfodau*, druids, and – to quote again from *Under Milk Wood* – 'the memorial of peoples in the region of Llareggub before the Celts left the Land of Summer and where the old wizards made themselves a wife out of flowers', could be the mirror of the Bowen Manse in 1944. Orchwy Bowen's two sons were giants of Welsh bardism: Euros Bowen, notable for his experimentation in the thousand-year-old tradition of the unique Welsh artform of *cynghanedd*, and twice winning the National Eisteddfod crown; and Geraint becoming the principal historian of the Gorsedd of Bards and serving as the Archdruid of Wales from 1979 to 1981.

The prologue by the *Under Milk Wood* narrator echoes the opening paragraphs of *Quite Early One Morning*. In both, a slumbering town is observed in the early hours. In the former we observe 'night in the four-ale, quiet as a domino; in Ocky Milkman's loft like a mouse with gloves'; in the latter we see 'the milkman ... still lost in the clangour and music of his Welsh-spoken dreams'. However, in contrast to the comparatively dispassionate neutrality of the *Under Milk Wood* narrator, in *Quite Early One Morning* it seems to be Dylan himself who does the observing, and reacting passionately to the drama of the small hours as he 'walked through the streets like a stranger come out of the sea, shrugging off weed and wave and darkness ...'.

In a letter to Pamela Hansford Johnson dated 15 October 1933, Dylan responds to her query regarding the meaning of his name: 'My unusual name – for some mad reason it comes from the *Mabinogion* and means the "prince of darkness" ...' (*The Collected Letters*, 25). The remnants of the Dylan legend are found in the Fourth Branch of the Mabinogi. Born to Arianrhod daughter of Dôn, he was named Dylan:

As soon as he was baptized he made for the sea. And there and then, as soon as he came to the sea, he took on the sea's nature and swam as well as the best fish

in the sea. Because of that he was called Dylan Eil Ton – no wave ever broke beneath him. The blow which killed him was struck by Gofannon, his uncle
Sioned Davies, The Mabinogion (Oxford University Press, 54)

Llyfr Taliesin contains an elegy to Dylan Eil Ton and some writers on Celtic Mythology claimed to have found evidence of the existence of an earlier myth depicting Dylan as the god of darkness, in contrast to Lieu, the god of light (e.g. Charles Squire, *The Mythology of the British Islands* [London: Blackie & Son, 1905]). This claim is now generally refuted by Welsh Celtic scholars.

The naming of Dylan must have caused quite a stir in suburban Swansea in 1914. Whereas Dylan is a popular name today, it is believed that the newly born son at 5 Cwmdonkin Drive was the first to be named Dylan in modern times. It may be the case that the poet's fame is partly responsible for the current popularity of the name. When the boy first attended the primary school he must have been asked, if not pestered by his fellow scholars, about the unusual name and its meaning. Dylan's father, D. J. Thomas, a scholar in Welsh literature, would have been well acquainted with the Mabinogi. It was probably the father who would have informed the son of the 'prince of darkness' embellishment to Dylan's legend, he having possibly found reference to it in the above mentioned Charles Squire tome.

But there is much conjecture as to why D. J. chose the name. In her history of the Welsh theatre, *Y Theatr Genedlathol yng Nghymru*, Hazel Walford Davies offers a plausible answer. D. J. was an ardent supporter of Howard de Walden in his campaign to establish a Welsh National Theatre. In July 1914, an opera by Howard de Walden, *Dylan, Son of the Wave*, was being performed in the Drury Lane Theatre in London. Subsequent reviews of the opera appeared in the Swansea local press and D. J. would have read them. A few months later his son was born, and he was named Dylan.

In the Pamela Hansford Johnson letter, the twenty-year-old Dylan seems to relish the 'prince of darkness' tag. The *Quite Early One Morning* reference seems to signify another level of consciousness regarding the name. Here, the thirty-year-old poet deliberately embodies the mythical Dylan figure, but this time he is not entering the sea to join the fish, but coming 'out of the sea, shrugging off weed and wave and darkness …'. The remnants of the Dylan legend are being revisited and augmented by a new voice. In less than a decade the thirty-nine-year-old Dylan adds a new chapter to the legend by adopting the role of the *Cyfarwydd* (the traditional Welsh storyteller, usually an itinerant court entertainer under the patronage of the medieval Welsh Princes and later of the Gentry) when he takes part in the first public performance of *Under Milk Wood* in New York on 14 May 1953. And sadly, during those turbulent months leading to his premature death on 9 November 1953, only days after his second public performance of the role of the *Cyfarwydd* in *Under Milk Wood*, the 'prince of darkness' tag takes on a sinister significance. Towards the end of the prologue and the voice's introduction to Captain Cat, we sense that Dylan Thomas had foreseen the dark end of his new Dylan legend:

Only you can hear and see behind the eyes of the sleepers, the ... wishes and flight and fall and despairs and big seas of their dreams ... Captain Cat ... asleep in his bunk ... dreams of never such seas as any that swamped his S.S. Kidwelly bellying over the bedclothes and jellyfish-slippery sucking him down salt deep into the Davy dark where the fish come biting out and nibble him down to his wishbone ...

Captain Cat's dream is a negation of the Mabinogi Dylan legend. Instead of the seafarer enjoying his confident swim with the fish, he is horribly devoured by them.

In the explanatory notes to the Davies/Maud definitive edition of *Under Milk Wood* the phrase 'Davy dark' is explained as a dual reference, one to the evil spirit of the sea ('Davy Jones's locker' being an idiom for death at sea) and the other to the coal miners' safety-lamp, the miners' survival kit to warn them of the presence of deadly gasses. Knowing Dylan's enthusiasm for double meanings, one could accept the relevance of both references in this context, the pitch-darkness of the forces of evil and the darkness of the coalface lit by a small flame of survival. Dylan's mood during the last years of his short life was a mixture of both darknesses. On the one hand, due to his precarious lifestyle he knew that he was playing a game with death; at the same time he intended to create a long poem which would be entitled *In Country Heaven*. The three published completed poems which would be parts of the long poem, 'In Country Sleep', 'Over Sir John's Hill' and 'In The White Giant's Thigh', reveal a robust confidence in survival despite the inevitability of death. A flicker of light was to be seen in the utter darkness.

The *Cyfarwydd* was to provide yet another twist to the Dylan legend. Here is a précis of Dylan Thomas's description of the unfinished title poem:

The poem is to be called 'In Country Heaven'. The godhead, the author, the milky-way farmer, the first cause, architect, lamp-lighter, quintessence, the beginning Word, the anthropomorphic bowler-out and blackballer ... He, on top of a hill in heaven, weeps whenever ... one of his worlds drops dead ... And when he weeps, Light and his tears glide down together, hand in hand ... Country Heaven is suddenly dark. Bushes and owls blow out like candles. And the countrymen of heaven crouch together under the hedges and ... surmise which world ... in the skies has gone for ever. And this time, spreads the heavenly hedgerow rumour, it is the Earth. The Earth has killed itself. It is black, petrified, wizened, poisoned, burst; insanity has blown it rotten ... The poem is made of these tellings. And the poem becomes, at last, an affirmation of the beautiful and terrible worth of the Earth. It grows into a praise of what is and what could be on this lump in the skies. It is a poem about happiness.
Quite Early One Morning, 156–7

For Dylan, the prime manifestation of the world's insanity is the dropping of atom bombs on Hiroshima and Nagasaki. (In addition to *In Country Heaven*, he intended to write a libretto to the music of Stravinsky in a work reacting specifically to these tragedies.) And the idea of the insanity of the world recalls the early intended title for *Under Milk Wood*, *The Town Was Mad*. It also underlines the fact that *Under Milk Wood*, written during the travails of the Second World War, reflected under its light rompishness a dark aspect of life. Llareggub is both comic and tragic, both beautiful and terrible.

However, the quality of truth is not only confined to honest reactions to the realities of historical fact but is also present in myth. In the intended *In Country Heaven*, Dylan Thomas works his magic to produce the dramatic entry of the god of Light into the world of the prince of Darkness. The myth-maker, Dylan Thomas, intended to bring Dylan and Lleu together in a tense truce.

Fate decided that Dylan's *In Country Heaven* remained unfulfilled. And he would not live to see the world still reacting to the dangers of insanity during the worldwide human and civil rights movements of the 1960s. Protests against yet another insane war in Vietnam escalated across the globe. Frequently, the non-violent protests focused on the rights of minorities. In Wales, the fate of Welsh as a minority language produced a civil rights reaction led by the Welsh Language Society. The identity of Wales in relation to the British state had a prominence in a debate led by Plaid Cymru. In 1966, Gwynfor Evans won his famous victory in Carmarthen, to become the first-ever Plaid Cymru Member of Parliament. The advocates of Britishness, cunningly led by George Thomas, the Labour Welsh Secretary of State, devised a ploy to counteract the resurgence of Welshness. The eldest son of the Queen of England was sent for a few weeks to learn a smattering of Welsh and fragments of Welsh history in Aberystwyth before being invested as the Prince of Wales at a ceremony in Caernarfon in 1969. In contrast to the many exciting victories of the 1960s on behalf of oppressed peoples and nations, at the end of such a memorable decade Wales suffered the indignity of having to celebrate a blatant falsehood. Wales's last rightful prince was Llywelyn; he had been slain in 1282, and his head publicly displayed in London by a triumphant Edward I, an ancestor of Prince Charles.

Meanwhile, on the cultural front, Wales had been mourning the loss of one of its foremost poets. Dylan Thomas had died in New York on 9 November 1953. In August 1958 the Carmarthenshire Community Council sponsored a Dylan Thomas Festival in Laugharne, where in 1949 Dylan and his family had finally settled to live in The Boat House. The Laugharne Players, a company of amateur actors drawn mostly from the county of Carmarthen, performed *Under Milk Wood* in a marquee during a week-long festival. From the outset it was intended as a triennial festival; consequently the 1961 production was followed by another in 1964. Then, the director, an established theatre and television Welsh language dramatist, Gwynne D. Evans, invited me to consider translating *Under Milk Wood* into Welsh. As I had played the part of the First Voice from the beginning, the play was very familiar to me, and all the characters, directed so sensitively by Gwynne and played so enthusiastically by an experienced team of actors, had become my fond acquaintances. I accepted the challenge. *Dan y Wenallt* was first performed in Talacharn on Friday 4 August 1967 as part of the fourth triennial Dylan Thomas Festival. After reflecting on its favourable reception it was planned to stage further performances in the 1970 Laugharne festival, but that festival never took place. Significantly, however, *Dan y Wenallt* was performed at the 1968 Barry National Eisteddfod, bringing Dylan's work, for the very first time, into this major Welsh language festival.

Back in 1950, what has come to be known as the 'Welsh rule' was first adopted at the Caerffili National Eisteddfod, and the Eisteddfod has adhered to the rule without exception to the present day. During the 1940s, after a period of deliberation, it was decided by the governing body that the National Eisteddfod existed in order to celebrate and nurture the Welsh language. In 1950, the National Eisteddfod was invited to Caerffili, an anglicized area, on that very basis. There was some opposition to the Welsh rule, some of it ferocious. Ness Edwards, the local Labour Member of Parliament and President of the Day on the last Saturday of the festival, deliberately broke the rule by delivering his speech in English. He had initially intended to address his audience bilingually but in the end he decided not only to confine himself to English, but also to specifically attack the Welsh rule. This reactionary attitude is symptomatic of what could have happened from 1950 to the present day. English as the stronger language would have challenged the weaker Welsh for more and more attention and status in the deliberations of the Eisteddfod, effectively nullifying its *raison d'être*. To allow English to be used as an official language at the Eisteddfod would be as absurd as to sing *Hen Wlad Fy Nhadau*, the national anthem of Wales, in an English translation when the one strong aspiration expressed in the very last line is 'O bydded i'r hen iaith barhau' ('Oh may the old language endure')! Due to the Caerffili revolution, the Eisteddfod has been accepted over the last sixty-odd years as a celebration of literature, music, drama and visual arts through the medium of the Welsh language. But it is also a celebration for the whole of Wales where Welsh learners and non-Welsh speakers are encouraged by various means to enjoy the occasion. Over 150,000 visitors came through the turnstiles at the 2013 Denbigh National Eisteddfod.

When *Dan y Wenallt* was accepted as part of the official programme of the 1968 Barry National Eisteddfod, yet another bridge was built between the two main official languages of Wales. It would have been a cultural shock for D. J. Thomas, who had denied his son the opportunity to speak Welsh, to have seen his son's work celebrated in a festival specifically held to promote the use of Welsh. (It should be noted that at the beginning of the twentieth century Welsh was not an official language in Wales. Consequently the inferior status of Welsh had led the majority of the people of Wales to regard it as a hindrance rather than an asset; people who aspired to 'get on in the world' should not be lumbered with the burden of having to learn a dying language.)

But to return to the Laugharne triennial festivals, the scheduled festival for 1970 was never held. The sponsors, Carmarthenshire Community Council, decided to bring the festival forward to 1969 in order to make it part of the celebrations of the investiture of the Prince of Wales. I refused to take the part of the First Voice in the English performances, but, more significantly, I refused permission to perform *Dan y Wenallt*. I was determined that the 'community of Llaregyb' that had regained its Welshness should not tamely surrender it again in order to enhance Britishness. Such a surrender would have undone the whole purpose of the exercise.

Dan y Wenallt was published in 1967 by Gwasg Gomer; this was followed in 1992 by a new edition which included illustrations from the cartoon film version produced by S4C. It has also been broadcast on Radio Cymru and produced on stage on numerous occasions, including one national tour. As part of the 2014 Dylan Thomas centenary celebrations Gwasg Gomer has published a new version, specifically based on the Davies/Maud definitive edition, with an introduction by Walford Davies.

I pointedly use the word 'version' because I do not regard *Dan y Wenallt* as a translation of *Under Milk Wood*. In an appendix to his *Orpheus: A version of Rilke's 'Die Sonette an Orpheus'* (Faber and Faber, 2006) Don Paterson discusses the difference between a translation and a version:

> A translation tries to remain true to the original words and their relations ... It glosses the original, but does not try to replace it. Versions, however, are trying to be poems in their own right; while they have the original to serve as detailed ground-plan and elevation, they are trying to build themselves a robust home in a new country, in its vernacular architecture, with local words for its brick and local music for its mortar ... Charles Simic once memorably remarked that poems are translations from the silence. For a version to be any kind of real poem, it must first reinhabit that extra-linguistic silence the original poem once itself enjoyed ...
>
> *Orpheus*, 73–5

A translation simply explains and interprets the original; it does not attempt to replace it. *Dan y Wenallt* is not a translation but another version of *Under Milk Wood*. It tries to be a 'play for voices' in its own right. That is why to call *Dan y Wenallt* 'better than the original', as some well-meaning critics have done, is an irrelevance.

The very first stage direction in *Under Milk Wood* is 'Silence'. It is the silence before the artistic creative event. In that silence I heard a community awakening from dreaming in Welsh (like the milkman in *Quite Early One Morning*). I decided to break the silence by giving that community the ability to realize those dreams; I heard a community suddenly stirred by its newfound ability to communicate in Welsh, to remember, love, laugh, chatter, sing, cry, to live life to the full in Welsh. And I decided to bring the characters to life by giving them a specific dialect; it was my very own Sir Gâr (Carmarthenshire) dialect. I regarded this as a justifiable choice, since the main inspiration for the play, Talacharn, is in Sir Gâr. In that sense it became my community. And I heard and saw it growing in its self-confidence to demand that Welsh be recognized as an official language in Wales. And consequently, I saw my community adopting a zero tolerance of any tokenism regarding both the Welsh language and Welsh nationhood. That is why I urged my community to reject the political cynicism of the Charles Investiture.

Languages, like their users, have their strengths and weaknesses. The process of creating a version should at times involve taking advantage of the strength of one language over another's weakness. Here is one instance of my taking such an advantage. In the prologue to *Under Milk Wood* the Narrator says: 'Time passes. Listen. Time passes'. The idea of listening to the passage of time reminded me of the Welsh idiom, 'mae amser yn cerdded' (time is walking). Moreover, I was also reminded of the Welsh language's advantage over English in the availability of words for the chronology of days. In English there are only three – yesterday, today, tomorrow – whereas in Welsh there are six: echdoe, doe, heddiw, yfory, trennydd, tradwy (literally translated: the day before yesterday, yesterday, today, tomorrow, the day after tomorrow and the day after the day after tomorrow). Since the Narrator invites us to listen to the 'walk of time', five of the six words were included in order to enhance the sound and rhythm of the steady tread of time.

Following the decision to locate the play in Sir Gâr, the dialect sometimes produced interesting nuances of meaning. One such example was interpreting the meaning of Captain Cat's commentary: 'Who's that talking by the pump? Mrs Floyd and Boyo talking flatfish. What can you talk about flatfish?' My interpretation of 'talking flatfish' was that it was a chatter about nothing in particular, an insubstantial exchange. My Welsh word for such an insubstantiality is 'fflwcs'. ('Pwy sy'n cloncan ar bwys y pwmp? Mrs Ffloyd a Dai Di-ddim yn trafod fflwcs. Beth all dyn weud am fflwcs?') What I did not know at the time was that the Welsh word for 'flatfish' in Llansaint – a village in the same county as Talacharn – is 'fflwcs'! I often wonder whether Dylan knew this.

It is a matter of conjecture how much Welsh Dylan knew, and, more specifically, his knowledge of Welsh literature, especially of the *cynghanedd* tradition. *Singing in Chains*, by Mererid Hopwood (Gwasg Gomer, 2004), provides an excellent introduction to the artform of *cynghanedd*. The title, taken from the last line of 'Fern Hill', signifies the nature of *cynghanedd*. The word simply means 'harmony'. As a musician has to learn the rules of the craft of harmonizing before composing a musical multipart piece, similarly a poet wishing to write in *cynghanedd* would first have to learn the metrical rules of the craft. Some would argue that rules stifle creativity. But on the other hand, once the rules are mastered by an artist, as Mererid Hopwood says, 'it is a discipline that liberates the creative spirit. It does not hold this spirit back. On the contrary, it gives it wings' (*Singing in Chains*, xii).

Dylan seems to have stumbled accidentally upon the very nature of *cynghanedd* in the last line of 'Fern Hill'. There is no evidence that he acquainted himself, as did Gerard Manley Hopkins, with the rules of *cynghanedd*. (Hopkins learned Welsh in order to gain a thorough understanding of the mysteries of the unique artform.) On the other hand, Dylan's poetry is often coloured by a style similar to the strict metre construct of *cynghanedd*. The meticulous use of rhyme and the conscious search for alliteration often provide the poems with a musicality and a rhythm akin to *cynghanedd*. In the *Prologue* poem to *The Collected Poems*, the 102 lines have an intricate rhyming pattern whereby the first line rhymes with the last, the second line with the penultimate line and so on until the very middle of the poem is a rhyming couplet. Its form is reminiscent of the *cywydd*, one of the most popular measures of *cynghanedd*, which consists of a series of rhyming couplets, with alternate accented and unaccented seven-syllable lines.

Numerous lines of *cynghanedd* are found in Dylan's poems. In *Singing in Chains* Mererid Hopwood explains the meanings of the technical Welsh terms for the different types of *cynghanedd* I have listed in the following selection:

Where blew a flower may a flower no more (*cynghanedd sain gadwynog*)
Weighed in rock shroud is my proud pyramid (*cynghanedd sain gadwynog*)
My world was christened in a stream of milk (*cynghanedd draws*)
Though the town below lay leaved with October blood (*cynghanedd sain*)
Do not go gentle into that good night (*cynghanedd draws*)
Nor heed my craft or art (*cynghanedd draws*)
When the morning was waking over the war (*cynghanedd sain*)
To the burn and turn of time (*cynghanedd sain*)
Oh as I was young and easy in the mercy of his means (*cynghanedd sain*)
Though I sang in my chains like the sea (*cynghanedd draws*)

Since the last line of 'Fern Hill' is both a description and also an example of *cynghanedd*, in my Welsh version I felt obliged to offer the last line in *cynghanedd*: 'er i mi ganu yn fy nghadwyni fel y don' (*Nawr*, 101). It has been my privilege to publish, in the same volume, Welsh versions of 'A Visit to Grandpa's', 'Do Not Go Gentle Into That Good Night', 'After The Funeral', *Quite Early One Morning* and *Return Journey* (abridged). My versions of 'Once It Was The Colour of Saying', 'And Death Shall Have No Dominion' and 'The Hunchback In The Park' have been published in my latest book of poems *Cymanfa* (Gomer, 2014).

In my Welsh version of 'A Visit to Grandpa's', the ability of Dylan's grandfather to speak Welsh is restored. The visit's location was the village of Johnstown on the outskirts of Caerfyrddin (Carmarthen), where D. J. Thomas had been born and bred in a Welsh-speaking home. It is a fact that his father did not deny D. J. the ability to speak Welsh. My Welsh version of the short story re-establishes that fact. On the other hand, in my Welsh version of 'Do Not Go Gentle Into That Good Night', I have imagined Dylan pleading with his father in Welsh, a verbal exchange deliberately denied him by his father. The child Dylan was even sent to elocution classes in order to erase all traces of a Welsh accent! The irony is that this Welsh language exchange in my version never took place. But it prompts me to ask this question: had Dylan Thomas been given the ability to speak Welsh, would it have added another significant dimension to his work, as it has done to the works of the likes of R. S. Thomas and Emyr Humphries?

Part of the fascination of the centenary celebrations is that there are so many unanswered questions still to be asked concerning Dylan's work. Although my question will inevitably have to remain unanswered, I cannot avoid asking it time and time again. It has as haunting an attraction as Dylan's final couplet of 'Should lanterns shine':

The ball I threw while playing in the park
Has not yet reached the ground.

Drifting with Dylan

Owen Sheers

For the last two days a succession of poets have sat down to speak with me, often with admiration and sometimes surprise, about the poetry of Dylan Thomas. All of them held copies of his *Collected Poems* as they spoke. Each of those copies was different, the changing fonts and artwork testament to the enduring appeal of a poet who, despite the obscurity of much of his work – or perhaps because of it – has always, somewhere, at some time, found a popular readership.

For some of the poets, the books they held were editions from their school days, the poems inside annotated in their teenage hands. Beside a stanza of 'Fern Hill', a younger Jo Shapcott had written a note on how the poem's accumulation of 'ands' gifted it the tone of a child's remembered storytelling. A younger Simon Armitage, meanwhile, sitting in a bedroom in Yorkshire, had attempted to boil Thomas's percussive poems down to meaning, labeling their margins with the fundamentals of life: 'love', 'birth', 'death'.

The poets were all talking to me as contributors to a documentary I'm making about Dylan Thomas's poetry; about, as much as possible, the poems rather than the poet. The note of surprise surfacing through many of their comments betrayed a consistent trait of rediscovery – a reappreciation, decades later, for the craft and daring behind the poems that had once captivated them as teenagers.

I say once, because with Thomas, it seems, the captivation on first exposure to his acoustically seductive poems is often followed by a drift. He is a poet who kick-starts the engines of countless young readers and writers, only for many of them to ride off into the distance without him. Having been infected by him with words and what they can do, they leave Thomas, often in search of a poetry more directly inherited from spoken speech, with less octane in its performance and more lived experience in its veins.

Intoxication is not love, and to meet the poems of Dylan Thomas as a teenager is a heady mix, the potency of which can't be sustained indefinitely. Here are poems of extraordinary emotional immediacy, more visionary communication than description, which move us as a melody might: without full narrative understanding, but with all the force and power of our instinctive tides. They are poems of such richness that only so many can be taken at once.

With other poets, reading a succession of their poems is often to hear their voices gather depth and timbre, each poem drawing you further into their idiolect and vision. But with Thomas his poems were written to stand alone, as if each had always existed, not created but discovered. To read more than three or four in a row can, therefore, be a frustrating experience, a movement from amazement at the penetration of his work, to a creeping sense of the craft becoming crafty. From being moved, to feeling the poet doing the moving. With increased familiarity there is an apparent devaluation of originality. Never, it should be said, in relation to the poetry of others, but only ever in relation to Thomas's other poems. With Thomas his strengths are also often his weaknesses, and this is a case in point. The distinctiveness of his voice is why we go to him. But it can also be why we turn away, as if such elemental, sonorous music should be a rare ore, and to mine it repeatedly is to push both our, and the poet's, luck.

So I understand why lovers of Thomas tend to fall for him, then drift from him. But I also understand why they come back. And why, like the poets who spoke with me for the documentary, the nature of their appreciation might alter over the years. For me, returning to Thomas as an adult was to see anew the craftsmanship of poems I'd originally received as fluid, spontaneous outbursts of language. It was to appreciate the intimate work of his syllabic structures, the patterns of his rhymes and half-rhymes and the fabrics of assonance and consonance that weave sails of sound from his words. Someone once said – maybe even Thomas himself – that he wrote 'at the speed of a glacier'. And this, I think, is one of the pleasures of returning to Thomas after time away from his voice. To witness, especially after you've tried working in words yourself, the skilfulness with which he translates that glacial speed of composition into the rhythmic pulse and drive of the finished poem.

Unlike Jo Shapcott or Simon Armitage, I was never taught Dylan Thomas at school – it was another Thomas, R. S., who first excited my mind to poetry – but it still feels as if he's always been there, right from the early days of my reading life. An oscillating presence, sometimes waning, then swelling back into significance. Which is, I think, the best relationship to have with Thomas. He was, after all, a tidal poet, a poet of the estuary's daily pull and shift. So to have him wash in and out of my poetic life has always felt appropriate.

But like the tide, however many times I send him away, he always returns. Often it's been external influences that have brought him back. Being asked to read 'Fern Hill' at a young friend's funeral; finding myself on the Carmarthenshire coast, my mind suddenly occupied by 'heron-priested' shores and 'palavers of birds'; or requests from one of the anniversaries that still circle about his life and his work.

At other times though, it's been me who's returned to him, and I hope for the best of reasons too. Simply because there is something in his poems that feeds an elemental part of us; something we don't find elsewhere, however far we roam and graze in the world of poetry. A unique, visceral and musical voice, speaking not so much about intimate truths of human nature, as truths about what it means to *be* human; to be creatures of apperception, to be alive and dying. A bardic voice, in the truest sense, singing, via Thomas's 'bone island', the songs of us all. A voice, as Louis MacNeice once said, describing his own first exposure to it in the 1930s, that was 'astonishingly new and yet went back to the oldest of our roots – roots which had long been ignored, written off, or simply forgotten'. Eighty years later, and a hundred years after his birth, for all our drifting away and back to him, Thomas's poems are, somehow, still here, still new, and still reminding us of what we've forgotten.

Dylan Thomas: Music and Truth

Gillian Clarke

My copy of the *Collected Poems of Dylan Thomas* is the 1955 hardback edition. The Author's Note is dated November 1952. By the time I bought it, the poet was two years dead. I wrote my name, Gillian K. Williams, on the first clear leaf of the book in my best schoolgirl handwriting, in blue ink, with my Conway Stuart fountain pen. The book today is slightly worn, much read, and puzzled over, the first collection of contemporary poetry I ever bought. The paper cover of the *Collected* is slightly dog-eared but intact, and the pages, darkened at the outer edges, still bear the few pale pencil marks, messages to myself sent all those years ago.

In June 1955 I was just eighteen, had left school and was preparing for my first term reading English at Cardiff University. Some years earlier I had listened, enthralled, to a production of *Under Milk Wood* on the BBC Welsh Home Service. I remembered then how, a year or two earlier, my father, a sound engineer with the BBC in Cardiff, had come home and talked of meeting a poet that day who was a young genius who had brought beauty, chaos and careless manners into the studio. I remember him describing one such incident to my mother. The poet had spilt a glass of beer over himself, and my father, who was six feet tall, happened to have a spare pair of trousers in his office. Dylan, five foot seven, 'tall for a Welshman', as he somewhere described himself, had to fold over the turn-ups many times in order to walk.

By the time my father took me to a stage performance of the 'play for voices' in a Cardiff theatre, the words had already begun to take their place in my mind: phrases, sentences, sequences of cadence accented like the speech of my paternal grandmother and aunts in south-west Wales. Both the language of the narrator's speech and the way the characters spoke carried in precisely recorded detail the tragedy, comedy and banality of life around them in much the same way that my father's family gossiped, giggled, complained and quarrelled at home in Cardiff, or Carmarthenshire, or on the farm in north Pembrokeshire. Never until then had I recognized my country in a work of literature, heard great poetry spoken with a Welsh accent, or encountered the English words of a Welsh writer. There was a 'proper' way to write, and Welsh-English was not thought appropriate except as caricature. My education had taught me that all great poetry was the work of dead Englishmen. In the cinema Welsh characters were portrayed as 'thieving gypsies' or police constables, never as ordinary people, never as heroes, never normally, bloodily human. None featured in stories or poems in children's literature. I and my people were invisible. The radio broadcast of *Under Milk Wood* was a revelation to me, and it caused a stir in the listening audience. It opened a door between Wales and the world.

What those characters in *Under Milk Wood* did was voice the innermost thoughts, guilty secrets, shames and desires of the inhabitants of the town of Llareggub in voices that spoke as my own tribe did. Lonely people, Captain Cat, and Rosie Probert, Myfanwy Price alone in her bed in Cockle Row dreaming of her lover, Mog Edwards, the 'draper mad with love', their dilemmas sad and funny so you laugh and cry at the familiar humanity of it all, and reader, listener, whether Welsh or no, could laugh at finding their own slightly ridiculous selves in the poetry, whoever they were, wherever they lived, however they spoke.

On a recent journey, as the London train pulled out of Carmarthen, the train manager announced a welcome over the tannoy that was way beyond essential information and in a manner so poetic, nuanced, musical that I caught the eye of a fellow passenger and smiled, and we both said together, 'The Reverend Eli Jenkins!'. There was something of the 'We are not wholly bad or good / Who live our lives under Milk Wood' about the manner of the announcement. The cadences of rural Carmarthenshire, which sounded the depths of the poet's imagination at the time when he wrote *Under Milk Wood*, endure in the aural harmony of ordinary west Wales speech today. As the train curved out of the station that day and along the wide estuary of the Tywi and the shining sands, mudflats and currents of his landscape, there beside the train stretched 'the heron-priested shore', with its cockle-pickers, its dogs biting the waves. Dylan took from and gave back to the landscape and the language, until the place speaks the poetry as much as the poetry voices the place. More importantly, by being true to the local and particular, his words tell not simply local but universal human truths. Auden's famous words surely apply to Dylan Thomas, that it is 'a poet's hope to be, / like some valley cheese, / local but prized everywhere'.

So I was startled awake to the world of contemporary poetry, on hearing *Under Milk Wood* for the first time back in the fifties, because what I heard, on the radio and off the page, was the authentic sound of a world I knew, but heightened and transfigured into word-music. The non-Welsh reader could trust it the way I trusted James Joyce's account in *Portrait of the Artist as a Young Man*, in *Dubliners* and in *Ulysses*. It is clear Dylan had read Joyce, and was encouraged by those texts to trust his own ear for the voices he heard in his own local version of the world. Because I knew this language, knew it to be authentically, accurately recorded, I knew that here was a version of the real world made familiar by the sound of common speech, yet transformed by the power of poetry. As in the earlier language of Joyce, we trust it because it is true, local, non-standard English, modified by Dylan's perfect ear for the music of words. We believe it, whoever and wherever we are. Because it is true to life, it is universal.

Is it a play? Is it a poem? It seems obvious to me now: it is a long poem for voices, and radio its perfect medium. I once heard a critic condemn it as 'a shallow little melodrama'. I pondered this for a few years, my young judgment shaken. Older, I know the critic was wrong. Powerful writers, especially those who write at a moment of change, a transition of style, who alter the way a generation reads, hears and writes, create their work fearlessly as if no one were listening. They tell us the truth, not mere factual truth, but a truth that the writer hears, observes, and that rises from the subconscious mind and is not trying to impress. This is not writing a few feet distant from a clean white page, filtered by education, the rules of grammar and the polite front parlour of poetry. It is writing from the gut. Caution and the conscious brain are not on guard. Prevailing fashion does not man the gates of the imagination. Edna O'Brien has said that she writes as if no one is going to read her work. Another poet who influenced Dylan, Gerard Manley Hopkins, assumed that his own work would never be published, and that only one or two friends would ever read it. It is the power of such fearless focus that gives us writers like Hopkins, Joyce, Dylan Thomas and, more recently, John McGahern. We are lucky to be allowed in. We are guests in the writer's attic. We are not admiring the cleverness of their conscious craft, but overhearing them talk to themselves in the privacy of the page. Such writers work with the word in the white fire of the mind, and dare to place on the page those fragments that the imagination catches when the conscious self is not standing guard to censor every word.

Dylan Thomas was born into a community where, several generations earlier, and in past centuries, the people had learned to read English through the means of the King James Bible, and an even earlier generation had become literate through the translation of the Bible into Welsh. The Bible, which had brought literacy to Dylan's ancestors, had been the only book available to most people, and its language and stories continued as familiar currency in the Nonconformist community in which he was raised. It had provided myth, verse, word-music, phrase and metaphor for generations of his people, and his poetry is enriched by the easy use of its language. The opening phrase of *Under Milk Wood*, which I heard that long-ago night on the radio, is biblical in its reference and intonation: 'To begin at the beginning'. It and the ensuing paragraph are quoted often enough to have become part of the contemporary mind, remembered by all listeners and readers:

'It is spring, moonless night in the small town, starless and bible-black',

words almost sung under the breath like a lullaby to the final words of the sentence:

'the sloeblack, slow, black, crowblack, fishingboat-bobbing sea'.

The word-play lights up that famous opening speech, the joining of words, 'sloeblack', 'crowblack'; the discovered double meanings in familiar words, as in 'the lulled and dumbfound town', silent but overheard in its dreams, discovered in its darkness, 'the organplaying wood'; the double entendre of 'the jolly, rodgered sea'. Listen also to the *cynghanedd* of 'widows weeds', 'slow, asleep', and 'salt and silent black', a familiar poetic in a Welsh-speaking community where every child would be taught to recite in the local *eisteddfod*.

Cynghanedd is a traditional component of Welsh poetry at least fifteen centuries old, and still a powerful music in contemporary Welsh poetry. It is based on alliteration, not of a single repeated consonant, but of several repeated in sequence. Keats achieved a moment of *cynghanedd* by chance, in 'faery lands / forlorn'. Listen to f, r, l, n repeated. Poetry was an oral art for centuries, so it is what you hear, not what you read that counts in *cynghanedd*. The poetry of Dylan Thomas was above all oral. It is word-music. It was second nature to him to steal the music of the two tongues he heard around him.

From the 'fishingboatbobbing sea' until the closing paragraph/verse beginning 'The thin night darkens. A breeze from the creased water sighs the streets close under Milk waking Wood', I was a bewitched teenager shaken by words that seemed to me then to be the very sound of the time and place called here and now, jewelled by those old references and rhythms still familiar to us in my own generation.

The poet's Note, dated November 1952, which prefaces the *Collected Poems* declares, at first without irony, though with a note of irony tossed in at the end: 'These poems, with all their crudities, doubts, and confessions, are written for the love of Man and in praise of God, and I'd be a damn fool if they weren't.' This might seem to be a surprising statement coming from such an irreverent person as Dylan, yet there is much textual evidence to prove his respect for the sacred. The poems are rich with biblical echoes, allusions, and the poetry of hymns and sermons, unsurprising in the culture and education that raised the poet, son of a grammar school senior English master, in the west Wales of the time, but there are times when he is not just quoting, but believing. Much of the poetry has a quality of awe, 'love of Man' and 'praise of God' that lights the language and lifts the verse. He stole imagery and language from everywhere, and his poetry had treasure to draw upon, not only in the colourful speech of his people, but in the still-powerful traditions of eloquence in Nonconformist preaching, the ancient culture of the Eisteddfod, and of fourteen centuries of Welsh poetry. It was all grist to the poet's mill.

The Author's Prologue to *Collected Poems*, written in 1952, warns the reader of what is to come. Nothing I had read had prepared me for this wild weather of words, so *Under Milk Wood* was a kind of initiation:

> This day winding down now
> At God speeded summer's end
> In the torrent salmon sun,
> In my seashaken house
> On a breakneck of rocks

English Literature studies at school and university led my generation steadily through its history from Beowulf to Edward Thomas – who had also shaken off the shackles of the prevailing style for his generation. I now knew the rules could be broken, must be broken now and again so that poetry can renew itself, while holding true to the music and the centuries-long journey of poetry. Word-music and the lovely muscular syntax of English are essential, or it is not poetry. Dylan rarely loses either. Rules are broken by painters, sculptors, composers in every age. Even as artists were stepping out of the frame, Dylan Thomas was shaking apart the sentence, making new words, giving familiar words new work to do, and finding word-links to surprise us into seeing his world – the language of poetry should always surprise – and all this within a sound-frame of music, iambics, internal rhyme and end-rhyme, often influenced by *cynghanedd,* that particular Welsh use of alliteration, which he surely heard in the *eisteddfodau* of his childhood, and which he certainly took in later through the poetry of Gerard Manley Hopkins, who learned Welsh and studied *cynghanedd.* Hopkins's poem in praise of Christ, 'The Windhover', begins:

> I caught this morning morning's minion, king-
> dom of daylight's dauphin, dapple-dawn-drawn Falcon, in his riding
> Of the rolling level underneath him steady air, and striding

Note the consonantal sequences of *cynghanedd* in 'morning morning's minion', and 'steady air – striding'. These lines, and sounds, are surely in Dylan's head as he writes 'claws' and 'gallows' (the c echoing the g) in the following:

> Over Sir John's hill,
> The hawk on fire hangs still;
> In a hoisted cloud, at drop of dusk, he pulls to his claws
> And gallows, up the rays of his eyes the small birds of the bay
> And the shrill child's play
> Wars

The rhyme continues to the stanza's last word, which rhymes 'heron' with 'headstone'.

The poem that opens his *Collected Poems*, and the lines that open that poem, warned the eighteen-year-old me of what he was about to do with language:

> I see the boys of summer in their ruin
> Lay the gold tithings barren

The scene is agricultural, the 'gold tithings' acres of ripe corn, the tenth part of a harvest due to the parish, laid waste. That part was familiar enough. It is both literal description and metaphor. Then:

> Setting no store by harvest, freeze the soils;
> There in their heat the winter floods
> Of frozen loves they fetch their girls,
> And drown the cargoed apples in their tides.

Dylan rips up the picture and remakes it, reloading familiar words with new meaning, images from Carmarthenshire's autumn fields, or in any rural place at the end of summer, 'setting no store by harvest', 'tithings', 'store', 'the cargoed apples' (loaded into the trailer behind a tractor, or maybe floating in a river and borne downstream), 'the boys of summer' who squander their harvest on the pursuit of pleasure. He rips up the sentence, as Hopkins does, yet, as in the work of the expressionist painter, we think we 'understand' it all the same.

Not only in the dialogue in *Under Milk Wood*, but in the seashaken, breakneck-of-rocks language of his poetry and prose too, I find something of Welsh-English about it, especially the breakneck parts, the passion and the pace. Speak fast, speak fierce. Turn grammar upside-down. I recently heard of a south Wales mother calling an errant child with 'Come you by 'ere or you'll go 'ome lost'.

Out of all the wildfire of his creativity, *Under Milk Wood*, the stories and the poetry at its best bring music and truth, and truth and music. The poems perplexed me when I first read them, and some of them still do today. They are not always successful. They work the language to its limits, stretching it until it breaks. The early poems are trying what has not been tried, and the poet often loses his reader. Yet others are among the most powerful, beautiful examples of the music and truth of poetry, and even in those early poems, after struggling with the confusion of 'When once the twilight locks no longer / Locked in the long worm of my finger' I come to 'Only When the October Wind', and I am with him to the end in his list of weathers and sea and natural things that excite him into poetry. Here the excitement is more powerful than grammar. This early poem presages the great poems that were to come later: 'Fern Hill' that closes *Deaths and Entrances,* and the group of fine poems from his last collection, *In Country Sleep* – poems such as 'Over Sir John's Hill', 'Poem on His Birthday', and probably the finest villanelle ever written, 'Do Not Go Gentle Into That Good Night'.

These poems, and perhaps a dozen others – too short, safe and mean a list, in my opinion – are those usually quoted as his great poems, and most of the rest are left to silence. They are 'difficult'. However, I would like to share my admiration for a poem from his first collection, *18 Poems*. 'Before I Knocked' is musically formal, lyrical, syntactically conventional, lit by awe and also irreverence, and above all it surprises. It begins 'Before I knocked and let love enter / With liquid hands tapped on the womb', with the lovely nuanced meaning of 'tapped' after 'liquid', and continues with this perfect word-music:

> I who was shapeless as the water
> That shaped the Jordan near my home
> Was brother to Mnetha's daughter
> And sister to the fathering worm

'My father in his dome' in the next stanza is, of course, God, and father. Is the one 'shapeless as the water' the just-conceived Dylan himself? I assumed so until I reached the final stanza, when the question is answered, and I read the whole poem again in its light. This child was 'born of flesh and ghost', and was 'mortal to the last / Long breath that carried to my father / The message of his dying christ'. He closes the poem with a message for

> You who bow down at cross and altar,
> Remember me and pity Him
> Who took my flesh and bone for armour
> And doublecrossed my mother's womb.

The final brilliant line is a shock, the visual image and nuanced meaning of 'doublecrossed' powerful indeed. In the *Collected Poems,* 'Before I Knocked' immediately precedes 'The force that through the green fuse drives the flower / Drives my green age', his famous poem about the green energy of youth, the life force which also drives ageing, and death. So one of his finest and best-known poems was also one of his earliest, one of the *18 Poems*.

Under Milk Wood woke me up. The poet was one of our own. The poems, to which I came a few years later, were a brave new world, and their power to surprise and inspire has endured. My re-reading, after too long away, has dazzled me again.

Reading Dylan Thomas

Griff Rhys Jones

I got to know Dylan Thomas about ten years ago. It was at a reading.

I knew him of course – slightly. I had read his best-regarded poems. I had watched several versions of *Under Milk Wood* (under those ever-present down-lights), and my first when I was at school more than forty-five years ago. I had even helped anthologize him. I was never 'taught' him though. I never knew him. I never really made his acquaintance.

There is something great and lasting about poems we are force-fed when we are young. We never forget the taste. I wish I had learned Dylan Thomas by rote then. We scarcely understand how fresh the white pages of our unclut-tered brains are until we try to learn poetry in old age. I have boned up on stuff recently: whole poems and plays, scripts, 'pieces to camera' and even patter songs, but they have all sluiced through the drain holes of my memory almost immediately after use. Only the mother's milk of poetry seems to stick to me forever. Bits of *Hamlet* adhere like burrs. But what about Dylan?

My passing knowledge of Dylan Thomas was put to the test. Geraldine James had asked me to read aloud at St John's in Smith Square. Was it a Christmas event? I can't imagine. Can't remember. If it was, why was I asked to read 'Do Not Go Gentle …'? Perhaps Geraldine suspected that people should be encouraged to overeat and die pulling crackers, but none the less, the poem that I knew of but had never read properly was sent over.

Now I had to read it out loud, to a big room. It's a bitter test, of both the reader and the poet. Here was a place, a London church, and like a lot of London churches rather too big for its purpose. Here was a nave and a great domed ceiling. Here was a need for a measured firm delivery. And I started off trying to get a handle.

'Do not go *gentle* in to that good *night*'.
Nope.
'Do not *go* gentle into that *good* night'.
Nope.

If you are reading poetry aloud in an echoing vault, you need to know how the poem works. What are its bones? You can't just deliver it conversationally, as some people, particularly academics, might prefer. It just becomes a blur. In a big space you are forced to partly 'sing'. It has to become an incantation to overcome those echoes. And the poem needs to be good. You need to become a bit of an actor laddie and you have to enjoy those sounds and the rhythms.

So I worked it through. The beat seemed to be on the *not*. It must be. To get the rhythm, it needed to be marked. That decision changed the emphasis and started to unravel the strengths and underlying framework – and, indeed, the genius – of the poem.

Most poets, when they read their own poems, do tend to emphasize the inner music of the poem, the beat they felt, the rhythm that they chose, the structure of the thrust of the poem. Sometimes they sound daft doing it. (Listen to crackly recordings of Tennyson.) But they made this frozen music and they want to highlight the structure that they wrought into it. Dylan Thomas was no exception. 'A little fruity' is one of the kinder descriptions of his reading. Clearly he loved sound. He revelled in orotundity. But the cadences are nothing without rhythm and the clackety-clack of the feet tapping through his verse.

Reading this great poem aloud opened it up for me. Like Shakespeare, its meaning became clearer. Gradually it echoed and underscored the sentiment.

The line seems to have five beats, doesn't it? But they are sparingly strung through the words. If I looked forward, I could easily pick it up on the third line, 'Rage, rage ...', where I suddenly heard the insistent drum that is actually there throughout, but it is muscly, demanding and complex – almost tongue-twisting.

'Do *not*' became important. It became emphatic. It needed space somewhere around that early phrase. It defied being swallowed. The poem itself required that the reader took sides. Once I recognized that, then the snare-drum plosive consonants at the end of the first line began doing their work: '... *thattt* good *nightttt*'.

Already, in the first three lines, I needed to swing my tongue into the sounds, and the sounds are there, backing the sense. And the proper fury, the passion of the writer is beginning to ring around the hall. This is the defining quality of poetry. The music is delivered via the words themselves. The argument of the poem (and this poem delivers a really powerful message) is utterly backed up by the underlying tempo.

There is no real mourning, either. The repeating refrain makes it far from elegiac. The song line starts to break through. It becomes a barrel organ of rhythm and rage: life itself barking back at death. 'Rave, rage, bay, late, grave, gay, blaze, pray' – the scattering of those flat 'ay' notes is not random but insistent. They form a skeleton that controls and supports the whole argument.

'Good night' then? Why is it 'good'? The central repeating incantation of the poem has irony, doesn't it? 'Good night' is, after all, a politeness, a 'time for bed', 'off we go' sort of phrase, held up to be contrasted with the black vacancy of death. But it also recognizes the traditional 'good' in itself – heaven is in that 'good' night. Isn't it? Rest is in that 'good' night. Perhaps. But it is a pallid alternative to the rage. 'Good night' is already thick with meaning and possibilities.

Reading this poem aloud, I began to appreciate Dylan's command of his medium. Each idea at the beginning of each refrain is picked up and banged down. Try it. Read it to yourself. Note how the complex heartbeat at the core of this poem lies in each of those opening and defining adjectives. The beat demands that they have to be hammered home and therefore distinguish each class of men. In the fourth line you have to use that '*though*'. It is crucial to the sense that follows. But then we hear the other thoughts. '*Good* men ...' then '*Wild* men ...' then '*Grave* men ...' – the differentiated adjectives, each on the crest of the line, structure the poem. Each one rings out its idea. But Dylan undercuts his own rigid song by the sudden break of the last stanza 'and *you* my father' – where a different, broken timing suddenly trips up the steady repeating bang. It deliberately wrong-foots us and takes us to a new place, like a lump in the throat.

This poem is not just technically complex, it is technically perfect. The villanelle form with its repeated refrain and dancing rhyme is complicated enough to begin with, but this poem plays with a doubly complex structure of rhythm, assonance and sprung rhythm. As I read it I realized that it was masterful. A bossa nova of a poem.

It also hugely accessible. This is a complex and unique philosophical proposal (great poems often are). Here is one that we instantly cleave to. We surrender to this cry. Life requires us to 'burn', 'rave', 'rage', 'dance', 'sing', 'bless', 'curse'. This is vigour and, given the comet-like trail that Dylan himself blazed, here is something of the essence of the man himself. It is such an exciting, vibrant poem. One to secrete, and one that led me on to find out more after that first deep encounter.

He wrote these words on the death of his father, with his own death not more than a year ahead. And if anyone wants Dylan Thomas to be a polite word-painter, a safe, reassuring poet, then they should consider them well. These are the thoughts of a rebel, a defier, a Canute, a howler. These are the words of one who wants to live at extremes: drowning, cursing, raving and blazing.

Do not go gentle into that good night,
Old age should burn and rave at close of day;
Rage, rage against the dying of the light.

Though wise men at their end know dark is right,
Because their words had forked no lightning they
Do not go gentle into that good night,

Good men, the last wave by, crying how bright
Their frail deeds might have danced in a green bay,
Rage, rage against the dying of the light.

Wild men who caught and sang the sun in flight,
And learn, too late, they grieved it on its way,
Do not go gentle into that good night.

Grave men, near death, who see with blinding sight
Blind eyes could blaze like meteors and be gay,
Rage, rage against the dying of the light.

And you, my father, there on that sad height,
Curse, bless, me now with your fierce tears, I pray.
Do not go gentle into that good night.
Rage, rage against the dying of the light.

Contributors

Peter Blake was born in 1932 in Dartford, Kent. He studied at Gravesend School of Art before earning a place at the prestigious Royal College of Art, London in 1956. His love of art flourished as he built up a respectable portfolio of work through extensive travels across Europe and beyond. Inspiration was drawn from his surroundings, influencing much of his work, and he began to produce collages incorporating iconic figures. Alongside these Blake also worked with found objects such as photographs, cigarette packets and matchboxes. The concept of found art was an aspect that excited Blake and the notion of finding beauty within banal everyday objects greatly appealed. In 1983 Peter Blake became a CBE and in 2002 received a knighthood for his services to art. His long and respected career is admirable and his contribution to the art world is truly inspiring. Even today, Blake's work retains its popularity and a contemporary aesthetic is maintained with every new piece created.

William Christie is Professor of English Literature at the University of Sydney and Pro-Dean for Research in the Faculty of Arts and Social Sciences. He is President of the Romantic Studies Association of Australasia and a Fellow of the Australian Academy of the Humanities. As a teenager, he stumbled upon Ralph Maud's edition of the notebook poems of Dylan Thomas in the State Library of New South Wales and, throughout a long career as a scholar and university teacher, has maintained an interest and affection for the poet's work. He joined the Dylan Thomas Society of Australia when it was formed in the 1990s and was for many years its president, which was when his imitation *Under Mulga Wood* was written. He is currently completing a literary life of Dylan Thomas.

Gillian Clarke has been National Poet for Wales since 2008. She is President of Ty Newydd, the Welsh Writers Centre, which she co-founded in 1990. Her recent collection of poems, *Ice*, was shortlisted for the T. S. Eliot Award 2012. In December 2010 she was awarded the Queen's Gold Medal for Poetry, and in 2012 the Wilfred Owen Award.

Trefor Ellis works as a buyer for a large oil company. In his spare time, he sings with the London Welsh Chorale in the tenor section. He was married to Dylan

Thomas's daughter Aeronwy from 1973 until her death in 2009. He has two children, Huw and Hannah, and two grandsons, Oscar and Charlie.

Paul Ferris is a journalist, biographer and writer. He has always worked as a freelance journalist, except for a short period in the early 1950s when he worked for the *Swansea Evening Post*, the same paper Dylan had contributed to 20 years previously. He has written articles for many newspapers and magazines and was the *Observer*'s radio critic for 35 years. His plays and documentaries have appeared on BBC radio and TV. His published books include novels and biographies, among them lives of Freud, and Dylan and Caitlin Thomas.

Jo Furber is Swansea Council's Literature Officer and is based at the Dylan Thomas Centre, where she directs the year-round arts programme and annual Dylan Thomas Festival, and curates its permanent Dylan Thomas Exhibition. She earned an MPhil from Swansea University in 2003, and continues to publish widely; her research interests include contemporary poetry and Dylan Thomas. She has taught English at Swansea University and delivered an Arts Management module on University of Wales Trinity St David's MBA course, and regularly lectures on Dylan Thomas and cultural tourism.

John Goodby holds a Chair in Poetry and Poetics in the Department of English at Swansea University. He is a critic, poet, translator and arts organizer. As an authority on Dylan Thomas, he has edited the new annotated edition of the *Collected Poems* (2014), is author of *The Poetry of Dylan Thomas: Under the Spelling Wall* (2013), and acts as Director of the Dylan Thomas Research Project, as well as advising the British Council, BBC, AHRC, Literature Wales and other bodies marking the centenary of Dylan Thomas's birth. His books of poetry include *Illennium* (Shearsman, 2010), and he was the winner of the 2006 Cardiff International Poetry Competition. He co-organizes the Hay (2009–12) and Alloa (2012) Poetry Jamborees with Lyndon Davies, and in 2011 he founded the Boiled String series of poetry chapbooks.

Paul Jackson is a Senior Lecturer in History at the University of Northampton. He has published a wide range of research on twentieth-century British intellectuals and ideologues, focusing on their interest and connection with fascism. This includes analysing anti-fascist figures such as Dylan Thomas. His publications include the book *Great War Modernisms and 'The New Age' Magazine* (2012), and he is currently writing a new monograph on British neo-Nazism after 1945. Finally, he is also part of the 'Thomas Family', having married Hannah Ellis in 2010.

T. James Jones, whose bardic name is Jim Parc Nest, is a former Archdruid of Wales. He is a published poet and dramatist, and a National Eisteddfod crowned and chaired bard. A native of Newcastle Emlyn, Carmarthenshire, he now lives in Cardiff with his novelist wife, Manon Rhys. He is the foremost translator of Dylan Thomas's poetry and prose into Welsh, the most important of which is his Welsh version of *Under Milk Wood*, *Dan y Wenallt* (Gomer, 2014).

Hilly Janes is a freelance author, editor and journalist. Born and brought up in Gower, South Wales, close to Dylan Thomas's home town of Swansea, she is the daughter of the late Alfred Janes, an artist and close friend of the poet, of whom he made several portraits. While Thomas died before she was born, Hilly learned to love from an early age works like 'Fern Hill', *Under Milk Wood* and *Return Journey*, which reflected the landscapes and characters she grew up with. After the Janeses moved to London in the 1960s they returned to Swansea every year for holidays and to see the close family friends that Thomas and her father had grown up with. An award-winning journalist, Hilly has worked for many national newspapers and magazines as a features editor and writer, with staff posts on *The Times*, the *Independent* and *Prospect* magazine. She lives in London with her husband and two children, but can't stay away from Swansea and Gower for long.

Andrew Lycett is an English biographer and journalist. After studying history at Oxford University, he worked for two decades as a foreign correspondent, specializing in Africa, Asia and the Middle East. Since the mid-1990s he has concentrated on writing biographies. Among his works are lives of Colonel Gadaffi, Ian Fleming, Rudyard Kipling, Dylan Thomas, Sir Arthur Conan Doyle and, most recently, Wilkie Collins. He is a Fellow of the Royal Society of Literature.

Cerys Matthews, singer, songwriter, author and broadcaster, won Gold at the 2013 Radio Academy Awards for her weekly BBC show which she programmes and hosts. Her singalong book 'Hook, Line and Singer' (Penguin, 2013) was a *Sunday Times* bestseller, and 2013 also saw her debut at the Proms at London's Royal Albert Hall. She is a columnist for the world music magazine *Songlines*, a judge for the Dylan Thomas Prize and the Forward Prizes for Poetry 2014, patron of the Dylan Thomas Society and Ballet Cymru and is regularly seen presenting art and culture features for BBC's *The One Show*. Cerys was the founder member of multi-million-selling band Catatonia, sings with Tom Jones on perennial winter favourite 'Baby it's Cold Outside' and is Vice-President of the homeless charity, Shelter. Her best-selling collection of Welsh folk songs 'TIR' (Land) was followed up in 2013 with a sister album, 'Hullabaloo'.

Roger McGough is poet, performance poet, broadcaster, children's author and playwright. He has worked as a teacher, was a member of a comedy, poetry and music trio called The Scaffold whose version of 'Lily The Pink' reached number one in the UK singles chart in 1968. He was also responsible for much of the humorous dialogue in The Beatles' animated film 'Yellow Submarine'. He presents the BBC Radio 4 programme *Poetry Please*. Roger was awarded the CBE in June 2004 and is a patron of the Dylan Thomas 100 festival.

Antony Penrose is the son of the American surrealist, fashion and combat photographer Lee Miller and Roland Penrose, surrealist artist and biographer. He is the director of the Lee Miller Archive and the Penrose Collection located in his parent's former home, Farley Farm House, Chiddingly, now a house museum. He has written numerous books, articles and two plays on the subject of his parents and their associates including *The Lives of Lee Miller* (Thames & Hudson, 1988), *Roland Penrose: The Friendly Surrealist* (Prestel, 2001) and has broadcast on radio and television. He is also a curator of photography and an artist in his own right.

Philip Pullman was born in Norwich in 1946, and educated in England, Zimbabwe, and Australia, before his family settled in North Wales. He received his secondary education at Ysgol Ardudwy, Harlech, and then went to Exeter College, Oxford, to read English. He worked as a teacher, and taught at various Oxford Middle Schools before moving to Westminster College in 1986, where he spent eight years involved in teaching students on the B.Ed. course. He has published nearly twenty books including the children's books *Count Karlstein*, *The Ruby in the Smoke* and *His Dark Materials* trilogy. His books have been honoured by several prizes, including the Carnegie Medal, the Guardian Children's Book Award, and the Whitbread Book of the Year Award – the first time in the history of that prize that it was given to a children's book. In 2002, Philip was recipient of the Eleanor Farjeon Award for children's literature and in 2005 he won the Astrid Lindgren Award.

Griff Rhys Jones was born in Cardiff. He has worked in television in comedy and documentaries as an actor, writer and producer and was recently the executive producer of A Poet in New York, a BBC drama about the death of Dylan Thomas. He has written several books and many TV shows.

Peter Ross was born near Newport, Gwent in 1941. He studied at Newport Art College between 1958–62, and at Bristol between 1962–63. Most of his working life has been spent as an art teacher though he has painted since leaving art college and exhibited widely. In recent years his interests as a painter have veered towards memories and influences from his past including the life and works of Dylan Thomas.

Michael Sheen was born in Newport, Wales, and began his career on stage before making a successful transition to the big screen. He made his West End debut in 1991 opposite Vanessa Redgrave in *When She Danced* and his Broadway debut in 1999 playing Mozart in Peter Hall's revival of *Amadeus*. He won the 2003 London Evening Standard Award for Best Actor for his role in Peter Morgan's *Frost/Nixon*, and was nominated for a BAFTA for his acclaimed portrayal of Kenneth Williams in the BBC's *Fantabulosa!* He has played British Prime Minister Tony Blair in three TV dramas directed by Stephen Frears, and has starred in films including Ed Zwick's *Blood Diamond*, Ridley Scott's *Kingdom of Heaven*, Tim Burton's *Alice in Wonderland* and Woody Allen's *Midnight in Paris*, as well as Ron Howard's film adaptation of *Frost/Nixon* which received an Academy Award nomination for Best Picture. He returned to the London stage in 2011 to play *Hamlet* at the Young Vic directed by Ian Rickson. Michael also created, co-directed and starred in *The*

Passion of Port Talbot, a live three-day continuous event for National Theatre Wales, which netted him and co-director Bill Mitchell a nomination for Best Director for a UK Theatre Award 2011 and was adapted into a film in 2012.

Owen Sheers has written two poetry collections, *The Blue Book* and *Skirrid Hill* (Somerset Maugham Award) and a verse drama, *Pink Mist* (Hay Festival Poetry Medal 2013). His non-fiction includes *The Dust Diaries* (Welsh Book of the Year 2005) and *Calon; A Journey to the Heart of Welsh Rugby*. His novel *Resistance* was translated into ten languages and made into a film in 2011. His work for theatre includes National Theatre of Wales's *The Passion* and *The Two Worlds of Charlie F.* (Amnesty International Freedom of Expression Award). Owen wrote and presented the BBC's *A Poet's Guide to Britain*. He has been a New York Public Library Cullman Fellow and Writer in Residence for the Wordsworth Trust and the Welsh Rugby Union. His most recent novel *I Saw A Man* will be published in 2015.

David N. Thomas was brought up in south Wales. After trials for Swansea Town football club and a stint as an *Evening Post* copy boy, he settled for Balliol, the LSE, and then a bracing apprenticeship on the streets of inner London. He has published widely with Routledge on community development and social welfare. His books on Dylan Thomas include *A Farm, Two Mansions and a Bungalow*, two volumes of *Dylan Remembered* and *Fatal Neglect: Who Killed Dylan Thomas?*, all published by Seren. He lives in Powys, and is working on a book about the poet's afterlife, *Jump Aboard! 1954–2014*.

M. Wynn Thomas is Professor of English and Emyr Humphreys Professor of Welsh Writing in English, CREW (Centre for Research into the English Literature and Language of Wales), Swansea University. He is the author of over 20 books, in Welsh and in English, on the two literatures of Wales and on the poetry of the USA, the latest of which is *R. S. Thomas: Serial Obsessive*. Sometime Visiting Professor at Harvard, he is a Fellow of the British Academy and of the English Association and is Vice-President of the Learned Society of Wales.

Jeff Towns opened Dylan's Bookstore in Swansea in 1970. Jeff spent years locating Dylan Thomas materials and has an extensive personal collection. He has met, and become friends with, many of Dylan Thomas's contemporaries, leading academics, critics and biographers, and handled the archives of some of Dylan's closest friends. Jeff has helped many clients build their own Dylan Thomas collections, as well as building a substantial collection for Kyoto University in Japan and the 'Word & Image' Exhibition in Swansea's Dylan Thomas Centre. He has worked with numerous TV and radio documentary-makers and filmmakers as both a contributor and a consultant. He has toured with a show, 'The Two Dylans', in which he discusses the impact Dylan Thomas had on Bob Dylan and the Beat generation in the 1950s and early 1960s in New York City and beyond. His publications include a previously unknown Thomas poem 'Letter to Loren', four Dylan Thomas walking trail booklets and, most recently, a book about Dylan Thomas's favourite pubs.

Jon Tregenna, born in Llanelli, has TV script-writing credits with the BBC, S4C and ITV. He co-created a re-imagining of *Under Milk Wood* in Laugharne – *Raw Material: Llareggub Revisited* – for National Theatre Wales/BBC (May 2014); wrote an eBook on *Under Milk Wood* for the BBC (Oct 2014), and an update of the same play entitled *Buggerall*. Jon has recently completed his first novel, *No-one Ever Grew Up Wanting To Be A Car Salesman*. He lives in Laugharne, Carmarthhenshire and manages the iconic Brown's Hotel.

George Tremlett sat on the Greater London Council from 1970 to 1986 and left politics to concentrate on selling books and writing. He has written 30 books, 18 of them on rock'n'roll music, several on social themes and *Caitlin: A Warring Absence* (co-authored with Mrs Caitlin Thomas, Secker & Warburg, 1986); *Dylan Thomas: In the Mercy of His Means* (Constable, 1991) and *The Death of Dylan Thomas*, which he wrote with the American brain surgeon James Nashold (Mainstream, 1997). In 1982, Tremlett and his wife Jane settled in Laugharne where they own and run Corran Books.

Daniel G. Williams is Professor of English Literature and Director of the Richard Burton Centre for the Study of Wales at Swansea University. He was educated at the University of East Anglia, Harvard University and Cambridge University (King's College). He is the author of *Ethnicity and Cultural Authority: From Arnold to Du Bois* (Edinburgh University Press, 2006) and *Black Skin, Blue Books: African Americans and Wales* (University of Wales Press, 2012). He has edited *Slanderous Tongues: Essays on Welsh Poetry in English 1970–2005* (Seren, 2010), *Canu Caeth: Affro-Americaniaid a'r Cymry* (Gomer, 2010), co-edited (with Alyce von Rothkirch) *Beyond the Difference: Welsh Literature in Comparative Contexts* (University of Wales Press, 2004), and edited a collection of Raymond Williams's writings, *Who Speaks for Wales? Nation, Culture, Identity* (University of Wales Press, 2003). He is general editor of the Welsh-language cultural studies series 'Safbwyntiau' (2012–) and co-edits (with Kirsti Bohata) the CREW series of monographs 'Writing Wales in English' (both University of Wales Press). He is also editor of a special edition of *Comparative American Studies* on 'The Celtic Nations and the African-Americans' (2010) and a special edition of *Keywords* on 'Raymond Williams in Japan' (2011). He was a Leverhulme Trust funded Visiting Professor at Harvard University in 2012, and Director of the Centre for Research into the Literature and Language of Wales from 2007 to 2010. He is also saxophonist with the jazz-folk sextet Burum, who have recorded two albums: *Alawon: The Songs of Welsh Folk* (Fflach, 2007) and *Caniadau* (Bopa, 2012).

Rowan Williams was born in Swansea in 1950 and educated at Dynevor School. After studying Theology at Cambridge, he did research at Oxford in Russian religious thought, and taught in Yorkshire, Cambridge and Oxford before becoming Bishop of Monmouth in 1992, Archbishop of Wales in 1999 and Archbishop of Canterbury in 2002. He is now Master of Magdalene

College, Cambridge, and Chancellor of the University of South Wales. He has written several books on theology and related subjects and has published four books of poetry.

Clive Woosnam, the son of a coalminer, was born and raised in the Rhondda Valley of South Wales, and loved poetry and choral music from an early age. When schoolteachers replaced coal as the Rhondda's main export, Clive migrated to Sydney to teach at one of its best-known schools, Newington College, for 35 years. He is a founder member of the Dylan Thomas Society of Australia and has been its president for ten years. He has been president of the Sydney Welsh Choir for 21 years, and has been awarded an Order of Australia Medal for his contribution to education and the arts.

Photographers

Lee Miller was painted and photographed by some of the greatest artists of her day, Picasso, Dora Maar, Man Ray, Edward Steichen, and Roland Penrose, and in return she photographed them and some of the greatest moments in the history of the 20th Century. Her modelling career started when she was accidently discovered by Condé Nast in New York. Steichen made her into what we would today call a super model, but she announced she would 'rather make a picture than be one' and went to Paris to study photography with Man Ray. Her photographic career spanned working in Paris, New York and Egypt, before she returned to England with her husband-to-be Roland Penrose and resumed working for Vogue. She became a war correspondent and then, famously, a combat photographer. In the post-war years she continued to photograph her old friends, Picasso, Max Ernst, Man Ray, Joan Miró and a host of other figures from the worlds of art and literature. She died in her Sussex farmhouse, having reinvented herself as a Surrealist gourmet cook.

Nora Summers was born in Bristol in 1892. She went to Bristol School of Art before enrolling at the Slade School in London from 1907 to 1910. Her interest in art continued and her paintings were exhibited in such places as the Chenil Gallery, Chelsea, the New English Art Club and the Walker Art Gallery, Liverpool. Later in life she enjoyed photography and took iconic photos, including those of Caitlin and Dylan Thomas.